Anti-Roman Cryptograms
in the New Testament

Studies in Biblical Literature

Hemchand Gossai
General Editor

Vol. 127

PETER LANG
New York • Washington, D.C./Baltimore • Bern
Frankfurt am Main • Berlin • Brussels • Vienna • Oxford

Norman A. Beck

Anti-Roman Cryptograms in the New Testament

Hidden Transcripts of Hope and Liberation

Revised Edition

PETER LANG
New York • Washington, D.C./Baltimore • Bern
Frankfurt am Main • Berlin • Brussels • Vienna • Oxford

Library of Congress Cataloging-in-Publication Data

Beck, Norman A.
Anti-Roman cryptograms in the New Testament:
hidden transcripts of hope and liberation / Norman A. Beck. – rev. ed.
p. cm. — (Studies in biblical literature; v. 127)
Includes bibliographical references (p.   ) and index.
1. Rome in the Bible. 2. Cryptograms in the Bible. 3. Opposition (Political science)
in the Bible. 4. Bible. N.T.—Criticism, interpretation, etc. I. Title.
BS2545.R65B43   225.9'5—dc22   2009035447
ISBN 978-1-4331-0656-9
ISSN 1089-0645

Bibliographic information published by **Die Deutsche Nationalbibliothek**.
Die Deutsche Nationalbibliothek lists this publication in the "Deutsche
Nationalbibliografie"; detailed bibliographic data is available
on the Internet at http://dnb.d-nb.de/.

The paper in this book meets the guidelines for permanence and durability
of the Committee on Production Guidelines for Book Longevity
of the Council of Library Resources.

© 2010 Peter Lang Publishing, Inc., New York
29 Broadway, 18th floor, New York, NY 10006
www.peterlang.com

Printed in the United States of America

To ESTHER

and to our children MATTHEW, DAVID, AND LAURA,

and to our grandchildren DILLON AND KYLA

Contents

Series Editor's Preface xi

Acknowledgments xiii

Introduction 1
    Cryptograms As Messages of Hope and Liberation
        for the Oppressed 1
    The Example of Hidden Transcripts in the Songs of
        African-American Slaves 2
    Recent Studies of the Political, Economic, and Social Situation
        in First Century Galilee and Judea 6
    Brief Observations Regarding Cryptograms in the Israelite Scriptures 8
    Demons, Satan Figures, and Cryptograms in the Jewish Pseudepigrapha ... 12
    The Two Basic Theses of This Book 14
    Methodology—Criteria Used in Identifying Hidden Transcripts
        of Hope and Liberation Within the Newer Testament 15
    The Outline to Be Followed 20

I. Anti-Roman Cryptograms of the Jesus of History 21
    A Survey of Recent Publications About the Jesus of History 22
    A Reconstructed Scenario of the Life of the Jesus of History 30
    Options Open to the Jesus of History and to Other Jews
        in Galilee and Judea at That Time 32
    The Jesus of History As a Jewish Messiah Figure
        with a Religious-Political Agenda 35
    Jesus' Teaching About the Kingdom of Adonai, Not of Caesar 41
    Conclusions 45

II. Anti-Roman Cryptograms in the Letters of Paul and
    in Other Pauline Literature 47
    Philippians—"Jesus Christ [Not Caesar] Is Lord" 55
    Paul's Life Situation When He Wrote His Letter to the Philippians
        and His Letter to Philemon 57
    The Life Situation of Those in Philippi to Whom Paul Wrote 58
    The Principal Expression of Faith Professed by Paul in This Letter 59
    Possible Meanings of the Word "Lord" Intended by Paul in This Letter ... 59
    "Jesus Christ Is Lord!" As an Anti-Roman Cryptogram 61
    1 Thessalonians—Satan Hindered Us and the Tempter Tempted You 62

1 Corinthians—the Rulers of This Age, Satan, and
the Beasts at Ephesus 63
2 Corinthians—Satan and the Thorn in Paul's Flesh,
a Messenger of Satan.. 66
Romans—Be Subject to the Governing Authorities;
Soon the God of Peace Will Crush Satan under Your Feet 70
Colossians—Delivered from the Dominion of Darkness........................... 74
Ephesians—Stand Firm Against the Wiles of the Devil 75
2 Thessalonians—The Activity of Satan, the Evil One 77
1 Timothy—Delivered to Satan; Avoiding the Devil 79
2 Timothy—Rescued from the Lion's Mouth 80
Conclusions... 81

III. Anti-Roman Cryptograms in the Synoptic Gospels 83
In "the Gospel of Jesus Christ" (Mark) and Continued
in Matthew and/or in Luke... 86
In the Temptation of Jesus Accounts.. 86
In the Proclamation of the Kingdom of God.. 90
In Exorcism Stories and in Other Healing Stories 93
In the "Lord's Prayer" in Matthew and in Luke 100
In the Stories About Herod the Great and Other Rulers
As Representatives of Roman Power in Matthew 103
In the References to the Lists of Roman Rulers and
to the Roman Census in Luke 104
Conclusions... 105

IV. Anti-Roman Cryptograms in John and in the Johannine Epistles ... 107
The World of Darkness 111
No Power Unless Given from Above.. 113
Conclusions... 113

**V. Anti-Roman Cryptograms in Revelation, 1 Peter, and Acts: Three
Vastly Differing Responses to Severe Roman Persecution 115**
Revelation—the Great Harlot, Babylon the Great, the Beast Rising from
the Sea, the Beast That Rose from the Land, the Devil Himself......... 124
1 Peter—Honor the Emperor, but Watch Out! That Devil Is Prowling
Around Like a Roaring Lion, Seeking Someone to Devour................. 134
Acts of Apostles—the Romans Are Fair and Just; Turn Away
from That Satan-Devil and His Savage Wolves Who Are
Tearing Up the Flock... 136
Conclusions... 141

VI. Anti-Roman Cryptograms in the Remaining Newer Testament Documents: Hebrews, James, Jude, and 2 Peter 143

Hebrews—Destroying the Devil Who Has the Power of Death 143

James—Stand Firm Against the Devil, and the Devil
Will Flee from You 145

Jude and 2 Peter—Lordship for Jesus Christ (Not for Caesar) 146

Conclusions 146

VII. Conclusions, Implications, and Future Agenda 149

Notes 153

Bibliography 175

Index of Authors 185

Series Editor's Preface

More than ever the horizons in biblical literature are being expanded beyond that which is immediately imagined; important new methodological, theological, and hermeneutical directions are being explored, often resulting in significant contributions to the world of biblical scholarship. It is an exciting time for the academy as engagement in biblical studies continues to be heightened.

This series seeks to make available to scholars and institutions, scholarship of a high order, and which will make a significant contribution to the ongoing biblical discourse. This series includes established and innovative directions, covering general and particular areas in biblical study. For every volume considered for this series, we explore the question as to whether the study will push the horizons of biblical scholarship. The answer must be yes for inclusion.

In this second edition of Norman Beck's *Anti-Roman Cryptograms in the New Testament*, the author explores the essential role of cryptograms in the time of Jesus and the early church. Beck proceeds with two principal theses: (1) that the Jesus of history and his earliest and closest followers during his lifetime and during the decades after he had been crucified by the Romans not only had a deep longing for eternal life but also a strong desire for liberation here on this earth; (2) that in the Christian Scriptures there are significantly more hidden transcripts, anti-Roman cryptograms of hope and liberation, for "freedom now" within this life than has been realized during most of the past nineteen centuries. In this extensive study, Beck argues persuasively that cryptograms are pervasive in the New Testament, found within the Gospels, Paul and Revelation. The argument in this regard is that cryptograms were not in any way peripheral but central for an understanding of hope and liberation in a context of Roman oppression. Beyond the scholarly examination of these theses, this volume provides a fine insight in the manner in which cryptograms are used in modern contexts of oppression. In particular he notes the use of cryptograms in American slavery. This second edition will continue this important discourse.

The horizon has been expanded.

Hemchand Gossai
Series Editor

Acknowledgments

First Edition

The research and the writing of this book have been supported generously by Texas Lutheran College, its administration, and staff. It is a pleasure also to express my gratitude to Mr. Marvin Selig, Mr. Clyde Selig, and the Structural Metals, Inc. Foundation of Seguin, Texas, for major Research Grants during the years 1987–1994.

Numerous scholarly colleagues read extensive portions of the manuscript during its development and provided valuable comments and suggestions. I am especially grateful to my closest colleague in the Department of Theology at Texas Lutheran College, Dr. Thomas Wilkens, for the encouragement that he consistently provided and for his expertise in the areas of Liberation Theologies and Social Ethics. It was in the context of team-teaching courses with him in Religion and Culture Today and in Biblical Interpretation that many of the ideas presented in this book were conceived and developed. Hundreds of our students also contributed graciously to this book in classroom discussions and in essay response papers.

Finally, I express sincere thanks to the Editor of The Westminster College Library of Biblical Symbolism, Dr. Peter W. Macky, for his patient guidance and comments, to the editorial staff of Peter Lang Publishing, Inc., and to Ms. Sondra Wiedenfeld and Ms. Christi Anderson for the typesetting.

Second Edition

This second edition provides an opportunity to acknowledge and respond to publications that have appeared since the release of the first edition of this work, to incorporate numerous additions and improvements resulting from insights provided by others, and to add further acknowledgements.

There has been a significant increase of interest during the past few decades in the political and economic conditions that prevailed during the development of the Newer Testament documents. Since much of the terminology being employed regarding the anti-Roman cryptograms in the Newer Testament now utilizes the term "hidden transcripts" in reference to coded messages in written form, I have changed the subtitle of this second edition from "Symbolic Messages of Hope and Liberation" to "Hidden Transcripts of Hope and Liberation."

It is a pleasure to acknowledge the ongoing assistance and encouragement for this work provided by Texas Lutheran College (now Texas Lutheran University), and by Structural Metals, Inc. (now incorporated into Commercial Metals Company). The initiative and partnership of the editorial staff of Peter Lang Publishers, Inc. is greatly appreciated. Finally, I am grateful for the valuable insights and suggestions for this second edition provided by Derek L. Knox, a very impressive young scholar who will make major contributions in this and in related fields of research in the future.

Introduction

Cryptograms As Messages of Hope and Liberation for the Oppressed

When people suffer prolonged political, economic, social, and religious oppression, it is not unusual for them to develop cryptic coded messages of hope and liberation by which they provide encouragement to one another. In most instances, these messages are transmitted orally. When the oppressive conditions persist for extended periods of time, and when some of those who are being oppressed are literate, leaders among the oppressed may risk transmission of some of these messages in written form in order to reach more people.

These messages of hope and liberation must be coded in ways in which their message and their intent are shielded from the perceptions of the oppressors. The messages are intended only for those who "have ears to hear." The messages utilize the language of faith, of salvation, of Deity and of adversaries of Deity, and are important in building and maintaining communities of faith. Words that are commonly used within the faith milieu of the oppressed people are given new and double meanings. The earlier meanings of these words are also maintained, partly through inertia and partly to protect the cryptograms from detection by the oppressors. In order for these cryptograms to escape detection and to accomplish their intended purpose among the oppressed, they must be used sparingly. Their hidden meanings must not be too readily apparent. The cryptograms must be mixed with other material that is not cryptogrammic, especially when they are expressed in written form.

Also, for the protection of the oppressed, the literature into which the cryptograms are incorporated will frequently include in prominent positions admonitions to respect the authority of the oppressors, even to honor them as having power delegated to them by the Deity. These admonitions to respect and honor the oppressors fulfill an important function as foils. They induce the oppressors and others who have never experienced oppression to think that the oppressed people are supporters of the status quo and that they are satisfied with their present conditions. Nothing, of course, could be farther from the truth. The illusion of satisfaction is essential, however, for the protection of the oppressed from even greater oppression. Only in situations in which leaders among the oppressed come perilously close to losing all hope of survival is this illusion of satisfaction discarded.

A variety of forms and genres are used by the oppressed in sharing and communicating their messages of hope and liberation. Genres used include legends, fables, parables, riddles, and reports of visions and dreams, with frequent applications of number and animal imagery and symbolism. The messages are also placed into folk songs, and pseudonymity of authorship is common, partially in order to protect the identity of the composers and partially because so many different people are involved in the process of their composition over extended periods of time. In many instances, a highly respected figure from a prior period within the religious tradition is said to be the author. This is done in order to gain a larger hearing for the message, but more importantly because oppressed people know that oppressors cannot seize, torture, and kill persons who are already dead. Since the intent is to hide the messages from the oppressors, but to uncover them for the oppressed who desperately need these messages of hope and liberation, these messages are properly labeled as apocalyptic in the literal sense of "that which is uncovered for those who need to see."

Coded messages of hope and liberation are still being used by oppressed people today. Their messages could be studied and compared to similar messages in earlier times. Research and publication of current practices of the sharing of cryptograms among oppressed people, however, would expose oppressed people contemporary to ourselves to further oppression and would nullify their expressions of hope. It would be morally unconscionable, therefore, to engage in such research and publication.

The Example of Hidden Transcripts in the Songs of African-American Slaves

Perhaps the best example of the use of hidden messages of hope and liberation from a relatively recent but not contemporary period of time that is available to us in the U.S.A. today is the example of African-Americans' songs. During the years from 1619 until 1865, they developed songs to communicate messages of hope for freedom from slavery and for the possibility of freedom from slavery via the "Underground Railroad." Let us look briefly at some of the coded messages of hope and liberation in the freedom songs developed and utilized by African-Americans during the years prior to 1865.[1] We shall do this in order to honor the memories of a proud and brave people and to show appreciation for their descendants who are living now. This will also help us to recognize code words used in similar ways by early Christians and incorporated into the Newer Testament canon.

Theoretically it would have been possible for descriptions of the use of coded messages of hope and liberation by African-Americans to have been published soon after slavery became unconstitutional in the U.S.A. at the conclusion of the American Civil War. Many decades passed, however, before detailed descriptions of these freedom songs were published. After many generations of slavery, oppression, and poverty, African-Americans generally had neither the resources nor the desire to explain their secret codes to the non-African-American public. Some former slaves undoubtedly explained the meanings of the coded words included in their songs to their children and grandchildren. Others merely sang their songs and preferred not to talk about their experiences as slaves, and not all of their children and grandchildren were interested in the old ways. The road to economic and social recovery was long and tortuous. The physical and economic mobility of the African-American sharecropper was not much greater than that of the slave. Progress was slow. Since, in many instances, people who had not been slaves remained basically indifferent and hostile to the former slaves and to their descendants, even when explanations of the secret codes in the slave songs were published there was little market for them. As a result, most of the significant publications regarding the coded words of hope and liberation in the songs of the African-American slaves that are now available date no earlier than 1939 or were reissued after 1939, and although this literature is now fairly extensive, relatively few people who are not themselves African-Americans are familiar with it.

The earliest books published on this subject were focused on the Underground Railroad and on the lives of individual African-Americans rather than on detailed analyses of the cryptograms in the songs.[2] Later writers went beyond this to place the coded words into groups with similar meanings and to develop and to publish their interpretations of the coded words and messages in the songs of the African-American slaves as they relayed their coded messages from field to field and from one plantation to another.[3] Our studies of these analyses of African-American slave songs help us to see that the code words used in cryptograms, whether sung, spoken, or written, must have two distinct though related messages. One meaning must be obvious to everyone who might hear or read them, the oppressors as well as the oppressed. This serves as the decoy to foil the oppressors, who in their privileged positions characteristically consider the oppressed people to be incapable of developing complex, nuanced messages and transmitting such complexities from person to person and from group to group. The other meaning, the hidden message, is intended to be perceived only by the oppressed and by those who can be trusted to help the oppressed. Analyses of the African-American slave songs indicate how ingenious the slave leaders were and how, in most instances, they used religious and biblical terms to encode political realities. The plantation owners had been reluctant to have the biblical messages shared with the slaves, but willing for this to occur so long as the verses within the Newer Testament that the slave owners considered to have the most relevance, especially the admonitions that slaves obey their masters in Colossians 3:22–24 and in Ephesians 6:5–9, were emphasized. They did not perceive that the slaves would focus on the Exodus from Egypt accounts in the Older Testament.

A short selection of code words used in the freedom songs of African-American slaves is given in Figure 1 so that we may have a better understanding of the slave songs and be alerted to similarly coded words with double meanings in the literature of oppressed early Christians. Perhaps the most widely used and best known of all of the slave songs that contained cryptograms is "Swing Low, Sweet Chariot":

> I looked over Jordan, an' what did I see, comin' for to carry me home?
> A band of angels comin' after me, comin' for to carry me home.
>
> If you get dere before I do, comin' for to carry me home,
> Tell all my friends I'm comin' too, comin' for to carry me home.

As these words were passed from field to field and from plantation to plantation, the slave owners, as was intended, thought that the slaves were happy in their other-worldly dreams and speculations. Actually, however, the slaves were planning redemption in *this* world. They were spreading the message that Harriet Tubman or some other "conductor" was in the area and that tonight, for those who were willing to take the risks, there was an opportunity to take the Underground Railroad north to freedom. In the words of Kim and Reggie Harris,

> In coded spirituals, the slaves expressed longing for freedom, calls for meetings, plans, methods of escape and other hidden signals. The masters and overseers restricted the slaves to only reading the Bible, and mistakenly believed that a singing slave was happy. This (the biblical text) provided the fugitives and their helpers on the *Liberty Line* with many useful code words and a means of transmission that was most effective.[4]

More specifically, Kim and Reggie Harris continue by pointing out that the spiritual, "Sinner, Please Don't Let This Harvest Pass,"

> urges the sinner (slave) to take the opportunity to escape. Planning and executing an escape was difficult. Most slaves did not know the safest routes to travel or the more intricate methods of avoiding capture. To have an *agent* or *conductor* of the Underground Railroad come to the plantation or the area was a chance not to be missed. Most of the help given to fugitives came after they had traversed the difficult *middle passage* and crossed the Mason-Dixon Line. Middle passage was the term used for the route of travel between slavery and freedom in the North.
>
> ("Sinner, Please Don't Let This Harvest Pass") was sung as a song of hope for those frightened of making the long journey. On the evening before an escape, their religious faith gave dignity to the real possibility of meeting death on *John Brown's Trail*.[5]

Figure 1

Code Words	Biblical Reference	Underground Reference
Moses	the biblical figure who led the early Israelite people from slavery in Egypt to freedom in the promised land	Harriet Tubman, the Moses of her people and of her enslaved brothers and sisters
Pharaoh	the title of the rulers of the ancient Egyptians who held the early Israelites in bondage	the slaveholder on the plantation who held African–Americans in bondage
Egypt	the land of slavery for the early Israelites	the land of slavery for the African–Americans in bondage
The Promised Land	the land of Canaan, believed to be promised to the Israelites by the Lord	Canada and in some instances ultimately Africa
Heaven	the condition of eternal life and happiness for the redeemed of the Lord	freedom from slavery and from all of the mental and physical suffering associated with slavery
Home	a place of one's own where a person can relax	freedom from slavery, either in Canada or back in Africa
The River Jordan	the river in Canaan over which the early Israelites passed in order to enter into the promised land	the Ohio River and beyond it the Niagara River joining Lake Erie and Lake Ontario
The Great Day	the day of resurrection and of entry into eternal life	the day when freedom in Canada was achieved at last
Sinner	a person who breaks the commandments of God and is in need of redemption	a slave who desires redemption from slavery
The Harvest	the gathering of the crops from the field	escape from slavery
Breaking Bread Together on Our Knees	receiving the Christian Eucharist	meeting at the eastern edge of the slave quarters before sunrise in order to plan or to attempt an escape from the plantation
The Chariot	the means of transportation that took Elijah into heaven in the 2 Kings 1:11 account	the means of transportation to freedom on the Underground Railroad
Angels	messengers of God in biblical stories	persons who risked their lives in order to guide and assist slaves running to freedom
Satan	the personification of evil, the semi-divine adversary of God	everyone who was cruel and inhumane to the slaves

The slaves who made up their minds to escape were proud and used the song "Steal Away" to alert family and friends of the decision.

A slave girl alerts another of her escape plans with the song "Let Us Break Bread Together." They plan to meet before sunrise on the east side of the slave quarters.

As J. Garfield Owens[6] puts it, slaves had to conceal from the slave masters their deep determination to throw off the yoke of slavery. They artfully disguised their ambitions, therefore, by making it appear that they were only waiting for the chariot to "Swing Low" and carry them, like Elijah, into heaven. They wanted to be carried from or to "Steal Away" from the oppressive, dehumanizing world of slavery to the glorious campground of freedom, freedom first of all here on this earth among their brothers and sisters, and then freedom forever as a heavenly goal. When the slave masters heard them singing about the campground, they thought, "Oh, how beautiful are their songs!" "How hopefully they speak about heaven." Similar observations are made by John Lovell, Miles Mark Fisher, James H. Cone, Krista K. Dixon, Charles L. Blockson, Kim and Reggie Harris, and O. Fred Cravens.

Recent Studies of the Political, Economic, and Social Situation in First Century Galilee and Judea

Within the past few decades, numerous descriptions of the political, economic, and social situation in Galilee and Judea during the first half of the first century C.E. have been published. For the purposes of this present study, among the most notable of these is Klaus Wengst, *Pax Romana and the Peace of Jesus Christ*.[7] Wengst notes that the view of the period that has been glorified as the "*Pax Romana*" and accepted for nearly two thousand years all too uncritically by most Western historians is a view that Wengst describes as "from above." It was developed by Roman historians in order to please their wealthy patrons and to extend the privileged position of their wealthy patrons as long as possible. Its depiction of the beneficial results of the Pax Romana obscures the harsh reality of life faced by most people during that period. Wengst is interested in the view "from below" gleaned from the less literary fragments of evidence that have survived from the lives of ordinary people of that time.

When Wengst examines the evidence from the lives of ordinary people who lived within the boundaries of the Roman Empire, he finds that the conquest of a land by the Romans was accompanied by measures that resulted in the economic exploitation of its people by the Roman rulers. The exploitation of the people of the provinces was designed for the benefit of the city of Rome and especially for the benefit of the richest people there. The Pax Romana guaranteed the preservation of the existing social order in which the privileged status of the "upper" classes both in Rome and in the provinces was to be maintained at all costs. Wengst shows that it was a primary goal of the Roman rulers to transfer war and its evil consequences to the periphery of the empire so that in Rome itself there was "peace."

Wengst writes that for wealthy members of Roman society the Roman system of law and justice was exemplary. They and the Roman historians who articulated their perspective reaped the benefits of that system. The quality of Roman justice, however, diminished rapidly as one moved from Rome itself to the far reaches of the Roman Empire. The inhabitants of recently conquered and rebellious regions had no civil rights. They were to be controlled as effectively as possible and with the least expense possible. In the eyes of the Roman provincial administration in Jerusalem, there can be no doubt that the Jesus of history, when he eventually came to the attention of the ruling forces, was perceived not as a gentle, benign comforter of innocuous peasants, but as a dangerous political rebel whose words and actions might give the restive populace encouragement to revolt. Therefore, according to Wengst, Jesus' message of hope and imminent liberation meant a liberation from oppressive Roman power at that time, as well as a liberation beyond death. This message appeared to the Roman rulers to be a threat to the Pax Romana in Jerusalem and a threat to their lives. Since to the ruling powers Jesus and his message of "the kingdom of God" rather than "the kingdom of Caesar" in the volatile political climate in Galilee and Judea at that time disturbed the Pax Romana, it would be necessary to remove Jesus from the scene. For the sake of the Pax Romana, therefore, Jesus was seized during the night in the Garden of Gethsemane. He was tortured privately nearly to the point of death that same night behind the walls of the Roman praetorium. Then what was left of him after the floggings by the Roman soldiers was crucified publicly outside the walls of the city of Jerusalem for maximum deterrence against others who might engage in similar activities.[8]

Whenever the social, political, and economic situation is oppressive over a prolonged period of time, whether this occurs among African-American slaves from 1619–1865, among Jews in Galilee and Judea after 63 B.C.E., or in any other time and place, the transmission of coded hidden transcripts of hope and liberation can be expected to occur. There will be some similarities in these hidden transcripts from one situation to another, but there will also be obvious differences. The development of these cryptograms will be unique in each situation. The development will be in a sense indigenous to each time and place. We shall see later in this present study that there are significant differences among the anti-Roman cryptograms that are apparent within the specifically

Christian Scriptures. Although the anti-Roman cryptograms obviously differed from one writer to another, we shall see that the most significant differences among the anti-Roman hidden transcripts that are apparent within the specifically Christian Scriptures are between those in the book of Revelation and those in the other portions of that literature.

Before we turn to the anti-Roman cryptograms of the Newer Testament, however, let us make a few brief observations regarding cryptograms in the Israelite Scriptures and look at demons, Satan figures, and cryptograms in the Jewish Pseudepigrapha.

Brief Observations Regarding Cryptograms in the Israelite Scriptures

There can be no doubt that the social, political, and economic situation of the ancient Israelites was oppressive over prolonged periods of time. Many of them suffered economic oppression because of the policies of their own kings, of whom David, Solomon, and Rehoboam in Jerusalem and Ahab in Samaria are only a few of the most obvious examples. All of the Israelites suffered both political and economic oppression over prolonged periods of time at the hands of the great world powers of Egypt, Assyria, Babylon, Persia, and Greece. When they lived outside of their own land, whether by choice or by coercion, they also suffered social oppression. It may be expected, therefore, that under these conditions they would have developed and transmitted innumerable hidden transcripts of hope and liberation, and that the sacred Scriptures that they formulated would be replete with such cryptograms.

We have no direct access, of course, to cryptograms that may have been transmitted orally by oppressed ancient Israelites. The sacred Scriptures (Torah, Prophets, and Writings) that they formulated and accepted as canonical are not replete with such cryptograms, although some hidden transcripts can be detected that have some similarities to the anti-Roman cryptograms in the Newer Testament. In order to facilitate this investigation, let us look briefly at some sample segments of these texts.

Within the narrative of Exodus 1 there are several indications that the tradition contained subtle expressions of hope for liberation from the pre-Israelites' position of slavery and servitude. According to this story, the new king of Egypt who did not know Joseph said to his people that the people of Israel were too many and too mighty (Exodus 1:8–9). Nevertheless, the more they were oppressed, the more they multiplied (1:12). The Hebrew midwives who were ordered to kill all of the male Hebrew babies said that the Hebrew women were so strong and vigorous that they delivered their babies easily and did not need to call the midwives to come to help them. The Israelite women were contrasted to the Egyptian women, who were implied to be weak and lacking in courage (1:15-19). Although these are not the elements of coded cryptograms, they are expressions of strength by a proud and spirited people, a people who will not be subdued by their oppressors. That there was no secret code utilized to conceal the identity of the oppressors is an indication that the story was written at a time when Israelites had little reason to fear the power of the Egyptians.

Economic oppression of the poor by wealthy men and women of the Northern Kingdom of Israel during the reign of Jeroboam II was addressed in Amos 3–9 of the Israelite prophetic tradition. The descriptive words such as "you who trample on the needy" (8:4) and "you cows of Bashan" (4:1) are not coded cryptograms, however, and Amos functions as a spokesperson for the Lord God and for the oppressed rather than as a person suffering economic oppression himself. Only in a very general way does the Amos prophetic tradition provide hidden transcripts that are similar to the cryptograms in the Christian Scriptures.

In order to give the powerful Babylonians no reason to increase their oppression of the political and religious leaders deported to Babylon in 597 B.C.E., during the period of the siege and capture of Jerusalem ten years later Ezekiel instructs his fellow captives to grieve and suffer silently rather than openly (Ezekiel 24:15–27). Analysis of the extensive oracles against various nations within the prophetic traditions, most of all a comparison of the oracles against the Egyptians and against the Babylonians, the two major powers in the oppression of the Israelites, is relevant here. Within the three largest of the prophetic documents: the Isaiah traditions, the Jeremiah traditions, and Ezekiel traditions, there are extensive condemnations of Egypt and of the Egyptian people (Isaiah 18:1–20:6; 31:1–3, Jeremiah 46:2–26, and Ezekiel 29:1–32:32). Within the same three traditions there are oracles against the Babylonians in Isaiah 13:1–22 and in Jeremiah 50:1–51:64, *but in the Ezekiel traditions there are no oracles against Babylon.* Although there are no oracles against Babylon in the Ezekiel traditions, there may be a cryptic reference to the Babylonians as the "wild beasts" who have devoured the unprotected sheep of the Lord God (Ezekiel 34:8).

Since Egypt was a major enemy of the Babylonians, Ezekiel and those who developed the Ezekiel traditions could freely speak and write elaborate condemnations of Egypt, but it would not have been wise for them as Israelite captives in Babylon to say or to write anything specifically against the Babylonians. Those who were knowledgeable and alert among the Israelite captives in Babylonia, however, would have been perfectly capable of thinking "against Babylon," when they spoke and when they heard Ezekiel and those who developed the Ezekiel traditions speak and write at least some of what they were speaking and writing "against Egypt." Babylonians, however, would be pleased to hear the Israelites speak and write condemnations of Egypt, and, similar to the owners of the plantations who heard the African-American slaves singing "Swing Low, Sweet Chariot," they would not understand the cryptogram, the hidden message.[9] *Within Ezekiel, chapters 29-32, therefore, there may be the most significant, subtle, and extensive hidden transcript within the Hebrew Bible.*

The bitter words of anger and desire for revenge against the Babylonians who had devastated Jerusalem and especially against the Edomites who had assisted them (Psalm 137) are not expressed in cryptograms. As in some of the examples previously listed, by the time that these words were put into written forms the persons and groups spoken against were no longer in power and were no longer a threat to the oppressed people. If cryptograms had been utilized earlier, they were no longer needed once the oppressors were themselves deposed. Therefore, in these instances the situation differs from that in the Christian Scriptures, in which the Romans remained in power throughout the process of development of early Christian oral as well as written tradition.

The oracle against Babylon in Isaiah 13 and the contempt shown for the king of Babylon and other haughty rulers in Isaiah 14 are also expressed openly, without coded language, indications that they were written at a time when Babylon had ceased to be a threat to the Israelites. The kings and the deities to whom the kings paid homage are said to be cut down to the ground, brought down to Sheol, to the Pit. The taunting songs of Isaiah 23–24, Isaiah 47, Jeremiah 50–51, and Ezekiel 26–27 are reflected in Revelation 18–19. Among these, it is likely that only in Ezekiel was the oppressive political power of the Babylonians still a factor at the time of the writing of much of Ezekiel, especially of the extensive oracles against Egypt in chapters 29–32. Therefore, the cryptogram of using the name of the earlier oppressive nation, Egypt, rather than the current one, Babylon, was necessary, even though this has not generally been noticed by later interpreters of the Ezekiel traditions. It is easily recognized, however, that the writer of Revelation used Babylon rather than Rome as the great harlot, drunk with the blood of the saints and martyrs of Jesus. The Roman Empire survived for many centuries, and the development of all of the Christian Scriptures occurred during Roman rule. Therefore, we should not be surprised that the written Christian sacred tradition includes hidden transcripts in which the word Babylon is used as a cryptogram for Rome, both in the book of Revelation and in some of the other documents in the Newer Testament.

The four horns of Zechariah 1:18-21 can be considered to be symbolic cryptograms of four mighty empires that have rooted up Judah, Israel, and

Jerusalem. Instead of mentioning the empires' names, the horn imagery was preferred, perhaps not because of fear of retribution from the empires, but merely because the horns of bulls and other wild animals were perceived to be frightful symbols of destruction.

Satan in Zechariah 3:1–2, as well as in 1 Chronicles 21:1 and Job 1:6–12, is only an adversary or prosecuting attorney whose task it is to bring accusations, and not a demigod. Therefore, Satan in these texts is not used as a code word to represent an oppressive nation.

Although the Daniel traditions are obviously comprised of two distinct segments (chapters 1–6 of *midrashim* based on authoritative sacred writings, more specifically *agadoth*, edifying teaching stories, and chapters 7–12 of visions or apocalypses intended to exhort), the symbolism that shall concern us here does not vary greatly from one segment to the other.[10] Most commentators agree that the same oppressive world empires (Babylonia, Media, Persia, and Greece) are represented symbolically by the four metals (gold, silver, bronze, and iron mixed with clay) of the image in Nebuchadnezzar's dream (Daniel 2) and by the four great beasts in Daniel's vision (Daniel 7). Both the image and the fourth beast are said to be crushed and eliminated by divine intervention, the image by the God of heaven who will establish a kingdom that shall never be destroyed (2:44), and the fourth beast by the Most High, who shall give the kingdom and the dominion to the saints of the Most High (7:26–27).

The hope that the most High God will establish an everlasting kingdom of sovereignty over all peoples, nations, and languages is strong within the Daniel traditions (4:3, 17, 25, 32, 34; 5:21; 6:26; 7:14, 22, 27). In the *agadoth* the most High God is depicted as intervening in the human predicament of the loyal and faithful Shadrach, Meshach, and Abednego by sending an angel, who is said to be "like a son of the gods" (3:25, 28). Later in the visions of the second half of the document God provides "one who is like a son of man" as a personal representative (7:13–14). While the goodness of God is personified in these ways, what we do not find in the Daniel traditions is an interest in a personification of evil in the form of a Satan, Devil, or demigod figure. Put succinctly by James A. Montgomery, "It is significant that no Prince of Evil is devised (in the Book of Daniel), a Satan or a Belial....The book is concerned with actual human history, and its arch-fiend is an atheistic king who, within a brief space, will meet his doom."[11]

Until that arch-fiend atheistic king meets his doom, however, his power must be respected. Certain precautions must be taken. One of these is the use of cryptograms to avoid direct reference to Antiochus Epiphanes. That despotic ruler is often given disparaging titles such as "a little horn" that shall be broken and "a contemptible person" who shall come to his end with none to help him. His name is never mentioned in the document.

The Daniel traditions were significant for the followers of Jesus who produced Mark and Matthew,[12] and most likely they were significant for the Jesus of history himself. Among the legacies that the Daniel traditions provided were the practice of representing oppressors as wild and savage beasts, an intense longing for the imminent kingdom of God that would replace the evil destructive kingdoms with which they had to contend, and a strong desire for religious and political liberation.

Within the Older Testament, therefore, the most significant hidden transcripts are subtle condemnations of Babylon in Ezekiel 29–32 and the more easily detected hidden transcripts against the Seleucid Greek empire and Antiochus Epiphanes in the Daniel traditions.

Demons, Satan Figures, and Cryptograms in the Jewish Pseudepigrapha

Many of the themes of the Daniel traditions were further developed within the Pseudepigrapha. Of particular interest here are the references to demons and Satan their prince in *1 Enoch* and in the *Book of Jubilees*, and the elaborate Eagle Vision cryptogram in *4 Ezra*.

In the portion of the Book of Noah incorporated into *1 Enoch* 6–36, in an elaboration of the Genesis 6:1–4 account, it is said that the angels, the children of heaven, saw the beautiful daughters of the men and women of the earth and lusted after them. Two hundred of these angels bound themselves together with an oath to choose wives from among these women and to beget children by them (*1 Enoch* 6:1–8)[13] They taught these women magical medicine and incantations. The women became pregnant and gave birth to great giants who devoured mankind (7:1–6). The giants promoted warfare and were corrupt in every way. As men perished, they cried out, and their cry was heard in heaven (8:1–4). Michael, Surafel, and Gabriel saw what had happened and brought the problem to the Most High (9:1–11). The Most High then provided directions to the good angels to protect Noah while Azazel would be bound hand and foot and cast into darkness, and the earth would be healed of all injustice, defilement, oppression, sin, and iniquity (10:1–11:2).

According to the *Book of Jubilees* which elaborated further upon the account available in *1 Enoch* and which O.S. Wintermute[14] dates 161–140 B.C.E., during the days of Mahalalel and Jared the angels of the Lord descended to the earth. These Watchers were supposed to provide instruction for the earth people and to guide them in the ways of sound judgment and uprightness (Jubilees 4:15). These Watchers, however, sinned with the daughters of men and mingled with them "so that they might be polluted" (4:22).The offspring of these unions were giants who promoted injustice and corruption over all of the earth (5:1–9). Their evil spirits were polluted demons which were said to be leading astray and blinding and killing the grandchildren of Noah (10:1–2). All of these demons were to be bound and taken to "the place of judgment" (10:3–7). At the request of Mastema, the chief of these spirits, however, the Lord God permitted a tenth of them to remain (10:8–9). These evil spirits are said to be worshiped by the nations (22:16–17). These deplorable conditions, however, can be changed. When children begin to study the Torah and seek the commandments of the Lord, when they return to the way of righteousness, the days of their lives will increase. They will live in "peace and rejoicing" and there will be "no Satan and no evil (One) who will destroy" them (23:26–29).

In the Similitudes (*1 Enoch* 37–71), Satan, referred to by various names, is the ruler of a kingdom of evil that opposes the kingdom of righteousness.[15] Satan is subject, however, to the power of the Lord of the Spirits (54:6). The demons of Satan often accuse those who dwell on the earth (40:7). These creatures misled Eve and showed children how to make instruments of death (69:6).

Although the accounts just cited from *1 Enoch* 6–11, the *Book of Jubilees*, and *1 Enoch* 37–71 use fallen angels, demons, and Satan figures to explain the origins of evil in this world and to express the belief that eventually oppression, unrighteousness, sin, and all evil will pass away, they are not focused on specific political situations. They are not primarily symbolic messages of hope and liberation from the Greek or Roman rulers or from anyone else whom we can detect. They are not cryptograms. *The Eagle Vision of 4 Ezra 11–12, however, is focused on a specific political situation; it is primarily a symbolic message of hope and liberation; it is a cryptogram. Moreover, it is an anti-Roman cryptogram.*[16] *It is the most elaborate anti-Roman cryptogram within the Pseudepigrapha.*[17]

There can be no doubt that the eagle which in the vision came up from the sea, the eagle with twelve feathered wings and three heads which spread its wings over the entire earth to reign over the earth and all who dwell on it, the eagle against which no one dared to speak, symbolically represents the Roman Empire. It is said to be what remains of the four beasts of Daniel 7, the one that has overcome all of the beasts of the past. Its winged form suggests that its power is seemingly air-borne; it covers more territory than the previous beasts. The vision provides a reinterpretation of Daniel 7 for its time; the political threat is now Roman rather than Greek.[18]

The Roman eagle is said to have "held sway over the world with much terror, and over all the earth with grievous oppression." It has "afflicted the meek and injured the peaceable," "hated those who tell the truth," and "loved liars" (*4 Ezra* 11:40-42). These are descriptions from the perspective of the oppressed, from below as Klaus Wengst puts it,[19] rather than as the Roman historians depicted the "Pax Romana" from above.

The date assigned for the composition of the Eagle Vision will depend on the interpretations given of the various wings and heads. Perhaps the author was deliberately obscure and cryptic in order to protect the author and the author's community. Perhaps the author was not entirely familiar with the particulars regarding Roman rulers from an earlier period. At any rate, there is enough information within the descriptions of the actions of various Roman rulers to suggest that the composition occurred at some time during the reign of Domitian (81–96 C.E.), or, as Bruce Metzger suggests[20] approximately 100 C.E. This places the composition within the period of the writing of the book of Revelation. Jewish antipathy for Roman rule had gone through more than a century of development by that time. Jesus and his Jewish followers lived their entire lives in that atmosphere of Roman oppression. They too, and their parents before them, must have longed for the time when, in the words of the composer of the Eagle Vision of *4 Ezra* 11:45–12:3, the Roman Eagle and its "terrifying wings," its "most evil little wings," its "malicious heads," its "most evil talons," and all of its "worthless body" would disappear and be burned away, and the entire world would be refreshed again.

These expressions of hope for liberation from Roman oppression within the then-present world of time and space bring us to the two basic theses of this book.

The Two Basic Theses of This Book

The first basic thesis of this book is that the Jesus of history and his earliest and closest followers during his lifetime and during the decades after he had been crucified by the Romans had not only a deep longing for eternal life with God beyond the limits of this world and its problems, but also a strong desire for liberation here on this earth from Roman political, economic, social, and religious oppression. Both of these desires were inherent in their experiences as Jews living under Roman rule. Pharisees, Essenes, followers of John the Baptizer, political activists, and many other Jews who were not specifically identified with any religious and political groups shared that longing. Their desire for "freedom then," at the conclusion of this life, as well as for "freedom now," during this life, links Jesus and his followers to other oppressed Jews, to African-Americans, to the campesinos of Latin America, and to many other oppressed ethnic and religious groups of every time and place.

The second basic thesis of this book, closely related to and supplying evidence for the first, is that within our specifically Christian Scriptures there are significantly more hidden transcripts, anti-Roman cryptograms of hope and liberation, for "freedom now" within this life than has been realized throughout most of the history of interpretation of the Newer Testament. This second thesis suggests that these coded messages of hope and liberation were intended to be such by the Jesus of history and by his closest followers. This thesis suggests that the code words utilized in these cryptograms had two distinct though related meanings, just as code words later had two meanings in the African-American songs. One meaning was quite obvious to anyone who might read or hear them. This served to make oppressors think that the messages were primarily "other-worldly." The other meaning was intended, as in the African-American songs, to be applied in "this world" and to be fully understood only by the oppressed.

I suggest in this book that gradually after the first generation of Jesus' followers died, and especially after Christianity became the officially promulgated religion of the Roman Empire, these hidden messages have generally been understood not as Jesus and his closest followers intended their own communities of faith to understand them, but as they intended the Roman oppressors to understand them. This book is designed to help take us back to the perspective of the Jesus of history and his earliest followers. This book is designed to help us increase our understanding of specific texts and of the political, economic, and social oppression experienced by Jesus and his closest followers. It is intended to be helpful to people who are severely oppressed politically, economically, and socially today. It is also intended to sensitize those of us, Christians and others, who are relatively affluent and have not ourselves experienced severe oppression. It is a purpose of this book also to motivate us to work for the freedom and the access to opportunities that are hoped for by the multitudes of suppressed and oppressed people of our time.

Methodology—Criteria Used in Identifying Hidden Transcripts of Hope and Liberation Within the Newer Testament

What rationale can and should be given for our study of hidden transcripts, concealed messages of hope and liberation within our early and developing Christian tradition? What insights can be gained from such a study? Why is this research and analysis necessary and in a very real sense mandatory for us?

Although it may always be appropriate to begin with the obvious, surface meaning of whatever we hear or read, when we discover or are shown by others that beneath the surface of an oral or written account there may be hidden transcripts of vital importance, it is imperative that we consider them. To do anything less would be an act of disrespect to the persons who developed the ideas in question, as well as an ill-advised refusal to use the abilities that we believe that God has provided for us. It would also cause us to miss the thrill and excitement of discovering something that previously we had not seen nor known.

Once we become aware that included within many of the songs developed and sung by African-American slaves within the United States prior to 1865 there were hidden messages of hope for freedom and guidelines for actions to take in risking an escape from slavery, we have an increased understanding of our history. Even more important, we are enabled to increase our appreciation and our respect for a very significant number of people within American culture and to enhance our feelings of self-esteem if we ourselves are African-American people.

As soon as we realize that the writer of the document within our Newer Testament that we call the Apocalypse or the book of Revelation was longing for the fall not of Babylon but of Rome and of those who profited greatly from Roman political and economic oppression, that entire document and, indeed, the entire Newer Testament becomes more fascinating and more meaningful for us.

How, then, shall we proceed? How can we provide for discussion not merely suggestions but also substantial evidence that embedded within the documents of the Newer Testament there are indeed numerous hidden transcripts, messages of hope and liberation? We recognize the limitations of our efforts. Even with the tools that we have through careful use of historical-critical methodologies, we have no "time machine" that would take us back into direct access to the life situations of Jesus and his earliest followers. Nevertheless, it is apparent from the documents included in the Newer Testament that Jesus and those who responded favorably to him were effective in their efforts by functioning somewhere between the extremes of docile submission to Roman authorities and attempts to use violent resistance to try to make the Roman military presence untenable for the Romans.

Although we cannot take a time machine back to first century Galilee and Judea and other regions of the Roman Empire of that time, observations of the responses of powerless people to their oppressors who are contemporary to ourselves can be made. For example, James C. Scott, based on his research that included two years of living among economically oppressed Malaysians,[21] notes that political responses of "subordinate groups is to be found neither in overt collective defiance of power holders nor in complete hegemonic compliance, but in the vast territory between these two polar opposites." Scott suggests that the vulnerability of subordinate groups does not permit them "the luxury of direct confrontation" with their oppressors. Instead, they "conduct what amounts to a veiled discourse of dignity and self-assertion." Scott affirms that "much of their political action requires interpretation precisely because it is intended to be cryptic and opaque."[22]

Scott labels as "public transcript" the records assembled and approved by the ruling elites and as "hidden transcript" the same situations from the perspective of the poor and oppressed. As William R. Herzog II depicts it,[23] the hidden transcript "contains what the oppressed say to each other and what they really think about their rulers but are too intimidated to express openly."

For excellent applications of Scott's research to our study of the life situations of Jesus and of Paul, see Richard A. Horsley, ed. *Hidden Transcripts and the Arts of Resistance: Applying the Work of James C. Scott to Jesus and to Paul*[24] and Horsley, *Jesus and Empire: The Kingdom of God and the New World Disorder*.[25] Christopher Bryan, in his *Render to Caesar: Jesus, the Early Church, and the Roman Superpower*,[26] also builds upon the work of James C. Scott. Bryan considers Jesus and his followers to have been resignedly accepting of Roman rule, though willing in some instances "to question or even challenge nonviolently the justice or appropriateness of its actions."[27] Bryan interprets Jesus as addressing the situations of "the poor" and of "the rich," rather than as one who was himself "poor" and consistently oppressed. Bryan contrasts his own perception of Jesus with that of Horsley and of John Howard Yoder,[28] both of whom picture Jesus to have been himself among the poor and oppressed and repeatedly opposing the Roman occupation, although nonviolently. My own position is somewhere between the positions of Horsley and Bryan, but much closer to that of Horsley.[29]

What criteria can be used in the identification and exposition of texts and transcripts within our Newer Testament that may have been intended by the Jesus of history and by the Apostle Paul and other followers of Jesus to provide messages of hope and guidance to those who were suffering severe economic and political oppression by the Romans and by zealous proponents of Roman Civil Religion? Within this current study, attention is focused on texts that include one or more of the following nine characteristics.

1. Texts in which "kingdom language" is used. References may be to the "kingdom of this world," "the kingdom of darkness," "the kingdom of God," or "the kingdom of Heaven." We will be aware that "kingdom language" is political language. The "parables of the kingdom" within the Synoptic Gospels will be of particular interest, as well as the petition "May Your Kingdom Come!" and related petitions within the "Lord's Prayer." We may have been told by our professors of homiletics in our seminaries that we must never bring political issues

into the pulpit. Certainly we must never endorse political candidates or political parties within our sermons and homilies. Nevertheless, we cannot lead our congregations in teaching and expositions of the parables of the kingdom used and/or attributed to Jesus and in praying the "Lord's Prayer" without engaging in political language, language that was political during the first century C.E. and has been political ever since, including also during our time.

2.   Texts, often closely related to the ones in which "kingdom language" is used, in which "the Lord," "the king," "the ruler of this world," and other designations of political power and control are used, either with reference to Jesus or to Roman rulers or rulers given political power by Rome. Even words such as "the shepherd" and "the shepherd of the flock" may fall within this category. This reminds us how easily followers of Jesus during centuries after the death of Jesus, especially followers of Jesus who after the fourth century have been comfortable and have had access to political and economic power, have missed the hidden transcripts that were intended by those who developed and first used these terms.

3.   Texts in which words such as "Satan," "the Devil," "the Evil One," "the Tempter," "the Beast," "the Lion," "a roaring lion," "the lion's mouth," "savage wolves," "wild beasts," "a legion," etc. are used. In this context, we will wonder why, apart from the question asked of Jesus whether it is in accordance with Jewish interpretations of the Torah for Jews to pay the required taxes "to Caesar" and the Lukan writer's placing the birth of Jesus during the reign of Caesar Augustus and the beginning of the activities of John the Baptizer during the reign of Caesar Tiberius, there are so few references in the Newer Testament documents to the Caesars who ruled over virtually all of the areas in which Jesus, Paul, and other followers of Jesus lived their entire lives. Were perhaps many of the instances in the Newer Testament in which "Satan," "the Devil," "the Evil One," etc. are mentioned references not so much to the religious concepts of a demi-god or evil angel expelled by God from heaven but instead are intended as political references to Caesars who ruled during the first and second centuries? When the writer of the Apocalypse depicted the Risen Christ as "the Lion of the tribe of Judah" in Revelation 5:5, may there have been a contrast intended between the "Lamb" slain but now alive and possessing ultimate power and Domitian or another Roman Caesar who wishes to be the "Lion" whom all will fear?

4. Texts, again related to the categories listed above, in which "demon possession," and "exorcisms" are prominent. Some, but perhaps not all, of the references in the Newer Testament documents to persons "possessed by demons" or "possessed by unclean demons" may be best understood as cryptic references to persons who are fully compliant and submissive to Roman power, especially when such persons may be seen not merely as isolated individuals, but as representative of groups of subdued peoples. This is what is described by Ched Myers[30] as "collective anxiety over Roman imperialism" and instances "in which the community's anguish over its subjugation is repressed and then turned in on itself."

5. Texts in which there are statements such as "Whoever has ears to hear, let that person hear!" or "Let the reader understand." In many instances, explicit statements such as these may be reminders that there is an encrypted message somewhere in this context that the oppressed hearer or reader should peruse. Because most of us are so far removed from the life situation in which these words were first used, we may not have been adequately aware of the significance of such statements.

6. Texts in which Latin rather than Greek words are used, as well as texts in which there is significant use of military imagery.[31] There was a potential danger that use of Latin words would alert Roman oppressors that a message was directed against them. This may have been a reason that the Matthean redactors avoided use of the word "Legion" as they shortened and modified the Mark 5:1–20 account in Matthew 8:28–34.

7. Texts in which words such as "Babylon," "Egypt," "the great harlot," and "the city that sits upon seven hills" are used. This criterion provides an opportunity to make an important distinction between texts in which the derogatory statements regarding the oppressive Romans are quite easily recognized, as they are generally in the book of Revelation, and texts in which the anti-Roman cryptograms are more carefully disguised and protected as they are in other documents such as the Apostle Paul's letter to the Romans, the Gospel According to John, Acts of Apostles, and 1 Peter. Hidden transcripts that are carefully disguised are the better cryptograms, because they are more difficult to identify. They are the ones that have in most instances been overlooked since the fourth century by followers of Jesus who themselves in many instances are economic and political oppressors.

8. Texts in which Jesus and/or his followers are said to be tempted to have power or to avoid persecution and death by submitting to someone who has great power. The temptation of Jesus accounts in Mark 1:12–13; Matthew 4–11; Luke 4:1–13 and in Gethsemane in Mark 14:32–42; Matthew 26:36–46; Luke 22:40–46, as well as the petition in the Lord's Prayer, "Lead us not into temptation," should be scrutinized here. In our life situations, when the word "temptation" is heard, we usually think about the temptations to eat too much or to drink too much, or to other temptations to indulge in activities that may be momentarily pleasurable but intrinsically harmful to ourselves and to other people, and not to the temptation of Jesus and his early followers in their life situation to try to escape persecution and to attain power by "bowing down" to Caesar and to Caesar's representatives.

9. The final criterion is to examine very carefully texts that are especially enigmatic, puzzling, difficult for us to find a purpose or meaning for them. Examples here would include "the thorn in Paul's flesh" that he describes as "a messenger of Satan" in 2 Corinthians 12:7 and the Legion of demons being permitted by Jesus to enter into a herd of hogs and rush over a steep cliff and be drowned in the sea in Mark 5:1–20 and parallels.

The Outline to Be Followed

These two theses and these nine interrelated criteria will be pursued and explored within this present study through an examination of specific Newer Testament texts, with the results of the investigation summarized in a final chapter. I shall begin with an attempt to reconstruct the scenario of the time of the Jesus of history and to identify, in broad terms, anti-Roman cryptograms that he may have used. This will be followed by chapters of possible anti-Roman cryptograms in the letters of Paul and in the epistles written in his name, in the Synoptic Gospels, in the Fourth Gospel and the Johannine Epistles, in the Apocalypse, 1 Peter, and Acts, and finally in the remaining literature of the Newer Testament.

This book is not a definitive study and report of every anti-Roman cryptogram, of every hidden transcript of hope and liberation from Roman oppression, within the Newer Testament. Instead, it is intended to encourage and to promote further study and analysis among scholars, as well as among all readers of the Newer Testament.

I. Anti-Roman Cryptograms of the Jesus of History

We shall never, of course, achieve complete objectivity in our search for the Jesus of history. Each of us has a personal stance, a point of view, a unique background of experience.[1] If we were to attempt to attain total objectivity in our search for the Jesus of history, perhaps by putting all available data into a computer and by programming the computer with computer-programmed programs, the printout of the Jesus of history that would emerge would in all likelihood be a mechanical robot with little resemblance to the man Jesus. The best that we can do is to use our methodologies with care, limit our subjectivity as much as possible, learn from the efforts of others who have engaged in the search, and respond to the criticisms of our peers.

Fortunately, we are able to learn much from the efforts of others who have engaged in the search for the Jesus of history. The original "quest" for the Jesus of history, the overconfident writing of "biographies" of Jesus based on the Gospel According to Mark that characterized the period from 1835–1918, got us started in the right direction, although it succumbed to its own excesses of subjectivity. The "new quest," or "second quest" that covered the period from 1953 until approximately 1979, attained more objectivity with Joachim Jeremias, Norman Perrin, and many others developing and using criteria of linguistics, multiple attestation, dissimilarity and coherence, etc. Although the new quest took us much farther than the original quest, we became aware eventually that the criterion of dissimilarity in particular separated the Jesus of history from his Jewish heritage in a way that was not acceptable. We realize now that since the early 1980s we have been involved in a still newer "third quest" in Jesus of history research.[2] One of the most significant factors in this third quest has been the application of sociological, political, and economic analyses of life in Galilee and Judea during the first century C.E., as mentioned on pages 6-8 of the Introduction above. As stated by John P. Meier, "To take into consideration the social environment in which Jesus moved is simply to take history seriously in all its human dimensions."[3] At the same time, as we utilize these sociological, political, and economic factors in our quest for the Jesus of history, we must guard against an undue emphasis on these factors that can distort our portrayal of Jesus himself.

In order to benefit as much as possible from the efforts of others who are engaged in this third quest, a brief summary of some of the features of recent publications about the Jesus of history and sociological, political, and economic factors that impacted his life is given here. This brief summary will also provide a context for the scenario of the life of the Jesus of history and for the analysis of anti-Roman cryptograms of the Jesus of history in the remainder of this chapter.

A Survey of Recent Publications About the Jesus of History

The survey begins with E. P. Sanders, *Jesus and Judaism*,[4] not only because this is one of the first and most important books in the third quest category, but also because Sanders effectively broke down the barrier that use of Norman Perrin's criterion of dissimilarity had built between Jesus and his own Judaism.

According to Sanders,

> Jesus saw himself as God's last messenger before the establishment of the kingdom. He looked for a new order, created by a mighty act of God. In the new order the twelve tribes would be reassembled, there would be a new temple, force of arms would not be needed, divorce would be neither necessary nor permitted, outcasts—even the wicked—would have a place, and Jesus and his disciples—the poor, meek, and lowly—would have the leading role. He had devoted followers who accepted his expectation, made it their own, and remained committed to a transformation of it after his death and resurrection. Further, he had a following among the masses. They were attracted both by his healings and by his message, which promised them a prominent place in the kingdom. Some, impressed by his message and power, saw him as a great figure from Israel's past, some, possibly, as "son of God." (319)

Sanders asserts that Jesus "fits into the general framework of Jewish restoration eschatology" and was "the founder of a group which adhered to the expectations of that theology." He says that "The execution of Jesus as would-be 'king of the Jews' shows us that others thought that he had claimed to be king" (321). Nevertheless, Sanders labels Jesus as "apolitical" in the sense that Jesus had no secular ambitions, had no "plan to liberate and restore Israel by defeating the Romans and establishing an autonomous government" (284-286). Although Sanders does not articulate the thesis that the Jesus of history utilized anti-Roman cryptograms, such a thesis is not incompatible with Sanders' portrayal of Jesus.

A. E. Harvey suggests that the Jesus of history was subject to historical constraints imposed by his own culture just as anyone else is subject to human factors and conventions. In his *Jesus and the Constraints of History*,[5] published three years prior to Sanders' *Jesus and Judaism*, Harvey presents Jesus as a Jew whose lifestyle and teachings are close to the lifestyle and teachings of the Pharisees, but with some significant differences as well. According to Harvey, like the Pharisees, Jesus offered a way of life in which religion would seem relevant to every activity; like them, he based his teaching on the will of God as revealed in the law; like them, he addressed much of his teaching to a public far wider than his immediate followers. But at the same time the differences are striking. On three matters that were of central importance to the Pharisees—a detailed code of observances, a careful selectiveness in the company they kept, and a concern for the authority of the tradition in which they stood—Jesus adopted a radically different stance. (51)

In Harvey's words, Jesus taught in a form that would "enable people to achieve a greater degree of religious commitment and satisfaction in the midst of the routine activities of ordinary life" (47).

Elisabeth Schüssler Fiorenza includes a characterization of Jesus in her feminist theological reconstruction of Christian origins.[6] That characterization is summarized in her words that the praxis and vision of Jesus and his movement is best understood as an inner-Jewish renewal movement that presented an alternative option to the dominant patriarchal structures rather than an oppositional formation rejecting the values and praxis of Judaism.

For Fiorenza, the patriarchal structures of oppression of the time of the Jesus of history included the Roman occupation of Galilee and Judea, but she does not focus her attention on the Roman forces. In spite of her careful avoidance of anti-Jewish statements, she does not concentrate on the most obvious center of male-dominated oppression of Jews, of Jesus, and of the early Christian movement, namely, the Roman military occupation forces in the eastern Mediterranean area. Certainly these forces were androcentric. In her analysis of the response of Jesus to the oppressive patriarchal-androcentric structures that Jesus faced, she says that

> Jesus' proclamation does not address critically the structures of oppression. It implicitly subverts them by envisioning a different future and different human relationships on the grounds that all persons in Israel are created and elected by the gracious goodness of Jesus' Sophia-God. Jesus and his movement set free those who are dehumanized and in bondage to evil powers, thus implicitly subverting economic or patriarchal-androcentric structures, even though the people involved in this process might not have thought in terms of social structures. (142).

Leonard Swidler in *Yeshua: A Model for Moderns*[7] continues in the "third quest" trend of insistence on the Jewishness of Jesus. For Swidler,

> Yeshua was a Jew, and an observant one, that is, he was committed to the keeping of the Law in the way that seemed best to him. Since he was a "rabbi," he taught others to do likewise. In brief, he did not come to dispense with or do away with the Torah, the Law. He came to carry it out. (44)

In agreement with Phillip Segal,[8] Swidler states that

Yeshua, far from being in intense opposition to the forerunners of the Yavneh rabbis and subsequent Rabbinic Judaism, was very like them, close to them, one of them, perhaps even a colleague in his youth of the founder of Rabbinic Judaism, Yohanan ben Zakkai.[9]

Although Swidler believes that "Yeshua had taught his followers to live a life that was intensely, interiorly, and in prophet-like concern for the oppressed, faithful to God's Torah" (15), Swidler does not pursue the issue of specific ways in which the Jesus of history may have expressed his "prophet-like concern for the oppressed."

Utilizing a synthesis of social anthropology, Greek and Roman history, and literary analysis of specific pronouncements, anecdotes, confessions, and interpretations of Jesus, John Dominic Crossan in *The Historical Jesus: The Life of a Mediterranean Jewish Peasant*,[10] concludes that the Jesus of history was a peasant Jewish Cynic. Interpreting Jesus "against the background of inclusive rather than exclusive Judaism," Crossan locates Jesus in a "peasant, oral, and popular philosophical praxis" involving "a way of looking and dressing, of eating, living, and relating that announced its contempt for honor and shame, for patronage and clientage" (421).

According to Crossan,

> (Jesus') work was among the farms and villages of Lower Galilee. His strategy, implicitly for himself and explicitly for his followers, was the combination of free healing and common eating, a religious and economic egalitarianism that negated alike and at once the hierarchical and patronal normalcies of Jewish religion and Roman power. And, lest he himself be interpreted as simply the new broker of a new God, he moved on constantly, settling down neither at Nazareth nor Capernaum. He was neither broker nor mediator but, somewhat paradoxically, the announcer that neither should exist between humanity and divinity or between humanity and itself. Miracle and parable, healing and eating were calculated to force individuals into unmediated physical and spiritual contact with God and unmediated physical and spiritual contact with one another. He announced, in other words, the brokerless kingdom of God. (421–422)

Of all of the portrayals of the Jesus of history that are examined in this survey, Crossan's Jesus of history comes closest to what is described above as putting all available data into a computer and programming the computer with computer-programmed programs. In this instance, the result is good. Nevertheless, the picture is still incomplete. There is still much data that is not included.

In *Jesus: A New Vision*,[11] as well as in his earlier *Conflict, Holiness and Politics in the Teaching of Jesus*,[12] Marcus J. Borg identifies Jesus as "a charismatic healer or 'holy person,' a subversive sage who undermined conventional wisdom and taught an alternative wisdom, a social prophet, and an initiator of a movement the purpose of which was the revitalization of Israel."[13]

According to Borg, Jesus was both a religious and political figure; he was both "deeply spiritual and deeply political."[14] In his words,

> Jesus' attitude toward Rome was not based on an apolitical stance, but on the conviction that in the political affairs of the world the judging activity of God was at work. Regarding his own society, he was intensely political in the sense which we have given to that term: he was concerned about the institutions and historical dynamic of Israel. The means which he used, including public revolutionary gestures, challenged current practice. The end which he sought was the transformation of the cultural dynamic of the quest for holiness into a cultural dynamic which would conform Israel to God's merciful activity.[15]

Thus, the picture of Jesus provided by Borg is congruent with the core of the first basic thesis of this present study, that Jesus had a strong desire for liberation from Roman political, economic, and social oppression. The coded messages of hope and liberation that form the center of the second thesis of this study could be included in what Borg depicts as "public revolutionary gestures" in the quotation cited above, even though that is not specifically Borg's intention. Such gestures were, of course, not revolutionary in the sense of advocating armed rebellion but revolutionary as a subtle means of giving hope to oppressed people.

Richard A. Horsley[16] suggests that Jesus shared with many other Jews of his time the perspective that soon God would judge the oppressive imperial rule of Rome and give dominion to God's people Israel. Moreover, Jesus was "convinced that God had already inaugurated the time of renewal and fulfillment" that would "end the spiral of violence as well as liberate and renew Israel."[17] Since God had begun to implement the political revolution that would remove the Roman presence, Jesus felt called to "proceed with the social revolution thus made possible by God's rule, to begin the transformation of social relations in anticipation of the completion of the political revolution" that only God could accomplish (324). The exorcisms that Jesus performed were indications that "Satan and the demonic forces were being defeated. Insofar as all historical conflict would be comprehended in the perspective of the struggle against Satan, since Satan was now being defeated, the days of Roman domination were numbered, and broader societal liberation and renewal were now possible" (190). Jesus, along with those who had composed the Qumran literature, envisioned the struggle between God and demonic forces as occurring on "three distinguishable but closely interrelated levels." The first level involved "the superhuman, divine-demonic world between God and

Satan." The second level was the level of "the people and their historical situation." The third level involved "the hearts of individual persons" (186).

In the Introduction to his first volume of *A Marginal Jew: Rethinking the Historical Jesus,*[18] John P. Meier lists some aspects of his current perception of Jesus. The following excerpt from his listing provides the general framework:

> Jesus, the poor layman turned prophet and teacher, the religious figure from rural Galilee without credentials, met his death in Jerusalem at least in part because of his clash with the rich aristocratic urban priesthood. To the latter, a poor layman from the Galilean countryside with disturbing doctrines and claims was marginal both in the sense of being dangerously antiestablishment and in the sense of lacking a power base in the capital. He could be easily brushed aside into the dustbin of death. (9)

The word "marginal" serves well as a unifying factor for Meier. Nevertheless, it seems apparent from the Gospel According to Mark that much of what the Jesus of history was saying and demonstrating publicly was what large numbers of his fellow oppressed Jews were also saying and thinking privately. Had he been as obnoxious as Meier depicts him, his movement would most likely have died with him. Perhaps Elaine Pagels' terminology of "dissident Jew"[19] would be preferable as a designation for the Jesus of history to Meier's "marginal Jew." As a "dissident Jew," the Jesus of history would have had the support of large numbers of other "dissident Jews." As a "marginal Jew" he would have had limited popularity and support. As a "dissident Jew," he would have operated within the structures of apocalyptic Judaism, using its symbols and the code words with which apocalyptic dissident Jews communicated. As a "dissident Jew," he could refer cryptically to Caesar or to Caesar's representative as "Satan" or as "the Evil one" and he would be understood by other "dissident Jews."

From the remaining books about the Jesus of history that might be included in this survey I have selected four: George Wesley Buchanan's *Jesus: The King and His Kingdom,*[20] Klaus Wengst's *Pax Romana and the Peace of Jesus Christ,*[21] A. Roy Eckardt's *Reclaiming the Jesus of History: Christology Today,*[22] and Richard A. Horsley, *Jesus and Empire: The Kingdom of God and the New World Disorder.*[23] I have placed these last in the survey because, in my opinion, of all of these books they come closest to the two theses of this present study.

George Wesley Buchanan's Jesus of history is a zealous political figure carefully designing plans and positioning himself to seize power at the opportune moment. He is far from the "marginal Jew" of John P. Meier. Instead, according to Buchanan, the parables and other sayings that have survived and been recorded in the Synoptic Gospels traditions indicate that Jesus was a highly committed leader among the Jews who was "pretending to the throne of Israel."[24] According to Buchanan,

Even though Jesus was convinced that God was prepared to give the Kingdom of Heaven to the Jews of his time with him as the new Messiah to sit on David's throne at Jerusalem, it was very important that the Romans not realize that he was at that very time recruiting followers and raising funds to undertake a movement that would evict the Romans from power. Therefore this movement had to be undertaken as quietly as possible without attracting undue attention from the Roman leaders until he was prepared to handle all the resistance they would provide. How could this be done? Somehow he had to be able to talk to mixed groups in such a way as to appear innocent to the Romans and their collaborators while at the same time communicating something more to those Jews whom he wanted to arouse to follow him. This was not difficult to do in relationship to the well-trained sectarians who were acquainted with the secret codes. This secret knowledge and these code terms were evidently taught as part of a catechism. To some groups it was called "the mysteries of the Kingdom of God" (Matt 13:11; Lk 8:10; Gospel of Thomas 62). (200–201)

Although I am not attracted to Buchanan's characterization of Jesus as a zealous political figure who was carefully designing plans and positioning himself to seize power, I agree fully with Buchanan's explanations of the use by the Jesus of history of coded forms of expression.

Klaus Wengst is well aware of the use of coded forms of expression directed against Rome and Roman power in Jesus' public proclamation,[25] as well as in the letters of Paul (78–79), in Mark 5:1-15 and its parallels in the Synoptic tradition (66), and in the book of Revelation (123–124). With regard to Jesus, he states that.

implicitly the central content of his (Jesus') proclamation, the imminence of the kingdom of God, amounts to a questioning of the Pax Romana: anyone who prays for the coming of the kingdom of God, expects it very soon, and sees the sign of its dawning in his own action has no faith in the imperial good tidings of a pacified world and human happiness in it; he does not regard this situation as the peace that God wants, but is certain that it will soon end. Such a basic attitude must not only be inferred from the confrontation between the kingdom of God proclaimed by Jesus and the reality of the Pax Romana; it is also attested by his explicit attitude to this peace. (55)

By addressing the Pax Romana from the perspective of the ordinary people who had to endure Roman rule rather than of the few in the upper economic stratum who benefitted so greatly from it, Wengst elucidates the "peace of Jesus Christ." Wengst does not separate the Jesus of history from the experience of other oppressed Jews living in Galilee and Judea. His presentation clearly supports the first basic thesis of this present work, that the Jesus of history had not only a deep longing for eternal life, but also a strong desire for liberation from Roman oppression.

According to A. Roy Eckardt, the Jesus of history was a "champion of Israel,"[26] a man who concerned himself with the total welfare and power of his people, and in the end gave his life for their sake. Eckardt expresses most succinctly three problems inherent in the Newer Testament, problems that more than any other factors have induced me to write both a previous work[27] and this present study, namely that

> First, implicitly as well as explicitly, the Apostolic Writings minimize the stark truth that the Eretz Yisrael (Land of Israel) of the time is under tyrannical foreign occupation, a tyranny that the Jewish people are, in fact, resisting and a situation that is productive of much popular unrest. The Jewish resistance to Roman oppression, centering in Jerusalem and Judea, extends across all segments of society. The Pharisees are often in the forefront, but the priesthood is involved as well. There are conditions of constant crisis. Thousands are slaughtered. Jesus' cross is one of hundreds, perhaps thousands. Second is the marked tendentiousness of the Apostolic Writings, especially in the matter of Jesus' trial and death. The Gospels were put together in their present form a full generation and more after the death of Jesus. They reflect apologetic interests and missionary designs vis-a-vis the people and even sometimes the leaders of the Roman Empire. A serious consequence of this situation is that the Gospels underplay the conflict that is raging between Rome and the people of Jesus, and they overplay and even distort contentions between the nascent church and the Jewish community. Third and most serious of all, the accounts of Jesus' last days contain historical falsehoods. The Christian evangelists, with their great concern to foster good relations with the Romans, do their best to establish the Jewish "rejection" of Jesus and to set "the Jews" and their leaders against Jesus.[28]

A. Roy Eckardt's statement that "the Gospels underplay the conflict that is raging between Rome and the people of Jesus" should not be limited to the Gospels. It is becoming apparent that most of the Apostolic Writings underplay that conflict. This present study is designed, in part, to identify segments of that conflict that have not been apparent to most Christians for many centuries because much of that conflict is expressed in subtle anti-Roman cryptograms. Most interpreters recognize the anti-Roman cryptograms that are in the Apocalypse because they are so near to the surface there and are so densely concentrated. In other portions of the Newer Testament they are expressed in much more subtle form and in most instances are widely scattered. Actually, we should probably consider the more subtle and widely scattered anti-Roman cryptograms of the New Testament to be superior in quality to the more obvious and densely concentrated expressions in the Apocalypse, since they much more effectively concealed their messages of hope and liberation from the Roman oppressors. Cryptograms that are easily identified by everyone are not good cryptograms. We might even question whether they should be called cryptograms at all!

Eckardt's parallel statement that the Gospels "overplay and even distort contentions between the nascent church and the Jewish community" should apply to the entire Newer Testament and not be limited to the Gospels, as I indicate in *Mature Christianity in the 21ˢᵗ Century*. His statement that "the accounts of Jesus' last days contain historical falsehoods" that have been identified by modern scholarship is the reason that I suggest in *Mature Christianity in the 21ˢᵗ Century* that in sensitive new translations of the Newer Testament into modern vernacular languages we relegate the most vicious anti-Jewish polemic of the Newer Testament to small-print status with appropriate explanations provided. What I suggest there, I have done in my *The New Testament: A New Translation and Redaction*.[29] I have translated with careful sensitivity the texts that include anti-Jewish polemic and the texts that relegate all women to an inferior status. I have printed the most vicious anti-Jewish segments and the portions in which all women are presented as inferior in small-type print status with explanations in footnotes and prefaces. I have rearranged the sequence of the documents as much as possible into the chronological order in which they were developed and written, beginning with 1 Thessalonians and ending with 2 Peter. I have also provided within an appendix to the translation a four year lectionary listing in which there are no texts that include vicious anti-Jewish polemic and no texts in which all women are relegated to inferior positions.

Richard A. Horsley takes his earlier insights several steps farther in his *Jesus and Empire: The Kingdom of God and the New World Disorder*.[30] He urges his readers to notice ways in which the Jesus of history has been "depoliticized" within much of our contemporary study of the Gospel accounts, reducing Jesus to being only "a relatively innocuous religious teacher" (13) who lived within a "depoliticized" Judea and Galilee (9–11) and a "depoliticized" Roman Empire (11–34). He suggests that on and during the days after September 11, 2001 "Americans experienced a rude awakening to a new world disorder" (4). Within the much more debilitating disorder forced upon the oppressed Jews of Galilee and Judea, Jesus condemned Rome and Rome's client rulers and "enacted God's renewal of the people" in the healings and exorcisms that Jesus performed (14). Specifically, Horsley wrote that

> In both his actions and teaching Jesus opposed the Roman imperial order and its effects on subject peoples. In prophetic proclamations and demonstrations directly against the imperial order, Jesus announced that both the Roman imperial rulers and their exploitative Herodian and high-priestly clients in Jerusalem stood under God's judgment. His mission in Galilean and other villages focused on healing the debilitating effects of imperial violence and on renewing the esprit de corps and cooperative spirit in communities disintegrating under the impact of the imperial order. (126)

Thus Horsley expands our understanding of the political and economic situation of disorder in which the Jesus of history acted and spoke and undergirds and strengthens our analysis in the present study of anti-Roman cryptograms in the Newer Testament as hidden transcripts of hope and liberation.

The brief survey here of twelve "third quest" studies that utilize sociological, political, and economic analyses of life in Galilee and Judea during the first century C.E. illustrates the great variety of perceptions of the Jesus of history that exists even when scholars use basically the same resources, operate with similar presuppositions, and employ similar methodologies. It indicates that our access to the Jesus of history, though indirect, is nevertheless considerable. The impact of his life on his closest friends and followers was obviously treasured and shared. His words and actions provided the primary impetus for the communities of faith that produced the Four Gospels and the other Newer Testament writings. Although these writings proclaim the Christ of faith rather than the Jesus of history, there is enough incidental historical information in them—combined with what can be gathered from recent studies such as those surveyed above of the social, political, and economic situation in Galilee and Judea during the first century of the common era—that we can with some confidence reconstruct not the life of the Jesus of history but at least a scenario of the life of the Jesus of history. By a scenario, I mean a brief sketch of Jesus within the social, political, and economic milieu in which Jesus lived.

Such a scenario is presented here. There will be inaccuracies, of course, in every reconstructed scenario of the life of the Jesus of history. Inaccuracies occur even when we attempt to reconstruct scenarios of contemporary or recent people and events. Nevertheless, reconstructed scenarios are helpful, especially when the subject is as important as the Jesus of history.

A Reconstructed Scenario of the Life of the Jesus of History

We can begin this scenario by stating that the Jesus of history and his father Joseph, his mother Mary, his sisters (whose names we do not know) and his brothers James, Joseph, Judas, and Simon[31] were probably busy much of the time producing, gathering, and preparing food for their own use. Like their neighbors, relatives, and friends, they were tilling the soil in small plots in the area immediately around the shelter in which they lived and on the stone-terraced hillsides near their village of Nazareth, growing herbs and vegetables and enough barley and wheat to make bread for their family. In addition, they probably had a few goats to tend and to milk each morning and evening and grape vines and olive and fig trees near their simple dwelling to add some variety to their diet. Most of their time, therefore, was spent in food procurement and preparation.[32] Joseph and his sons also constructed products from wood and from animal skins for their own use and to sell or trade, wherever possible, for a few other personal and family items that they could not make for themselves. [33]

Joseph and, when his sons became of mid-teen age, his sons, including Jesus, sought day labor. Taking woodcrafts that they had made during the many months each year when they were not tilling the soil or harvesting their meager crops, they would travel the few miles to the Roman town of Sepphoris, hoping to be hired at daybreak to earn a Roman coin by day labor, or, failing to obtain that, to sell or trade the best of their woodcrafts. Unfortunately, the days in which they and others might be hired to work in the fields and vineyards of the better lands controlled by the Romans were the same days in which they needed to be working in their own plots of land. Also, any coins that they might obtain from day labor or from selling or trading what they had produced were taken from them periodically by the dreaded tax assessor-collectors among their own people. These tax collectors procured the quantities that the Roman occupation forces required of them, and were permitted to keep whatever they obtained beyond their quotas.[34] Taxes imposed by the Romans were direct taxes collected on a per capita and land basis, as well as indirect taxes "comprised of all the tolls, duties, market taxes, inheritance taxes, and so forth, that could be used to extract even more out of the agrarian and commercial sectors."[35]

It is likely that throughout his childhood the Jesus of history heard his parents and their closest relatives and friends talk about how difficult it was to eke out even a subsistence level of living under such conditions. Since the more they worked the more was taken from them, there was little incentive to do anything beyond the minimum necessary for survival. Only the barest essentials of life were theirs. Everything else that had any market value was converted into coins by the tax collectors in Sepphoris, Tiberias, and Jerusalem, or carted away under supervision by the Roman military to be placed on Roman ships in Caesarea.

Roman justice, a matter of pride for Roman historians and for wealthy and powerful families in the city of Rome itself[36] was of no help at all to Jesus and to the people whom he knew in Galilee. There was no Roman justice when Roman guards accompanied the tax assessor-collectors to the homes of the poor to kill on the spot, or otherwise "persuade" householders who tried to prevent the seizure of their household goods. There was no Roman justice when Roman officers swept through narrow streets and crowded marketplaces on their horses, trampling on young children and aged people who could not get out of their way. There was no Roman justice when Roman soldiers (in violation of Roman military regulations) seized young Jewish women, violated them, and retained those whom they wished for their own use. There was no Roman justice when young Jews who attempted violent retaliation were caught, tortured, and crucified. There was no Roman justice for Jewish religious and political leaders who encouraged within the oppressed the hope that soon they would be free from Roman oppression. When their activity became known to the oppressive forces, particularly in Jerusalem, they too were seized, tortured, and crucified, together with the captured guerrilla fighters, as "rulers of the Jews" and enemies of the Roman State, which indeed they were. Roman justice did not extend to the oppressed Jews of Galilee and Judea.

Jewish religion was a source of hope, but not in its Jerusalem Temple form. The Jerusalem Temple was controlled by Annas, his sons, and his son-in-law Caiaphas, who cooperated fully with the Roman procurator Pontius Pilate. These ruling priests collected the half-shekel tax from male Jews and sold certified sheep and doves at inflated prices to those who wished to maintain the ritual sacrifices. Jewish religion was a source of hope at the family and community level, in private homes and in synagogues in which Torah and Prophetic tradition texts were discussed. Faith in Elohim as Creator and in Adonai as LORD was a significant factor for most Jews. Faith in Elohim as God Transcendent and in Adonai as God Active in history certainly characterized the Jesus of history. With his parents, relatives, and friends he must have discussed the implications of that faith and the options open to him and to other concerned Jews of that time and place. We know enough about the conditions that prevailed that we can list and describe briefly the choices that were available to Jesus and to others of that time and place, from the most passive and frequently taken to the most active and danger-filled.

Options Open to the Jesus of History and to Other Jews in Galilee and Judea at That Time

Most of the people of the land articulated their faith in God in terms of survival for themselves and for their families. They reasoned that there was nothing that they could do about the oppressive Roman presence in their land. Only Adonai could remove the Romans from their land, and that would occur only in Adonai's good time. After all, the Assyrians who had destroyed the Northern Kingdom were no longer a threat to them. The Babylonians who had destroyed Jerusalem had lost their power. The Persians who had controlled the entire area were no longer feared. Neither were the Seleucid Greeks. Eventually, the oppressive Romans would also leave their land. Until then, the most important factor was merely to survive.

Other Jews focused their attention on living their lives in accordance with the directions provided in the Torah. Since they realized that the Torah included large sections of civil code that had been designed for use in a situation of power in which Israelites had control over their own destiny, they had intense discussions over how they could apply these commandments in their own situation of powerlessness that differed so radically from the situation that had prevailed during much of the formative period of the Torah. Surely it was to be expected that Adonai would be pleased that they were trying to live under the present difficult conditions in accordance with the will of Adonai. They chose, therefore, to discuss at great length the appropriate application of the Torah in their daily lives, particularly in their families and in their homes.

Many devout Jews were chagrined by the ways in which their leaders of the Temple priesthood had literally sold out to the Romans their responsibilities to Adonai and to the people by cooperating fully with the Romans. Some of these devout Jews withdrew from Jerusalem and from other cities and towns and formed new communities in the desolate wilderness of Judea in which, they reasoned, they would have less contact with the oppressive Romans. They renounced the acquisition of personal property. They emphasized prayer and meditation and practiced ritual washings and ritual meals. Some of them returned occasionally to the cities and towns to encourage more active resistance to the Romans and to invite others to join with them in their communal lifestyle.

There were a few young Jews, older teenagers for the most part, who preferred a military solution. Growing up in a situation of violence, they chose violence as their primary response. If the Roman military would violently "rip off" the fruits of their families' labors and violate young women whom they knew and loved, they would retaliate with violence. Against the better judgment of their gravely concerned elders, they would sharpen their daggers and then by stealth approach isolated Roman guards on night watches. In some instances, they were successful, but only for the moment. If the Romans could catch them, they either killed these guerrilla fighters on the spot or tortured them nearly to the point of death and then crucified them. If the Romans could not catch them, the Romans seized a random number of older men from the area and killed them in front of their families, or tortured and crucified them. At times, according to Luke 13:1-2, Pilate even mingled the blood of Jewish men with the blood of animals that they were sacrificing. The option of violence was an active and danger-filled response. Most Jewish parents tried in every way possible to deter their sons from this course of action.

There were a few then, as there are a few in every oppressed society, who reasoned that "If you cannot beat them, join them!" Eventually the oppressors will go away, they thought. Until that time, they might as well use the system to their own advantage.[37] This also was an active and danger-filled response. The Roman oppressors did not fully trust these opportunists. Even though they forced them to submit fully to their authority and power, they realized that the opportunists were indeed opportunists and were never totally loyal to Rome. If the opportunists pledged loyalty to Rome and later broke that pledge, the lives of the opportunists were gravely endangered. The oppressed people, fully aware that the opportunists were adding to their oppression by cooperating with the Romans, treated the opportunists with contempt, avoiding social contact with them.

Even decades after the crucifixion of Jesus, when the Synoptic Gospels were composed, the opportunists were called "sinners" (*hamartoloi*), and were sharply contrasted to the "righteous" (*dikaioi*) oppressed.[38] As chief tax collectors and as the Temple hierarchy, these opportunists had to pay heavily in advance to the Romans for the privilege of being the chief tax collector in an area or of being in charge of the Temple operations. Having purchased these privileges, and repurchasing the privileges periodically, the opportunists were less subject to Roman taxation, and they were not accountable to the oppressed people of the land in their use of funds. As a result, the Chief Priest in the Temple and the chief tax collectors could become relatively rich, which was their reward for their complicity with the Romans. Nevertheless, the riches of these opportunists were never secure, since the poor oppressed people from whom their riches had been gleaned often tried to recapture what had been taken from them. Therefore, the chief tax collectors and the Chief Priest had to employ security guards to help them to protect their wealth. They could hire Roman soldiers, but Roman soldier security guards were expensive. As a result, they employed poor people from the ranks of the oppressed, even though they could not fully trust most of them.

The writers of the Gospel accounts call these security guards who were said to have talked with John the Baptizer and those who seized Jesus in the Garden of Gethsemane "a crowd with swords and clubs" (Mark 14:43; Matthew 26:47) and "soldiers" (Luke 3:14; John 18:3, 12), but today we would label them "goons." The opportunist Chief Priest and the chief tax collectors knew that if there were a revolt by the oppressed people that was initially successful, then the opportunists would be killed along with the Roman oppressors with whom they cooperated. Truly this opportunism was an active and danger-filled response to the political situation in Galilee and Judea.

One more active and danger-filled response can be identified in this scenario. It included elements from some of the other responses in that it provided hope for the people. It was a survival response. It drew heavily from the Jewish religious tradition. It included elements of prayer, meditation, ritual washings and ritual meals. Although it was a non-violent response, it risked violence at all times. Those who chose this option refused to cooperate with the

Roman oppressors, but they directly addressed their fellow Jews who did. This was the option taken by John the Baptizer, by the Jesus of history, and certainly by others before and after their time. It was the option taken by most Jewish messiah figures. Each, of course, exercised this option in an individual and unique way. Those who chose this option but failed to build enthusiasm among the masses of the oppressed soon faded into oblivion. Those who were successful in bringing to their fellow oppressed Jews the hope that soon Adonai rather than the Romans would be ruling over them were identified by the Romans or their surrogate rulers as a threat to their security. When this occurred, the Romans and their surrogates always seized, tortured, and killed these leaders from among the oppressed people in horrible ways, most commonly by public crucifixion, as a proven effective deterrent to discourage other Jews from assuming similar leadership roles.

Josephus in *The Jewish War* 2, 241, and 253 stated that the Roman procurators ordered the crucifixion of large numbers of Jews outside the walls of Jerusalem for the crime of rebellion against Roman authority. Such rebellion could be either overt military action as a guerrilla fighter or leader of a band of brigands, or relatively covert when religious and political figures such as Theudas, the prophet-redeemer from Egypt, and John the Baptizer criticized the Romans and their surrogates and gathered oppressed Jews into religious communities whose goals included political as well as religious liberation. As Ellis Rivkin puts it,

> Josephus chose Theudas and the Egyptian false prophet out of a seething prophetic brew. They were but two examples of the charismatics who flourished alongside the dagger wielding Fourth Philosophers, also called the Sicarii.[39]

Josephus gives us a feeling for the kind of chaos and anarchy that was prevalent and the kind of emotional and psychological disorientation that followed in its wake. He was not concerned with cataloguing an exhaustive list of charismatics. He selected a Theudas here, an Egyptian false prophet there as illustrative examples. He felt no need to name every prophet-like figure who stirred the people with visions of redemption.[40]

The Jesus of History As a Jewish Messiah Figure with a Religious-Political Agenda

During the past nineteen centuries, most Christians have shown little interest in the Jesus of history. They have been so involved with the Christ of faith apart from the Jesus of history that Jesus as a Jew, and especially Jesus as a Jewish messiah figure who was fully involved in the lives and concerns of his fellow

Jews in Galilee and in Judea, is a foreigner to them. Christians of my own Lutheran tradition with its "Two Kingdoms" theology and Christians living within the U.S.A. where the "Separation of Church and State" is a highly-valued dictum find it particularly difficult to understand that when John the Baptizer and the Jesus of history spoke about "The Kingdom of God" they and their fellow Jewish people with whom they were speaking were not making the same distinctions between the religious and the political realms that we try to maintain.

For so many generations we have been told that in the church—and most of all in the pulpit—we must never say anything political that many of us cannot imagine that Jesus himself might have addressed the political situation of his time. Many Christians today, especially in the U.S.A., reject the idea that Jesus and John the Baptizer might have spoken both privately and publicly against the Romans and against Roman rule in Galilee and Judea. When we add to this the fact that those who composed the documents that we call the Newer Testament expressed their anti-Roman thoughts and feelings in written form almost entirely in hidden transcripts that would not further jeopardize Christian lives within the totalitarian Roman State, we begin to understand how difficult it is for most relatively affluent Christians today, especially within the U.S.A. and other "First World" nations, to realize that the Jesus of history expressed himself in words of hope for political as well as religious liberation.[41]

Christians who have some familiarity with Jews and with Jewish worship practices, in which there are fewer distinctions between the religious and the political, are in a better position than other Christians to appreciate the political as well as the religious stance of the Jesus of history. Christians who have some awareness of daily life in Latin America, Africa, Asia, and other areas of poverty and oppression and of the Liberation Theologies that have been developed in those contexts have an additional very important resource that helps them to understand the political situation of the Jesus of history and of his followers.

During the years since the first edition of this present study was written, there has been a significant increase in the number of biblical scholars who realize that the message of the Jesus of history, while primarily religious, had very important political connotations.[42]

Many of these writers indicate that Jesus undoubtedly used words such as "Satan," "the Devil," and "the Evil One" that had what might be considered a religious referent as their primary meaning, but also had political connotations, especially for oppressed people living under near-totalitarian conditions. It is probable that Jesus also used more secular terms such as "pigs," "swine," and "wild beasts" in referring to military representatives of Roman rulers and "that fox" in reference to Herod Antipas. Certainly under those conditions his references to "the Kingdom of God" were political as well as religious. We are reaching the point at which we will realize that if the Jesus of history had not been anti-Roman in the political situation of Galilee and Judea of his time he would not have had the popularity that he experienced among the common oppressed people of the land and he would not have been crucified by order of the Roman prefect Pontius Pilate. This is consistent with criteria 1–3 as designated on pages 17-18 above.

It is not the contention of this present study that the Jesus of history was so involved in the political liberation of his fellow oppressed Jews in Galilee and Judea that he would have been perceived primarily as a political figure. He was first, last, and always primarily a religious leader in the tradition of the classic Israelite prophets such as Amos, Micah, and Jeremiah. The public proclamations of Amos, Micah, and Jeremiah that addressed political issues were probably made more explicitly than those of Jesus, because each of these three spoke in lands that were not directly occupied by a strong foreign power. The messages of Amos, Micah, and Jeremiah were more negatively critical of economically oppressive Israelite rulers than was the message of the Jesus of history. Because Israelite rule in Israel and in Judah was less totalitarian than the rule of the Romans in Galilee and in Judea, it was not as necessary for Amos, Micah, and Jeremiah to express their messages in the form of cryptograms as it was for the Jesus of history.

The use of hidden transcripts of hope and liberation was utilized by Ezekiel and others who like Ezekiel functioned in situations of direct foreign rule. The use of hidden transcripts is one of the characteristics of apocalyptic communications, the uncovering of a message to the understanding of the oppressed in a way that will not be apparent to the oppressors. Just as Amos, Micah, Jeremiah, and Ezekiel were primarily religious leaders rather than political figures, so also was the Jesus of history. A religious leader who expresses a message of hope and liberation to heavily oppressed people and who does this to a large number of people over a significant period of time is also a political leader. There have been prime examples of this during the past three centuries, especially among African-Americans in the U.S.A. and among native Africans in the Union of South Africa, Namibia, and Botswana.

In addition, it is not likely that everything that Jesus said had political connotations. It is sufficient to surmise that some of Jesus' sayings and parables included words that for perceptive oppressed people would have more than one possible meaning, one of which would be a cryptic message of hope and liberation. Of course, not all of Jesus' sayings and parables have been transmitted to us. Nevertheless, there are many sayings and parables of Jesus and stories about Jesus that were transmitted and further developed within the

Four Gospels traditions that appear to contain such double meanings and that can more adequately be understood as having such meanings. Such accounts are of interest in this present study. The intended meanings of many of these accounts will be reclaimed when we become aware of the cryptograms within them.

In the Synoptic Gospels, the memory is preserved that the Jesus of history functioned as a prophet similar in many respects to the classic Israelite prophets. We are aware that the classic Israelite prophets were religious leaders whose critical messages of judgment and hope had political connotations. Because Jesus is perceived by Christians as being much more than a prophet, as the divine and even pre-existent Son of God, it has been much more difficult to subject the message of Jesus to the same kind of scrutiny that has been applied to the messages of Israelite prophets such as Amos, Micah, Jeremiah, and Ezekiel. Nevertheless, the time has come in which such analysis can be done, as the writings of George Wesley Buchanan, Klaus Wengst, A. Roy Eckardt, Richard A. Horsley, Warren Carter, and most of the other scholars cited in note 42 above indicate.

The thesis that the message and stance of the Jesus of history, while primarily religious, also had political connotations helps us to understand many difficult texts in the Four Gospels. For example, we can see more clearly the reason that the mother of Jesus and his brothers are reported in Mark 3:20-35 to have been so anxious and apprehensive about what Jesus was doing that they walked from Nazareth to Capernaum to urge him, even to implore him, to return to his home and to cease being a public figure. The mother of the Jesus of history was understandably concerned about his safety when she learned that he was proclaiming publicly that soon Adonai rather than Caesar would be ruling over the oppressed Jews of Galilee and Judea. She was well aware that if he continued to do this he would soon be killed by the Roman authorities. They would not tolerate his message that the Kingdom of God would soon replace the present evil age of Roman sovereignty, and that every Jew in Galilee and Judea should repent of any thought or action of cooperation with the oppressors.

If Jesus was indeed moving from place to place from his base in Capernaum, proclaiming and demonstrating with his life that soon his fellow Jews would be free from Roman oppression, we should not be surprised that the mother and brothers of Jesus wanted so urgently to take him home. They would have been especially concerned because of the amazement and excitement of large numbers of Jesus' fellow young Jews who, according to the Mark 1:28–3:20 texts, were gathering closely around him.

It was not that Jesus' mother and brothers did not agree with what he was saying,[43] since it is probable that he was saying basically what his parents, their closest friends, and many other Jews who were heavily oppressed by the Roman occupation forces in Galilee and Judea were saying privately. The difference was that Jesus was saying and doing these things publicly and with a significant response. The crowds were amazed by his courage. His fame and reputation were spreading throughout the entire region of Galilee (Mark 1:28). People were coming to him from every direction (Mark 1:45). Very soon, the mother of Jesus feared, the Roman authorities would close in on him and he would be seized, tortured, and stretched out on a Roman cross! She had every reason to be anxious and apprehensive.

Not only Mark, but the other Synoptic Gospel accounts as well testify amply to the success that the Jesus of history had when he proclaimed his message of hope and liberation among his own oppressed people. When he urged his fellow Jews to turn from any cooperation with the oppressive occupation forces (except for payment under duress of the heavy taxes imposed on them) and to return to unconditional faith in Adonai within the best of their religious tradition, huge crowds of people heard him gladly, but with amazement and apprehension because of their fear of the Romans. That the Jesus of history was aware that as a Jewish messiah figure with a message that obviously had political connotations he was in constant danger of being seized, tortured, and crucified is clear from the accounts that indicate that as the crowds increased in size he proclaimed his message for the most part in desolate, remote areas where the Roman occupation forces were less likely to see what was happening. We realize that John the Baptizer had also proclaimed his message of judgment and hope in desolate areas for similar reasons, to extend the time as long as possible before Herod Antipas would order that he be seized. For the same reason, the Jesus of history repeatedly dismissed the crowds when they became so large that their presence would be brought to the attention of the Romans.[44] He wanted to share his message of hope and liberation with as many of his fellow oppressed Jews as possible before the Romans would end his proclamation and his life. That he was not afraid to be tortured and crucified is apparent in his decision to go to Jerusalem to proclaim there in the center of Jewish nationalism and Roman occupational power the same message of hope and liberation that he was proclaiming and demonstrating in Galilee. From the content of the Synoptic accounts it is likely that Jesus believed that while he was proclaiming and demonstrating the power of his message in Jerusalem with healings and exorcisms the Lord God would act in some wondrous way to redeem Israel from Roman oppression.

We see within the Synoptic Gospel accounts that as a Jewish messiah figure the Jesus of history had what we might call a dual mission. The first was a highly successful mission among many of his fellow oppressed Jews, who in the words of the Luke 15:3–7 parable were depicted as the ninety-nine sheep who were safe in the wilderness and needed no repentance. The other was a high-risk and only occasionally successful mission among the few relatively affluent Jews, affluent because they cooperated with the Roman occupation forces. His most notable success here was with a few tax collectors such as Levi (Matthew) and the Lukan Zacchaeus, and perhaps with a few prostitutes. When these "sinners,"[45] (given that designation by their fellow Jews because they cooperated with the Romans) repented and rejoined their oppressed families, there was great joy among the oppressed.[46] There was also great risk to the lives of these "sinners" who repented. A chief tax collector who broke a contract and pledge with the Romans might be sought out by the Romans and killed. A lower level tax collector might escape this fate if accountable only to a fellow Jewish tax collector. A prostitute who was considered to be desirable and who broke away from the grasp of Roman military personnel would be in danger of being seized again and even more severely mistreated by them. The Jesus of history, as a Jewish messiah figure who was urging these "sinners" to repent, risked severe retaliation by the Romans. The more successful he was in each aspect of his dual mission the greater was the danger to his life. Oppressors in every time and place are concerned, even paranoid, about serious threats to their positions and to their security. It is not surprising, therefore, that Jesus' mother was anxious and apprehensive and wanted him to return to private life in Nazareth.

The remainder of the account of the life of the Jesus of history as a Jewish messiah figure can be summarized briefly. After Jesus had proclaimed his message of hope and liberation in the areas of Galilee and surrounding regions in which Jews lived, he determined to go also to Jerusalem. His followers begged him not to go to Jerusalem as a public messiah figure because of the danger to his life and to theirs. He went to Jerusalem in spite of their fears and objections (Mark 8:31–38; 9:31; 10:32–34). In Jerusalem he proclaimed the same message that he had proclaimed in the northern regions. Annas, Caiaphas, and other members of the Temple hierarchy, who held their positions only because they were pledged to cooperate with Pontius Pilate and were far removed in lifestyle from the masses of oppressed Jews in Galilee and Judea, were fearful that there would be a revolt. They readily agreed with Pilate that what Jesus was saying and doing was a threat to their own security (Mark 14:l; Matthew 26:34; Luke 22:2; John 18:13–14).

Caiaphas, therefore, ordered some of the more trusted "goons," whom he employed to protect him and his wealth from his own people, to bring Jesus into custody so that they could deliver him over into the hands of Pilate (Mark 14:43). One of Jesus' followers, Judas Iscariot, confused, afraid and disillusioned, perhaps inadvertently helped the goons to locate Jesus in the Garden of Gethsemane during the night. During that same night, the Roman military tortured Jesus nearly to the point of death, as they always did to such persons in similar situations. Then the Romans crucified what was left of him publicly, as an example to the other oppressed Jews of what they did to anyone who would be a messiah figure among these conquered people, a "king of the Jews." Jesus' followers wept bitterly over their impotence, because they could not prevent his execution, wishing that he had never come to Jerusalem. A few of them tearfully placed his body[47] in a tomb and rolled the flat stone that sealed the tomb down its grooved path to its intended place.

Most of the Jews who had been given hope of freedom from Roman oppression by the Jesus of history sank back into deep despair after the Roman soldiers had crucified Jesus. Some of his closest followers, however, believed that his life and death had not been in vain, that he had died *for them*, and that God Transcendent had vindicated him by raising him from the dead. For them, and eventually for large numbers of others who had not been Jews, he became in their perception the most significant manifestation of God Active in History and Incarnate, the Christ of faith. This is also my perception.

Jesus' Teaching About the Kingdom of Adonai, Not of Caesar

From the tradition of the Synoptic Gospels, it is apparent that the message and actions of the Jesus of history centered on the person of Adonai and on the symbol of the kingdom of Adonai. Soon, Jesus proclaimed, Adonai and not Caesar would rule over the Jews. The rule of Adonai would be barely visible at first, like things hidden in the ground, like a tiny grain of mustard seed so small that it could scarcely be seen, like Jesus sharing his message initially among a few "believers" in obscure areas of Galilee. When planted in the soil of Israel, however, the rule of Adonai would grow and flourish like a mustard seed into a mighty shrub, so large that the birds of the air (Jewish people moving around like birds in the Diaspora?) would return to build their nests in it (Mark 4:30-32; Matthew 13:31-32; Luke 13:18-19). In a similar analogy, preserved for us in Matthew 13:33 and in Luke 13:20-21, he spoke about the rule of Adonai as still small and hidden, but multiplying and soon to have a noticeable impact, like yeast that a woman has placed into three measures of bread dough. The kingdom of Adonai would expand and multiply. Nothing, not even Caesar's kingdom with its power over almost the entire known world, could prevent the inevitable growth of Adonai's kingdom.[48]

It would not have been necessary for the Jesus of history to make explicit references to Caesar's kingdom with every reference to the kingdom of Adonai. It was sufficient to focus on the kingdom of Adonai in his sayings and parables, for in the political and religious milieu of Galilee and Judea of that time to speak about the kingdom of Adonai to Jews as heavily oppressed by the Roman occupation forces as they were was to speak political as well as religious language. As George Wesley Buchanan puts it, "(Both Jesus and his disciples) wanted the Kingdom of Heaven to come. This involved getting rid of the Romans."[49] According to A. Roy Eckardt, the words, "The time is fulfilled, and the kingdom of God is at hand; repent and believe in the gospel" (Mark 1:14), "plunge us right away into the political arena, since kingdom or reign is a thoroughly political concept."[50] The coming of the kingdom of Adonai, for which Jesus and his fellow oppressed Jews prayed fervently, could not occur until the Roman occupation forces departed. Only those few Jews who cooperated fully with the Romans and were relatively prosperous because of this cooperation would not pray this prayer, or if they would say the words they would mouth them as perfunctorily as many of us as Christians repeat the words "Thy kingdom come" in the Lord's Prayer today.

When it is said within the Israelite traditions that the Lord God "rules," the most common inference is to political, temporal freedom for God's people Israel. God's victory is earthly and experienced in the human realm. It is not simply spiritual or other-worldly. As Jews during the first century of the common era, Jesus and his closest followers would also have understood the "kingdom of Adonai" partially in political, this-worldly ways and not only in spiritual, other-worldly perspectives.

It is apparent from the Gospel accounts that the Jesus of history and his closest followers had deep concerns for the temporal lives of people, for their physical and mental health and stability. Healing accounts abound in the texts. Jesus is said to have had the power of God to resuscitate persons who had died, to restore them to life here in this present world of time and space. It is not likely, therefore, that Jesus would have failed to address the political, economic, and military oppression that caused so much of the suffering that he witnessed. Richard A. Horsley suggests that the healings that Jesus performed were "not simply isolated acts of individual mercy, but part of a larger program of social as well as personal healing," that Jesus was "healing the illnesses brought on by Roman imperialism."[51]

According to the book of Revelation, followers of Jesus within the Johannine community cryptically identified the Roman State as the Great

Harlot, the Beast Rising From the Sea and From the Land, the Devil Himself who was shedding the blood of so many of their members. In Paul's letters and in the epistles written later in his name there are numerous instances in which the words "Satan" and "the Devil" are used in ways that may have been intended as code words for Caesar. We shall see this also in 1 Peter, James, and in the Epistle to the Hebrews. It is likely, therefore, that the Jesus of history in his oral proclamation of the kingdom of Adonai also depicted Satan as active, or even incarnate, in the Roman presence in the land that should carry the name of Adonai alone.

Some of Jesus' parables of the kingdom, especially the parable about the weeds/tares/darnel in Matthew 13:24–30 and the Gospel of Thomas 57 discussed below in this section, seem to have been intended to pertain to the then current political situation of Roman occupation in the land of the good grain. This may represent in a sense the "tip of the iceberg" of such parables, since we can suspect that the majority of the parables of Jesus that had obviously political connotations may have been suppressed, in order to protect the lives of early Christians at the time when collections of Jesus' parables of the kingdom were put into written form.

At any rate, it is increasingly becoming evident in the more objective Christian scholarship on the life of Jesus that the reason that Pontius Pilate gave the order to torture and to crucify Jesus was that he perceived that Jesus and his message were a serious threat to Roman security in Galilee and Judea. It is not likely that Pilate was totally mistaken. Pilate gave the order to torture and to crucify Jesus for political security reasons, not because of Jesus' other-worldly theological statements. Had Jesus been entirely other-worldly in his emphasis, Pilate would have shown no concern. He might even have welcomed Jesus' efforts since then, to use Karl Marx's terminology eighteen centuries later, Jesus would have been providing an opiate for the masses of oppressed people. Jesus would have been deadening their senses with hopes for "a pie in the sky by and by."

Caiaphas and his supporters in the Temple hierarchy also cooperated with Pilate by providing the goons to seize Jesus in the Garden of Gethsemane, not because of Jesus' other-worldly theology, in which they in their privileged positions would have had little interest, but because they too perceived Jesus to be a popular political as well as religious leader among the restless Jewish populace.[52] Simply by using ordinary situations such as sowing and harvesting grain and preparing and baking bread that he and virtually all of the Jewish people of his area experienced regularly, Jesus was able to communicate his message of hope and liberation in cryptic ways that would be clear to those for whom it was intended, but hidden from the oppressive Romans. A sower, he said, probably many times in various regions in Galilee, goes out from his village to sow small strips of grain. Some kernels fall along the footpath, others among the stones of the rock terraces of the hillside, still others among the thorn bushes and thistles along the rocks, and some on the precious good soil. So it was also with the message of the kingdom of Adonai that Jesus was spreading throughout Galilee, punctuating it often with the apocalyptic refrain, "Let those who have ears to hear listen and understand this message of hope." It was probably not necessary for the Jesus of history to explain each time that when he referred to the wild birds that descended to the hillside after the sower had passed and quickly ate the grain that had fallen along the path that he was also referring to the activities of the Roman occupation forces and of the Jewish tax collectors who worked for them.[53]

There is one more parable of the Jesus of history about the kingdom of Adonai, however, that I shall comment upon here before concluding this chapter, and that is the parable about the weeds/tares/darnel (*ta zizania*) growing and remaining among the wheat until the harvest in Matthew 13:24–30 and the Gospel of Thomas 57, with the allegorized explanation in Matthew 13:36–43.

Robert H. Gundry,[54] suggests that on the basis of form critical analysis that Matthew 13:24–30 and 13:36–43 are Matthean compositions in literary form involving conflation of elements. Some are from the parable of the plant growing without human effort (Mark 4:26–29), and others from the parable of the sower who went out to sow his grain (Mark 4:1–20). The portion of the parable about the weeds/tares/darnel growing and remaining among the wheat coheres closely to the parables of the sower and of the mustard seed. Therefore, it is likely that the parables of the sower, of the mustard seed, and this portion of the parable of the weeds/tares/darnel are all based on reminiscences of Jesus' own message. In addition, the inclusion of the parable of the weeds/tares/darnel in the Gospel of Thomas with its somewhat separate existence and development in a shorter and perhaps more primitive form is another reason to consider it here.

The economic problem that is caused by the presence of *ta zizania* in wheat fields has probably been known wherever wheat has been grown, at least until recent times when more pure seed grain has been available. This weed, which in English we represent as tares, darnel, cheat, or chess, has stems that look like wheat stems until the heads of grain appear. It presents serious economic problems for many reasons. It cannot be detected as noticeably different from wheat stalks when both are still small and it would be less difficult to pull up the weeds. It takes up space and moisture that are needed by the wheat, especially in an area such as Israel in which both space and moisture are in short supply.

Finally, it produces an abundance of seeds that are noxious to animals and people. For these reasons, this weed provided a particularly appropriate illustration of the political situation in Galilee and Judea during the time of the public activity of the Jesus of history.

An enemy of the kingdom of Adonai, i.e., of Adonai and of the people of Adonai, had come during the night while the people had been sleeping and not been alert. This enemy had sowed tares/darnel/cheat/chess among the stalks of wheat. This enemy, also called "the devil" in the allegorical interpretation of the parable, is mentioned twice in this Matthean parable. In the context of political oppression in which the Jesus of history lived, it would not have been necessary for him to explain who had come during the night when the Jews had not been alert some ninety years earlier and sowed Roman soldiers among the good people of the land.[55] The identity of the enemy, the Evil One, the Devil whose sons were the tares/darnel/cheat/chess in the land, was well known, even if not often articulated publicly.

We can assume that there was also heated discussion, particularly between teenagers and their parents, over whether Jewish patriots should attempt to root up the noxious weeds by their own efforts. The answer of the Jesus of history to that question is clearly given in the parable. To attempt to root up the Roman military by the Jews' own efforts would result in the death of most of the "wheat." Not now, but soon, Adonai would cause the weeds to be gathered up and bound into bundles and burned. Along with patience and trust in Adonai would come hope and liberation, the certainty of victory.

The time of the obnoxious weeds growing among the wheat was the time of the present age of Roman oppression in the land of Israel within this present world of time and space. The goal was "freedom now," not the dissolution of the universe. The parables of the Jesus of history about the kingdom of Adonai are indications that the Jesus of history and his closest followers were not as "other-worldly" in their thoughts and mission as his later followers in the Christian Church came to be. This parable and the other portions of this chapter are consistent with the first basic thesis of this book and with criteria 1, 2, and 3 as designated on pages 29–30 above.

Conclusions

The conclusions reached during the course of this chapter are as follows. The scenario of the life of the Jesus of history can be reconstructed, not of course with anything like complete accuracy but sufficiently to provide a general background for our study of anti-Roman cryptograms that he may have employed. Among the various options that were available to the Jesus of history and to other Jews of that time, it is apparent that Jesus chose the option of proclaiming the message of hope to his fellow oppressed Jews that soon Adonai rather than the oppressive Romans would be ruling over them. The Jesus of history was a successful Jewish religious and political messiah figure, and his success brought him to the attention of Pilate, who gave the orders that he be seized, tortured, and crucified. The healing activities, the exorcisms, and parables about the coming kingdom of Adonai in Galilee and Judea are indications that Jesus had "this-worldly" as well as "other-worldly" concerns with respect to the plight of his own people. These conclusions support the two basic theses of this book as stated in its Introduction section above and are consistent with criteria 1–5 as stated on pages 17-19 above.

II. Anti-Roman Cryptograms in the Letters of Paul and in Other Pauline Literature

It is as a theologian, even as "the most important reflective theologian in the Newer Testament."[1] that the Apostle Paul is remembered. As a reflective and dynamic theologian, he is said by some to be among the most influential people who have ever lived.[2] Many Christians consider Paul to be the number two founder of Christianity, second only to Jesus. Some Christian scholars and perhaps most Jewish scholars designate Paul as the primary founder and articulator of the Christian faith. Christians generally define Paul as a pastor and writer of letters to nascent Christian house-church communities, a religious leader who was rarely if ever involved in what we might call politics and political affairs. For the most part, this is the way in which the Apostle Paul is remembered and presented when Christians gather for worship and study.

It was a departure from the norm, therefore, when G. B. Caird in his *Principalities and Powers: A Study in Pauline Theology* stated that the concept of principalities and world powers "reaches into every department of Paul's theology."[3] Caird pointed out that "the idea of sinister world powers and their subjugation by Christ is built into the very fabric of Paul's thought, and some mention of them is found in every epistle except Philemon" (viii). Caird cited Paul's references to the rulers of this age who crucified the Lord of Glory (1 Corinthians 2:6). He continued with Satan and the messenger of Satan who twice were mentioned as preventing or limiting the effectiveness of Paul's missionary activity (1 Thessalonians 2:18; 2 Corinthians 12:7). He added also the god of this age who has blinded the minds of those who do not believe (2 Corinthians 4:4), and the world-rulers of this darkness who hold the entire creation in bondage (Romans 8:19-25, 38-39). In addition, as Caird noted, the time will come when every principality and authority and power will yield to Christ (1 Corinthians 15:24) and every tongue in the heavenly places, on the earth, and under the earth will confess that Jesus Christ is Lord and every knee will bend to him (Philippians 2:10-11). Caird was interested also in what Paul and his followers meant by the elemental spirits of the world (Galatians 4:3; Colossians 2:8, 20), the ruler of the authority of the air (Ephesians 2:2), the world-rulers of this darkness (Ephesians 6:12), and the thrones, lordships, principalities, and authorities (Colossians 1 :16; 2: 10) (vii-x).

In Caird's opinion, the principalities and powers that crucified Jesus were both human and superhuman. Behind the Roman State and its representatives were angelic rulers, spiritual beings who shared with their human agents the responsibilities for their actions. It was for this reason, according to Caird, that Paul identified these powers as Satan and as representatives of Satan (15-7).[4]

I fully agree with Caird that the principalities and powers that crucified Jesus were Pontius Pilate, Herod Antipas, and Caiaphas. I agree also that the powers that Paul mentioned in 1 Thessalonians 2:18 and 2 Corinthians 12:7 as hindering him in his missionary work were the Roman State and its representatives. I can also say with Caird that for Paul, as the texts in question indicate, behind the Roman State and its representatives were angelic rulers, spiritual beings who shared with their human agents the responsibilities for their actions.

I go a step beyond Caird, however, with regard to the reason that Paul identified these powers as Satan and as representatives of Satan. It seems apparent to me that Paul used the general terms "principalities and powers" to refer to those who had crucified Jesus, rather than using the specific names of Pontius Pilate, Herod Antipas, and Caiaphas, because at that time it was prudent to avoid use of the actual names. I think that Paul referred to those who were hindering him in his missionary work as "Satan" and as "a messenger of Satan" rather than as the Roman State and as specific representatives of the Roman State. I think that Paul did this because it was absolutely essential that he use code words in communicating in writing something that negative about civil authorities within a totalitarian state.

The code words chosen by Paul ("Satan" and "a messenger of Satan") are indications that to Paul certain representatives of the Roman State, specifically zealous advocates of Roman Civil Religion, were "satanic." Paul thought that they were influenced by evil spiritual beings. These representatives of Roman power hindered Paul in his missionary activity.

That does not mean, however, that Paul was opposed to the Roman State when the Emperor and the Empire functioned properly as agents, under God, for the preservation of stability and order. Then, as most notably in Romans 13:1–7, Paul could urge his fellow early followers of Jesus to obey the laws of the Romans, to be subject to the governing authorities. Paul opposed certain Romans, not all Romans. Unfortunately for us and for our understanding of the situation at that time, Paul could not explain in writing which Romans he opposed and the reasons for his opposition to them. He used code words such as "Satan" and "a messenger of Satan" because these words would communicate what he wanted to say to his followers. If zealous advocates of Roman Civil Religion intercepted his writings, they would think that Paul had been writing about evil spiritual beings, not about themselves, when he used the word "Satan."

To take this argument one step farther, I shall suggest in this chapter that, as Caird noted, Paul and some of the later Pauline writers linked thrones, lordships, principalities, and other authorities together (Colossians 1:16; 2:10). Paul wrote about persons above the earth, on the earth, and under the earth worshiping the Risen Christ (Philippians 2:10–11). Paul wrote this because for Paul evil spiritual beings shared with their human agents the responsibilities for their actions. I shall suggest that Paul and the others did this to protect themselves and other early Christians from additional persecution by specific persons associated with the Roman State, while at the same time they were communicating important messages of hope for freedom from Roman oppression. By expanding the group of those against whom Paul and the others were writing to include spiritual beings not limited to this world, Paul and the others made their writings appear to be much less "political" than they actually were. By making their writings appear to be entirely "religious," they protected themselves, their intended readers, and the hidden transcripts from detection by their enemies.

Walter Wink defines the principalities and powers as "the inner and outer aspects of any given manifestation of power." He considers the inner aspect to be the "spirituality of institutions," the "inner essence of outer organizations of power." The outer aspect is the "political systems, appointed officials," all the "tangible manifestations which power takes." He says that the New Testament writers and their contemporaries depicted the principalities and powers in some instances as if they were "*these* centurions or *that* priestly hierarchy, and then, with no warning, as if they were some kind of spiritual entities in the heavenly places."[5]

Wink thinks that most people in antiquity "regarded the spiritual Powers as non-material, invisible, heavenly entities with specific characteristics or qualities." He says that these "Powers" were perceived to have been "the good creations of a good God." Since some of these creations were perceived to have rebelled against God and consequently to have "fallen," the ancients called some of those "Powers" angels, gods, and spirits, and others demons and devils (104).

From his perspective in the final decades of the twentieth century, however, Wink prefers to depict these principalities and powers, as stated above, as "the inner or spiritual essence, or gestalt, of an institution or state or system." In Wink's words, Satan is best described as the "actual power that congeals around collective idolatry, injustice, or inhumanity." For Wink, these principalities and powers "do not, then...have a separate, spiritual existence"

(104–5). He suggests that "If pressed, Paul would probably have readily conceded that spiritual forces did lie behind the Roman Empire. But when he wrote Rom. 13:1, he apparently was *at that moment* focusing on just those human authorities whom he describes later in the paragraph as wielding the sword and collecting taxes" (106).

Neil Elliott, using reader response methodologies, asks "how Paul's letters would have been heard by persons living under Roman rule" and notes that "Once we abandon the unwarranted and anachronistic assumption that Paul was opposed primarily to 'Judaism,' it may be possible to discern that he not only carried out his mission in the context of the Roman imperial world, but in preaching the gospel of Jesus Christ, was also opposing primarily the Roman imperial gospel of 'peace and security'"[6]

Before we move to a study of specific texts in which Paul and later Pauline writers may have employed anti-Roman cryptograms, it is important that we look briefly at what can be known of the circumstances of the final period of Paul's life. This is essential because, to have been killed in a state-sanctioned execution, Paul must have appeared to be a political threat to some persons who were associated with the Roman State and were in positions of power.

The task of recovering the circumstances of the final period of Paul's life is extraordinarily difficult. As Alan F. Segal expresses it, "Although we have considerable writings from Paul, his biography is incompletely known."[7]

The New Testament documents provide no direct record of his execution, nor of the circumstances that precipitated it. The reticence of these early Christian writers in this regard is itself evidence that the execution was political, that Paul was in some significant way perceived to have been a political threat to certain powerful persons associated with the Roman State.

One of the best summary evaluations of what we can know about Paul's life and the circumstances that preceded his execution is provided by Helmut Koester.[8] Only the final portion of Koester's reconstituted chronological summary can be cited here.

> Winter, 54–55: Ephesian imprisonment; writing of correspondence with Philippi, Philemon, and the letter preserved in 2 Corinthians 10–13.

> Summer, 55: Travel through Macedonia to Corinth; writing of the letter preserved in 2 Cor 1:1–2: 13; 7:5–16 and the collection letters, i.e., 2 Corinthians 8 and 9.

> Winter, 55-56: Stay in Corinth; writing of the letter to the Romans.

> 56: Travel to Jerusalem (Acts 20); preparations for the transfer of the collection Acts 21:15ff.); imprisonment of Paul

56–58: Imprisonment in Caesarea.

58: Replacement of Felix by Festus; Paul is sent to Rome.

58–60: Roman imprisonment (Acts 28:30).

60: Martyrdom of Paul.[9]

It should be noted, however, that Koester's chronological summary is heavily dependent on two suppositions that are questionable. One is that the letter of Paul to the Romans is the composition of Paul that we have that was written in closest proximity to the time of his execution. The other is that Acts of Apostles[10] can be used as reliable historical evidence for events that preceded the martyrdom of Paul.

Both suppositions employed by Koester also put too much emphasis on the Jews as the reason for the martyrdom of Paul. This is particularly the situation when Acts of Apostles—a play in which Paul is the most important character, a drama written in order to influence the thought of certain influential persons, rather than a short history of the early church—is given so much credence as a historical document. The writer of the Acts of Apostles literary drama used the names of persons such as Felix and Festus in this play, as is appropriate for a playwright. We must recognize, however, that not only are the narratives and the speeches in Acts compositions of the playwright; the itineraries are also. Giving prominence to Acts and to Paul's letter to the Romans distracts our attention to "religious" rather than "political" reasons for the death of Paul.

Fortunately, scholarship focused on the Newer Testament has been guided by its recognition of a multitude of significant differences between Acts and information in Paul's own basic seven letters[11] to look first to what Paul himself wrote about himself and to turn to Acts only as a supplement to be used with caution when seeking information about Paul. Koester's chronological summary reflects this caution. Additional caution, however, must be taken, especially in regard to information about circumstances leading to the execution of Paul. Methodologically, we should permit Paul himself to speak about the circumstances surrounding his impending execution rather than to turn to other writers who were much less specific about these matters, simply because they were less directly involved than was Paul in the circumstances surrounding his impending execution and because these other writers had other purposes for their writings.[12]

Methodologically, we should give priority to Philippians 1:1–3:1 and perhaps some attention to 2 Timothy 4:6–18 in our efforts to obtain information about the circumstances surrounding the impending execution of Paul. In Philippians 1:1–3:1

Paul looked back over his life and work and forward to the end of his life and to "the day of Jesus Christ." He wrote in Philippians 1:5 that he was thankful to God for the fellowship in the gospel of the Philippians from the first day that he had met them until now. He said in 1:6 that he was certain that the one who began such good work among them would continue it until the day of Jesus Christ. In 1:7–11 he wrote repeatedly about his affection for the Philippians, about the very close relationship that he had with them, about his earnest desire that no matter what happened to him their love would increase even more and more in understanding and in every kind of insight. Paul wanted them to be able to determine the things that are truly important, so that they would be morally acceptable and trustworthy for the day of Christ. This, rather than his letter to the Romans, has the characteristics and tone of Paul's "last will and testament."

Paul became even more specific in his references to the end of his life in Philippians 1:20–30. He wrote that it was his eager expectation and hope that in no way would he be prevented from demonstrating the value of the gospel. Even in his present situation of imprisonment and trial he wanted Christ to be magnified in whatever would happen to Paul's body, whether through his life or through his death. He indicated that the purpose of his dying is that gain should come to Christ. As is well known, he weighed the advantages of continuing his proclamation of the gospel in this present life over against the advantages of departing from this physical existence and being with Christ. Paul wanted the assurance that even if he himself would soon be executed, the Philippians would remain firm in one spirit, working together to enhance the faith experienced through the gospel.

Paul continued what he realized might be his final opportunity to express his concerns for the Philippians by urging them to have the same goals and purpose that he himself held, using the model of Christ Jesus for all of this (2:1–11). He wrote in 2:12–18 that the Philippians should with fear and trembling achieve their salvation in the name of Jesus Christ our Lord, so that they will be without blame and innocent, unblemished children of God in the midst of a crooked and perverted age, in which they will shine as stars in the world of space. All of this would occur, Paul hoped, after he could no longer be physically present with them or be able to write to them.

Even in the face of his impending execution, Paul wrote of his rejoicing over the proclamation of Christ (1:18, 19) and urged the Philippians to rejoice with him (3:1). He was willing to write as much as he could, and wanted to do so as a bulwark for the faith of the Philippians. Throughout Philippians 1:1–3:1

there is no reference to the Jews as a reason for his impending execution.[13] If the Jews had been the cause for his arrest and imprisonment, he would most likely have indicated that. The writer of Acts and the writers of the Four Gospels did not hesitate to blame the Jews for precipitating the death of Jesus. Paul, however, in Philippians 1:1–3:1 wrote only about the Roman praetorian guard, and in 4:22 about those of Caesar's household—clear though guarded references to those who had arrested him, were holding him, would be bringing charges against him, and would execute him.

Paul's carefully stated references to the Roman praetorian guard and to members of Caesar's household in Philippians1:13 and 4:22 are indications that he wanted the people in Philippi to whom he was writing to understand clearly who was holding him as a prisoner and would be charging him with an offense punishable by death. Paul does not, however, in Philippians 1:1–3:1 and elsewhere in Philippians indicate the precise nature of the charges being brought against him. If we expect Paul to speak for himself rather than to turn to the writer of Acts for reasons for his arrest and imprisonment, we shall have to do some reading "between the lines" of Paul's letters. As Pheme Perkins put it, "The grounds for the external opposition that led to the apostle's imprisonment (reported in Phil 1:1–3:1) are also unclear."[14] In this situation, I find the judgment of Klaus Wengst to be salutary. According to Wengst, "As it cannot be supposed that the accusation (against Paul) fell under the category of a criminal charge relating to property, and as the claim of Paul that he is accused as a Christian must be taken seriously, the accusation can lie only in the political sphere."[15] Some type of political factor must have been involved in Paul's message and in the results that he was achieving as an apostle of Jesus as the Christ. In Wengst's words, "Paul's proclamation must have been of such a kind or had such effects that it touched on this area (of the political sphere)" (202). In what way would the message of Paul and the results that he was achieving have touched the political sphere enough to warrant his imprisonment and execution? What can we find "between the lines" of Philippians 1:1–3:1 and elsewhere in Paul's seven basic letters that will help us to determine this?

While we shall address this question throughout the remainder of this present chapter, a few observations can be made briefly here. It is obvious that Paul was not urging anyone to rebel militarily against Roman rule. He was not an insurrectionist. This is certainly apparent in Romans 13:1–7, although that important text must not be read uncritically. At any rate, it would have been totally irresponsible for Paul to have advocated rebellion against Roman rule. Had he done so, he would have been executed immediately and would have further jeopardized the lives of those who were closely associated with him. We know from Philippians 1 that Paul did not want to increase the danger to his fellow believers. Paul could hardly have been uninterested in the political situation of Roman rule, but his letters indicate that he was primarily a religious leader, not primarily a political leader, just as the Jesus of history was primarily a religious figure rather than a political leader. We know from Paul' letters that Paul wrote primarily about God and about Jesus as the Risen Christ and Lord, not about Caesar and Roman rule.

It is well known that the Roman emperors permitted great diversity in the religious beliefs and practices of the people over whom they exercised control. For example, many Roman military personnel were devotees of the Mithra cult during the latter decades of the first century and throughout the second and third centuries.[16] This was apparently no problem so long as the devotees to Mithra bowed down to the image of Caesar whenever they were required to do so. These Roman military personnel who were devotees of Mithra were able to submit to Caesar as their Lord in physical, military matters while Mithra was their spiritually invincible Lord. As a result, the Roman Caesars were able to accept the devotion of their military forces to Mithra, and even, beginning with Commodus (180–192 C.E.) to participate in the Mithraic secret ceremonies themselves. In the opinion of Franz Cumont, the Roman rulers "found in its (the Mithraic) doctrines a support for their personal policy and a staunch advocacy of the autocratic pretensions which they were so energetically endeavoring to establish" (87–89).

The crucial difference here between Paul and other early leaders among the followers of Jesus and the devotees to Mithra is that Paul and the other early leaders among the followers of Jesus would not submit to Caesar as their Lord while the devotees to Mithra would submit in this way. Roman military personnel would, of course, be expected to submit to Caesar as their Lord on a regular basis. Leaders such as Paul among the followers of Jesus would not be asked to submit to Caesar as their Lord unless there was a specific reason to do so. This is an important key to our understanding of what Paul was communicating in Philippians 1:1–3:1. Paul does not explicitly state that he will be expected to submit to Caesar as his Lord when the trial/hearing that he anticipates in Philippians 1:20–24 occurs. He states, however, that he shall have to choose, presumably between submitting to Caesar as his Lord and defiantly affirming that he will acclaim only Jesus the Risen Christ as his Lord. Only to Jesus the Risen Christ will he bend his knee.[17]

As we read Philippians 2:1–11, it is difficult for us to think that Paul would have submitted to Caesar as his Lord, even to save his life. As a Jew from birth and now as an apostle of Jesus the Christ as his Lord, Paul would not do this. Even as Paul wrote Philippians 2:1-11, in which he articulated so clearly how he looked forward to the time when all would bend their knees, not to Caesar as

Lord, but to Jesus the Risen Christ as Lord, we can see that Paul had made his choice, the choice that would mark the difference between the continuation of his life here on earth and the end of his life on earth. By the choice that Paul made he would seal his fate at the hands of those who held him as a prisoner. It is for this reason that, unlike the majority of critical New Testament scholars, I think that Paul himself composed what we call the Christ-hymn of Philippians 2:5–11 as he was writing Philippians 1:1–3:1 rather than that he was quoting a Christ-hymn that had been written by someone else earlier.[18]

We should not think that every Roman of that time would have required some public act of allegiance to Caesar of Paul and of other early Christian leaders. Only those who were most closely associated with Rome and with Roman power would have required this. According to *The Martyrdom of Polycarp* account a century after the time of Paul's death, the venerable Christian bishop could have avoided death had he fled before the soldiers arrived or had he been willing to say, "Caesar is Lord," and to offer the required incense. Apparently, however, those who were ruling in the name of Rome wherever Paul was being held when he wrote Philippians 1:1–3:1 were likely to require something from Paul that, should he refuse to do it, would result in the sentence of death (Philippians 1:20–23). If this was taking place in Ephesus, it may have been zealous Greeks who had power only because of their Roman patriotism who would have been requiring some act of allegiance. These Greeks ruling in Ephesus in the name of Rome and at the pleasure of Rome, whom I call "zealous advocates of Roman Civil Religion" and perhaps whom the writer of Acts 19:31 called "Asiarchs,"[19] are the ones who would have required some act of allegiance of Paul.

It is because Philippians rather than Paul's letter to the Romans has the tone and characteristics of his "last will and testament" that I begin this study of specific texts in which Paul and later Pauline writers may have employed "hidden transcripts" of anti-Roman cryptograms with Philippians and focus attention first of all on the Philippians 2:5–11 Christ-hymn.

Philippians—"Jesus Christ [Not Caesar] Is Lord!"

What may be the most subtle anti-Roman cryptogram within the seven basic letters of Paul is his central affirmation that "at the name of Jesus every knee shall bend, in heaven and on the earth and under the earth, and every tongue shall confess that Jesus Christ is Lord, to the glory of God the Father."[20] This central affirmation of Paul's faith[21] has not generally been identified as a strong anti-Roman cryptogram for several reasons.

One reason is that most critical interpreters have considered the Philippians 2:5–11 Christ-hymn to have been a liturgical masterpiece that resulted from intense meditation by unidentified Christians earlier than or perhaps contemporaneous with Paul. Therefore, the specific life situation of its origin has not been available. A second reason is that since this central affirmation is included within a most basic Christological statement of Christianity, attention has been focused on how Christians perceive Jesus rather than on the affirmation as also an anti-Roman cryptogram. Finally, the words "not Caesar" are implied rather than explicitly expressed within the statement of faith. For Paul to have written "not Caesar" explicitly would have incited retaliation by the Romans and added greatly to the suffering of all followers of Jesus who were associated with Paul. Even in the spoken tradition, the words "not Caesar" were probably often implied by inflection in speaking rather than openly expressed, as I indicate here with italics for emphasis, "Jesus *the Risen Christ*...is *our* Lord!" or as we today might say, "our Boss!" For Jews who remained Jews, and that would have included most Jews of the late first century C.E., Adonai remained Lord as before. For zealous advocates of Roman Civil Religion during the time of the public activity of Paul, whoever was the Caesar at the time was the Lord or "Boss" for them.

When Paul and other leaders of the early church defined the Christian position in terms of "Jesus the Risen Christ is Lord for us," they made a clear and distinct departure from what had previously been the perception of the Jewish-background followers of Jesus and continued to be the belief of the Jews who remained Jews, that Adonai and only Adonai is Lord. This was also a clear and distinct departure from what was increasingly becoming the perception of the promoters of the Roman Imperial Cult that at least here on this earth everyone who lives within the borders of the Roman Empire must recognize that Caesar is Lord (Boss). Under what was for Paul a life and death situation as he faced a Roman court hearing that could easily result in a conviction leading to a state-ordered execution, Paul apparently was determining as he wrote Philippians 2:1–11 that at his trial he would boldly affirm that Jesus the Risen Christ is Lord. Paul was stating that Jesus the Risen Christ is Lord not only for all Christians, but soon will be Lord for everyone, particularly for those who were bringing charges against him, and eventually even for Caesar himself. In order to gain a better understanding of the "hidden transcript" anti-Roman cryptogram that may be implied within Paul's central affirmation of faith, let us look in more detail at this statement within the context of Paul's letter to the Philippians. This will provide additional context within which we can look more briefly at additional statements that may have been intended as hidden transcripts of anti-Roman cryptograms by Paul and by others who wrote later using Paul's name.

We shall begin this section with a closer look at Paul's life situation at the time that he wrote the major portions of his letter to the Philippians and his letter to Philemon, as we can reconstruct his life situation from information within these letters.

Paul's Life Situation When He Wrote His Letter to the Philippians and His Letter to Philemon

Some aspects of Paul's life situation when he wrote the major portions of his letter to the Philippians and his letter to Philemon can easily be discerned. Many others can not. We can not, for example, determine from these letters whether Paul was being held in Rome, in Ephesus, in Caesarea, or in some other center of Roman power within the Roman Empire. Neither can we pinpoint the date of their composition.[22] The references to the praetorium in Philippians 1:13 and to those who are in the domestic service of the emperor in 4:22 do not reveal to us the precise location of Paul's imprisonment. We can, however, discern from 1:7, 12–14, 17 that he was imprisoned by Roman governmental authorities and from 1:19–20 and 2:17 that he was being tried for an offense that was punishable by execution. Paul seems in 1:20, 2:17, and 3:10 to anticipate torture and public crucifixion like that which the Jesus of history had experienced, and this similarity to the torture and crucifixion that Jesus had experienced was obviously very important to Paul.

It is also quite clear from what Paul wrote that there was a close connection between the message that Paul was proclaiming and Paul's imprisonment, trial, and probable crucifixion (1:7, 12–14, 16, 20–22, 29–30; 2:17). We see that Paul tied his imprisonment closely to the proclamation and validation of the gospel already in 1:7. He wrote that his imprisonment and the charges brought against him had enhanced the spread of the gospel rather than hindered it (1:12–14). Paul wrote that in his imprisonment and trial he was in grave danger of death so that he would be able to demonstrate the value of the gospel, so that Jesus Christ would be magnified through what would happen in Paul's body, whether through his life or through his death (1:20–22). Paul's suffering was for the sake of Jesus Christ and because of what Paul was saying about Jesus as Christ (1:29-30). Even if Paul's life will be poured out as an offering in the service of the faith of the Philippians, Paul will do it gladly and rejoice with the Philippians because of their salvation (2:17).

Paul's life situation was such that he felt that he had some control over what would happen during his trial, whether he would be sentenced to die or be permitted to live. Perhaps this portion of his life situation may best be understood to mean this: if Paul decided at his trial to proclaim boldly and defiantly the gospel that Jesus Christ raised from the dead is Lord—rather than that Caesar is Lord—Paul could bring upon himself death by torture and crucifixion like that experienced by the Jesus of history and after that a resurrection to be with the Jesus Christ of faith. For Paul to do this, however, would not necessarily be best, or even good, for the Philippians who were known to be closely associated with Paul. Such a bold and defiant proclamation of the gospel by Paul could jeopardize the lives of the members of the Philippian congregation, or at least the lives of their most public leaders.

The Life Situation of Those in Philippi to Whom Paul Wrote

This brings us to a consideration of what can be known from Paul's letter to the Philippians about the life situation of the members of the Philippian congregation. They are said to have had fellowship in the gospel with Paul from the time that Paul had first met them (1:5-6). In Paul's imprisonment and in the proclamation and validation of the gospel they are all said to be praying for Paul and for his deliverance from imprisonment (1:19). He stated that it will be better for the Philippians if Paul will be released and be able to come to them than if he suffers torture and public crucifixion (1:24–26). Perhaps this would be better for them not merely because Paul would then come to them, but because if Paul were sentenced to death by crucifixion by the Roman governmental authorities, perhaps incited by Greek advocates of Roman Civil Religion, the people in Philippi who were most closely identified with Paul might also be arrested, tried, tortured, and crucified.

That the Philippians for whom Jesus Christ was Lord might have to suffer for the sake of Christ and have the same kind of struggle that Paul was experiencing is said in 1:29–30 to be a likely possibility. To this end, the Philippians are encouraged by Paul to make his joy complete by having the same attitude that he has, to experience the same kind of love, to be united with him in spirit, and to set their minds on the one important thing—to be one with Christ and with Paul, to be obedient as suffering servants even to the point of death on a cross (2:5–8). They are to do this so that they may with fear and trembling achieve their salvation through their death and resurrection in the name of Jesus Christ (2:12–13).

Paul states in 4:10–20 that the Philippians had risked their lives by sending a gift during Paul's imprisonment, perhaps a quantity of food or of money with which Timothy or Epaphroditus could purchase food for him. Because they have identified themselves with Paul so closely, their leaders may also be arrested, tried, tortured, and crucified if Paul is sentenced to death, especially if they, like Paul, boldly proclaim that Jesus Christ rather than Caesar is Lord.

The Principal Expression of Faith Professed by Paul in This Letter

The principal expression of faith professed by Paul in his letter to the Philippians is the statement that "Jesus Christ is Lord!" In the context in which Paul placed this confession of faith in the "Christ-hymn" of Philippians 2:6–11, Paul made it clear that he longed for the day in which every knee above the earth, on the earth, and under the earth would bend to Jesus Christ as Lord and every tongue proclaim Jesus Christ as Lord, just as it is written in Isaiah 45:23 that to Adonai every knee shall bend and every tongue shall confess. Paul's life situation and that of his readers suggest, therefore, that Paul longed for the day in which those who held him imprisoned would bend their knees to Jesus Christ and confess with their tongues that Jesus Christ and not Caesar is Lord of all.

We can be certain also that Paul looked forward to the day in which Caesar himself, who was obviously included among Paul's classification of "everyone above the earth, on the earth, and under the earth," would bend his knee to the name of Jesus Christ and confess with his tongue that Jesus Christ, not Caesar, is Lord of all. We should be aware that as Paul was writing his letter to the Philippians he was contemplating the situation that he would face soon when at his trial he would be ordered to bend his knee before an image of Caesar and to say that "Caesar is Lord." Paul knew that he must refuse to do this. In the document The Martyrdom of Polycarp, the explicit command to Polycarp to confess that "Caesar is Lord" to save his life from martyrdom is given, and Polycarp, like Paul, refuses."[23]

Possible Meanings of the Word "Lord" Intended by Paul in This Letter

In order to determine as much as we can about the meanings that Paul intended when he proclaimed in Philippians 2:11 that "Jesus Christ is Lord!" let us look at the use of the word *kyrios*. First we shall consider it in Greek composition other than the Septuagint prior to the time of Paul, then we shall look at the use of the word in the Septuagint, and finally at the use of the word in the life situations of Paul and of the people of Philippi to whom Paul was writing. In Greek composition other than in the Septuagint prior to Paul, *kyrios* (masculine) and *kyria* (feminine) are used to describe a person who has power and authority over other persons. A person who is said to be a *kyrios* or a *kyria* controls other people, usually as their master or owner. Those who are under the power and authority of a person designated as a *kyrios* or a *kyria* are said to be *douloi* or *doulai*, servants, subjected and subdued persons, usually slaves by birth or as a result of acquisition or conquest. The person who is said to be a *kyrios* or a *kyria* is the owner or possessor of people, places, and things. We see, therefore, that in Greek composition other than in the Septuagint prior to Paul the word "Lord" is primarily a political and economic designator. When the person designated as a *kyrios* or a *kyria* is said to have ultimate authority, the word also becomes a religious designator.

As is well known, it is in the Septuagint that the use of the word *kyrios* as a religious designator is most pronounced. Those who produced the Septuagint consistently chose to use *kyrios* to represent in Greek the Hebrew *tetragrammaton* for God Active in History. By selecting *kyrios* rather than a transliteration of the Hebrew word or the use of the Greek word *despotēs,* the Septuagint translators protected the Hebrew *tetragrammaton* from profanation in Greek usage and avoided the use of *despotēs,* a word that more easily than *kyrios* can suggest cruel and tyrannical qualities.

The selection of the word *kyrios* for the Hebrew *tetragrammaton* was particularly appropriate also for use in the Septuagint because within the civil religion of the Israelites prior to the destruction of the first temple the Hebrew *tetragrammaton* was not simply a religious designator. It was also a political designator. "Adonai" was perceived to be the master, the owner, the political as well as religious "Lord" of the Israelites. Their covenant with Adonai was similar in form to the covenants of that time between political leaders and their vassal princes. The perceptions of later Jews of Adonai as the "King of the Universe" is also both a religious and a political designator. Therefore, within the Israelite tradition both before and after 586 B.C.E. Adonai and *kyrios* are partly religious and partly political designators. Consequently, when within that tradition Paul wrote that the time will come in which every knee will bend in deference to the name of Jesus Christ and every tongue will proclaim that Jesus Christ is Lord, Paul was most likely also using the word *kyrios* as both a religious and as a political designator.

It is not possible for us to determine the extent to which enthusiasts of Roman Civil Religion were applying the word *kyrios* (or the Latin word *dominus*) to the Roman Emperor Nero at the time and in the place where Paul was being held when he wrote to the Philippians. According to Werner Foerster,[24] however, within the Roman Empire, "under a constitutional cover there triumphed in fact the type of absolute monarchy constantly associated in the Orient with the term 'lord.'" Foerster wrote that "The scene under Augustus reported by Suetonius shows us already that the relevant word was also very much in the air at Rome." Ethelbert Stauffer, in Christ and the Caesars, titled his chapter on Nero, "Nero the World Saviour." Stauffer wrote that late in Nero's life when he traveled to Corinth as an actor, he was received there "like a saviour from heaven, and acclaimed in the sports stadium as "Zeus the Liberator"[25] If Nero was honored as "Zeus the Liberator" in the Greek areas of the Empire, it is likely that he was also called *kyrios*, one who has dominical power in both the political and the religious sense.

"Jesus Christ Is Lord!" As an Anti-Roman Cryptogram

When we consider the vulnerable political situation of Paul imprisoned by Roman authorities at the time of his writing to the Philippians, what Paul wrote in Philippians 2:9–11 was not only a strikingly clear exposition of the gospel that he proclaimed, but also a daringly risky statement for him to make in written form. His statement of faith would have been even more daringly risky if Paul had written that every knee "including the knees of those who are holding me in prison, threatening to kill me, and including the knee of Caesar himself, will here on this earth bend in deference to the name of Jesus, and their tongues confess that Jesus Christ, rather than Caesar, is Lord!" That Paul did not specify whose knees he had in mind, but included them all within his depiction of every knee, and whose tongues, included within his designation of every tongue, suggests that Philippians 2:9–11 may have been intended by Paul not only as a strong statement of faith but also as a subtle "hidden transcript," an anti-Roman cryptogram. In this subtle way, within the context of this strong expression of faith, Paul was able to encourage his fellow-ministers in Philippi by assuring them that no matter what happened to Paul, ultimately his captors and even Caesar himself would have to submit to Jesus Christ as Lord.[26]

In view of this, it is likely that the other designations of Jesus the Risen Christ as Lord by Paul and by others throughout the Newer Testament documents were originally intended by their writers to be both religious and political, more than has generally been realized. After all, the Jesus of history had been tortured and crucified by the Romans in a political execution. The Romans had cruelly killed him, but now he was alive again! His tomb was empty! Jesus the Risen Christ (not Caesar) was truly the Lord, the Boss! In addition to this confession being the primary Christian statement of faith, the core statement of the so-called "Roman Symbol"[27] that evolved into the Apostles' Creed, it functioned also as an anti-Roman cryptogram until the time when the Roman State accepted Christianity as its state religion during the fourth century C.E. Adequately understood, this confession functions still today as a strong statement of faith and as a polemic against people in any nation who claim absolute prerogatives for their nation.

1 Thessalonians—Satan Hindered Us
and the Tempter Tempted You

Paul and the other writers of the documents that eventually became the Newer Testament obviously considered Jesus as the Risen Christ to be their Lord, the most important manifestation of God Active in History in their lives. Jesus the Risen Christ as their Lord represented everything that was good as they perceived good. They tried to live in accordance with this manifestation of good, and they tried to induce others to accept Jesus Christ as their Lord also and to live in accordance with this manifestation of good as well.

In 1 Thessalonians 2:17–18 Paul wrote that in spite of the great desire that he, Silvanus, and Timothy had to return to Thessalonica to visit their fellow believers there, *ho satanas* had hindered them, had prevented their return. Someone had opposed Paul and his fellow ministers and had prevented them from returning to Thessalonica. This opposition was obviously serious and life-threatening. It would have been irresponsible of Paul to have identified that person by name within a written document. Perhaps those to whom Paul was writing knew the identity of the adversary. By using the words *ho satanas*, Paul was able to communicate to his oppressed fellow believers that someone who was their serious adversary[28] was threatening the life of Paul and the others and had prevented their return to Thessalonica.

In 1 Thessalonians 2:17–18 Paul was most likely referring cryptically to some leader among the zealous advocates of Roman Civil Religion[29] who was threatening his life, or perhaps Paul was referring to Caesar himself. (In 1980 the Ayatollah Khomeini referred to the U.S. President Jimmy Carter as "Satan" after our poorly-implemented attempt to rescue our political hostages in Teheran had failed in the Persian desert. Saddam Hussein referred to the U.S. President George H. Bush as "Satan" during the Gulf War of 1991.) The words *ho satanas* to depict Paul's adversary served well, since if Paul's adversary gained access to Paul's letter it would appear to the adversary that Paul was writing about some supernatural, semi-divine, or divine being. This was exactly the impression that Paul may have intended to convey in 1 Thessalonians 2:17–18.[30]

The concept of "Satan" as an adversary of good people and of God, even as a demigod of sorts, may have been a part of Paul's thought process, as 2 Corinthians 11:14 ("even Satan disguises himself as an angel of light") indicates. The evidence from the basic letters of Paul, however, does not support the idea that for Paul Satan as a demigod was an important concept. In texts such as

Romans 8, for example, in which Paul wrote in considerable detail about the whole creation groaning as a mother groans while giving birth to her child, Paul mentions principalities and powers, sins of the flesh, death, and a myriad of other factors, but makes no mention at all of Satan as such. Examination of Paul's references to Satan indicates that for Paul Satan was both a powerful but rather remote demigod and a symbol for powerful human figures who were opposing and hindering Paul and those who were with him. No text brings this out more effectively than 2 Corinthians 12:7–10, the "messenger of Satan to hinder me" text, which will be analyzed below.

If Paul intended that those to whom he was sending 1 Thessalonians should understand that zealous advocates of Roman Civil Religion had prevented his return to Thessalonica, it is likely that his use of the word "tempter" in 3:5 was basically a synonym for the words *ho satanas* in 2:17–18. Both may have been references to the human adversary of Paul who was a threat to his work and to his life and was in a sense an agent of "Satan." The adversaries of Paul, however, would be led to think that Paul was writing about what they and we call the "Devil," or "Satan," a super-natural figure.

Helmut Koester[31] suggests that Paul in this letter "points to the coming of the day of the Lord as an event that will shatter the false peace and security of the Roman establishment" and that "Paul envisions a role for the eschatological community that presents a utopian alternative to the prevailing eschatological ideology of Rome."

Walter E. Pilgrim, *Uneasy Neighbors: Church and State in the New Testament,*[32] noting that Paul called those who proclaim "peace and security" agents of darkness, wrote that "'Peace and security' represents the propaganda machine of imperial Rome. Rome claimed to have brought peace to the world. But it was peace by bloody conquest, security by the sword. It was the fictional peace of the *pax Romana.*"

1 Corinthians—the Rulers of This Age, Satan, and the Beasts at Ephesus

Not only did Paul place a heavy emphasis on Jesus Christ rather than Caesar as Lord in this extensive letter; Paul also boldly, almost recklessly, spoke out in 1 Corinthians 2:6,8 against "the rulers of this age" who, he said, crucified the Lord of glory and are now doomed to pass out of existence. Paul said that these rulers have not understood the wisdom of God. If they had understood the wisdom of God, which is the wisdom that Paul claims to impart in this section of his letter, they would not have crucified Jesus. Many commentators have been influenced by the more cautious writer of the later Pauline epistle to "the

Ephesians" who in Ephesians 6:12 described the "world rulers of this present age" in non-human terms, not as people of flesh and blood. That writer identified these rulers as the "spiritual hosts of wickedness in the heavenly places." Paul himself, however, placed the blame for the death of Jesus exactly where it belonged, not on supernatural forces, but on cruel despotic human beings. Paul pointed out, in addition, that these cruel despotic human beings are mortal, "doomed to pass away."[33]

Paul did not, of course, identify "the rulers of this age" by name as Pontius Pilate and as the Caesar under whose authority Pilate functioned. Paul did not mention Herod Antipas or Caiaphas. It is logical to assume that Paul used the terminology "the rulers of this age" as a hidden transcript, as a cryptogram, in order to protect himself and his fellow Christians from Roman retaliation. Within the Christian community of faith, had Paul been asked to identify "the rulers of this age who had crucified the Lord of glory," we can be certain that Paul could and would have done so. As the Old Roman Symbol developed and evolved into the Apostles' Creed over the course of many decades and centuries, the more specific statement "suffered under Pontius Pilate" replaced Paul's cryptogrammic "rulers of this age."

Paul may indeed have believed and taught that behind, so to speak, the evil rulers of this age such as Pilate and Caesar there were "elemental spirits of the universe" (Galatians 4:3) and "world rulers of this darkness who hold the entire creation in bondage" (Romans 8:19–25, 38–39), as G. B. Caird suggests.[34] Many Christians hold views that are similar to that even today. It is important, nevertheless, to hold individual persons accountable for their actions and not permit them to pass on the blame to demonic, satanic forces. We are especially aware of this after Auschwitz and at a time when neo-Nazi groups seem to be proliferating. We must oppose evil actions and we must restrain those who perpetrate them. We must hold them accountable for what they do and have done. We cannot let them excuse their actions by saying that "The Devil made me do it," or to claim that they were guided by evil "elemental spirits of the universe" or "world rulers of this darkness who hold them in bondage. Had Paul and the early followers of Jesus with whom he was working been politically in positions of power such as we are rather than politically weak and vulnerable, Paul would most likely have identified "the rulers of this age who crucified the Lord of glory" and not have had to use hidden transcripts of subtle anti-Roman cryptograms.

It is essential that we as Christians today become aware of the anti-Roman cryptograms of the Newer Testament and recognize the reasons for their use. It is essential that we hold ourselves and others accountable for evil actions and not misuse Paul's anti-Roman cryptograms to pass responsibility and accountability for evil actions to some kind of other-worldly spiritual force.

Paul did use the word "Satan" twice in 1 Corinthians, both, however, in regard to personal and family problems rather than in what we might consider political situations related to the Roman State. The first of these uses occurs in his comments about the follower of Jesus in Corinth who was reported to be sexually involved with his father's wife (5:1–8), and the other pertaining to sexual activity within a marriage (7:1–7). Perhaps neither was intended in any way to function as a cryptogram. Paul may have been thinking in these two instances about the mythical supernatural being (Satan) who is said in the Similitudes (I Enoch 37–71) to have powers to tempt people to do things that are destructive and to destroy people's flesh. If Paul was indeed using the word "Satan" in part as a hidden transcript, an anti-Roman cryptogram in some instances, it was important and prudent for him to use the word in other instances primarily in the supernatural demigod sense as well. We should not suppose that Paul did not ever refer to Satan in the supernatural demigod sense. Neither should we suppose that Paul never used the word "Satan" in anti-Roman cryptograms. Both uses should be identified and the degree of one or of the other analyzed as well as we can with the resources available to us.

Therefore, we must be open to the possibility that Paul may have intended one or both of these uses of the word "Satan" to be in part at least a cryptic reference to Rome and to Roman power. Since Roman law as well as Jewish regulations provided the death penalty for this combination of incest and adultery, Paul's instruction in 1 Corinthians 5:5 to hand the offender over to "Satan" to be killed may have been a recommendation to deliver the man over to Roman authorities so that they could inflict the death penalty. Paul, however, could have expressed such a recommendation in direct, non-cryptic terms. Paul's use of the word "Satan" in 7:5 may also have been intended as a reference to Roman power and Roman ways that would tempt a man or a woman to be drawn away from the community of the followers of Jesus, but I do not think that it was. If Paul had intended either or both of these uses of the word "Satan" to be primarily a cryptic reference to Roman power and to Roman ways of living, he would have been foolish to have used the word "Satan" here, for to do so would be to expose one of his most important words used in anti-Roman cryptograms to possible identification by his Roman adversaries.

On the other hand, I think that it is much more certain that Paul used an anti-Roman cryptogram in 1 Corinthians 15:32 where he wrote that he had found it necessary for the sake of Jesus Christ to contend with beasts at Ephesus. If he had literally been fighting with wild beasts, he would not likely have survived to write another letter.[35] By "beasts" or "wild beasts" here he was probably referring either to Roman military personnel or to zealous advocates of Roman Civil Religion.

The practice of referring to military and political forces who are hurting you as "beasts" or "beastly" is common to many cultures and time periods. For example, Ignatius, bishop of Antioch, in his letter to the Romans 5:1 wrote a few decades after Paul's death that "All the way from Syria to Rome, by land and sea, I am constantly fighting with wild beasts (using the same verb that Paul had used in 1 Corinthians 15:32), being bound to ten leopards, which is a platoon of soldiers."[36] During the civil rights struggles of African-Americans in the U.S.A. city police and county and state officers who seemed to relish enforcing the Jim Crow laws were in some instances referred to as "pigs" by those whom they treated brutally. The Chinese student leader Wu'er Kaixi, after his escape to Hong Kong, called the top officials of his own government who had crushed the student demonstrations at Tiananmen Square during the summer of 1989 "wild beasts."

Just a few verses prior to 1 Corinthians 15:32, Paul had written in 15:24–25 about his hope that when Christ would come at the end of the age (of Roman political power?) Christ would destroy every rule and every authority and every power. Until that time, Paul and other early Christians had to contend with oppressive rulers and their representatives. Therefore, it is likely that Paul was referring in 15:32 to his struggles in Ephesus to avoid the machinations of *people* who were trying to kill him.

In 1 Corinthians 16:8–9 Paul wrote again about his adversaries in Ephesus, whom he said were many. Particularly in view of what Paul wrote in 2 Corinthians 12:7, which we shall look at more closely in the next section, it is likely that the "wild beasts'" of 1 Corinthians 15:32 were zealous advocates of the Roman Imperial Cult, the people who eventually caused his death and ended his personal proclamation of the gospel of Jesus Christ as Lord.

2 Corinthians—Satan and the Thorn in Paul's Flesh, a Messenger of Satan

As we turn to the composite document that was incorporated into the Newer Testament collection as 2 Corinthians, we come to what may be a reference by Paul to the most tenacious of these "wild beasts," a zealous advocate of Roman Civil Religion who more than any other person may have caused Paul's death. The reference, of course, is to the celebrated "thorn in Paul's flesh, the messenger of Satan (*aggelos satana*)," given to harass Paul, to keep him from becoming too elated by the abundance of revelations that he received.

Paul's hidden transcript cryptogram here may have been so well phrased that not only his enemies could not decipher it, but most of his friends in later generations also have not been able to understand its meaning.[37] Most of these friends in later generations have guessed that Paul's affliction, from which he sought relief through prayer three times without success, consisted of painful attacks of some type of illness. The summary of those guesses listed in Bauer-Arndt-Gingrich-Danker[38] includes epilepsy, hysteria, periodic depression, headaches, severe eye-trouble, malaria, leprosy, speech impediments such as stuttering or stammering, spiritual temptations caused by opponents, pangs of conscience, and other distressed states of mind.[39]

Some commentators, however, think that although the expression "thorn in the flesh" superficially suggests a problem within Paul's body, the problem was not deep within Paul's body or being, but was caused to Paul's body by something or someone external to Paul. A thorn that sticks to a person's flesh is a foreign substance. It is an intrusion that causes pain. It comes from a source outside the body. It hurts and irritates the body until it is removed. Jerry W. McCant, for example, argues that the thorn refers to certain persons, and thinks that it is highly probable that these persons were Christians within the Corinthian church because Paul wrote so much, especially in 1–2 Corinthians and Galatians, about fellow Christians who rejected his apostleship.[40]

McCant's suggestion is helpful in that it directs our attention to people and to social, religious, and perhaps political problems troubling Paul. Fellow Christians, however, may not have been the problem for Paul in this instance. Paul shows himself in his letters to be fully capable of cutting down, pulling out, and removing from his presence any fellow Christian believer whom Paul considers to be a detriment to the gospel that he lives and proclaims.[41] Because of the severity of the problem and in view of the many references that Paul makes within this composite letter to his sufferings and afflictions which he repeatedly compares to the sufferings and afflictions of the Jesus of history,[42] the "thorn in his flesh" was probably not a Christian. It is much more likely that the "thorn in his flesh" was someone outside of the fellowship of followers of Jesus, someone who was a dangerous enemy of Paul, a person over whom Paul had no power or control. Otherwise, Paul would have simply cut down, pulled out, and removed this person from his presence.

Perhaps in our attempts to reconstruct the scenario of what Paul was experiencing at the time when he wrote 2 Corinthians 12:7, we can be assisted by recalling some events that occurred in the cities of Phoenix and Tucson, Arizona, in our own country during the mid-1980s. Christians within several congregations in those cities, concerned about the plight of some refugees from strife-torn countries in Central America, particularly refugees who were pregnant and mothers of small children, were providing friendship and assistance of food, clothing, shelter, and medical care to some women among the refugees, even though the refugees were undocumented aliens. Officials of our Immigration and Naturalization Service, an agency of the Department of State of the executive branch of our federal government, in their zeal to carry out their assigned task of apprehending undocumented aliens who were refugees from certain countries in Central America and deporting them to their country of origin, paid at least one person to infiltrate a few small Lutheran Christian and Presbyterian Christian congregations in those two cities.

The informer, paid by this agency of our government, pretended to be interested in Bible study and discussion groups and other congregational activities, but never officially joined any of these congregations. After several weeks or months, he would no longer participate in these activities and would no longer be seen. Actually, he had come only to gather names, addresses, and phone numbers of members of these congregations who were providing assistance to the undocumented aliens. He had been instructed to gather other evidence that could be used against these members as he listened to conversations during Bible study and discussion sessions and to be able to identify these members by sight.

On the basis of this information, our United States Immigration and Naturalization agents arrested members of these congregations and within our federal courts charged them with serious violations of our laws. The officials of the American Lutheran Church and of the Presbyterian Church in the United States of America supported their accused members. After prolonged litigation, the church members who had helped women in need were convicted as guilty of breaking federal laws and regulations.[43]

If in our relatively free constitutional democracy, in which Christianity has a privileged place, there were people in positions of power who obviously with the approval of the then President of the United States paid persons, some of whom had criminal records in this country, to infiltrate mainline Christian congregations to gather evidence that was later used in our courts against women who were doing what they considered to be consistent with their Christian faith, it is possible that zealous advocates of Roman Civil Religion may have sent someone whom Paul would cryptically refer to as "a thorn in his flesh, a messenger of Satan," to shadow Paul to gather evidence that Paul was proclaiming publicly that not Caesar but Jesus Christ is Lord. When this person had gathered sufficient evidence that what Paul was doing was subversive to the Roman State, at least in the eyes of the zealous advocates of Roman Civil Religion, Paul may have anticipated that he would be arrested, accused of proclaiming someone other than Caesar as Lord, and if he did not renounce Jesus Christ as his Lord these people would kill Paul.

Paul may have sensed at the time when he wrote 2 Corinthians 12:7 that this person was an infiltrator, may have tried to "shake" him, and may have prayed three times that the Lord Jesus Christ would cause this person to leave, but without success. Evidence gathered by this person, this "thorn in Paul's flesh," this "messenger of Satan," may have been used against Paul later during the trial that Paul was concerned about when he wrote to the Philippians. Evidence gathered by this "messenger of Satan" may have contributed directly to Paul's death at the hands of these advocates of Roman Civil Religion who felt threatened by Paul's success among non-Jewish people in the Roman provinces of Asia, Achaia, and Macedonia.

If Paul and those with him continued to attract increasing numbers of non-Jews to this movement in which someone other than Caesar was hailed as Lord, the power of these promoters of the Roman Imperial Cult would be diminished. It would have made good sense to them, therefore, to make a preemptive strike against Paul, to kill him so that his followers would be frightened and would disperse. Their preemptive strike against Paul would be similar in some respects to the preemptive strike of the oppressive Roman occupation forces against the Jesus of history in Jerusalem. As Paul wrote in 2 Corinthians 2:11, he and the followers of Jesus in Corinth must do everything that they could to keep "Satan" (Rome, Caesar, and the advocates of Roman Civil Religion) from gaining the advantage over them, for, as Paul said, Paul and his friends at Corinth were not ignorant of "Satan's" designs. If we are correct in identifying these segments of 2 Corinthians as subtle anti-Roman cryptograms, we arc brought much closer to Paul and to his fellow Christians during the final months of Paul's life.[44] We also become more fully aware of their courage and are able to draw courage from their example even in our time.

Paul's interesting analogy in 2 Corinthians 11:12–15 between those whom he calls false apostles disguising themselves as apostles of Christ and Satan's disguise as an angel of light is also of interest here. It is one of the texts that most clearly indicates that Paul's thought included the concept of "Satan" as an adversary of good people and of God, as a demigod of sorts, as indicated above in our discussion of 1Thessalonians 2:17–18. Paul apparently assumed that his readers were familiar with legends that had developed around the mythological account in Genesis 3 about the temptation of Eve, which Paul had mentioned a few verses earlier in 2 Corinthians 11:3.[45] According to C. K. Barrett,

In the Apocalypse of Moses xvii.1 Eve herself recalls the event: "When the angels ascended to worship God, then Satan appeared in the form of an angel and sang hymns like the angels. And I bent over the wall and saw him, like an angel." In the related *Life of Adam and Eve* ix.1, Satan was wroth and transformed himself into the brightness of angels, and went away to the River Tigris, to Eve. The Slavonic text, xxxviii. 1, has "The devil came to me, wearing the form and brightness of an angel."[46]

This text is also direct evidence that Paul considered opposition to the Christian message as he proclaimed it to be of Satanic origin and that Paul perceived that Satan came disguised in various ways in order to gain an advantage over human beings. The opposition to Paul's message in this context is provided by what Paul calls false apostles disguising themselves as apostles of Christ, almost certainly a reference to Judaizing Christians, not a reference to advocates of Roman Civil Religion.

Romans—Be Subject to the Governing Authorities; Soon the God of Peace Will Crush Satan under Your Feet

When Paul wrote to followers of Jesus in Rome itself, the nerve center of Roman power, it was important for him to be as careful as possible to express any negative comments about Rome and Caesar in hidden transcripts, in cryptograms that would be especially subtle. It was also advisable for Paul to write something that was quite positive about Rome and its governing authorities so that if Paul's letter should come into their hands they would think that Paul and his friends were loyal supporters of the Roman authorities. This is exactly what we have in Paul's letter to early Christians in Rome, as the following analysis indicates.[47]

Few texts within the Newer Testament documents have been more important in the history of the Christian church than Romans 13:1–7 and its counterpart in 1 Peter 2:13–17 and 3:13. It is likely that these texts not only caused a significant reduction of Roman persecution of followers of Jesus prior to the time of Constantine over what the persecution might have been without these texts, but also that these texts made it much easier than it would otherwise have been for Constantine and his advisers to tolerate Christianity and then to make it in a modified form the official religion of the Roman state. From the time of Constantine until today, most Christians have responded to these texts in the way that Paul and the writer of 1 Peter wanted the Roman governing authorities to respond to them, that is, by thinking that Paul and the early Christians were loyal supporters of the Roman authorities and that they considered the Roman State, on the whole, to be just and beneficent. Romans 13:1–7 and 1 Peter 2:13–17 and 3:13 were very useful to Martin Luther, who used them selectively to his own advantage when on the basis of these texts Luther urged his followers to be supportive of the Elector of Saxony who was protecting Luther, but to be defiant of Charles V of the Holy Roman Empire and of the Pope in Rome who were opposing him. Tragically, during the twentieth century C.E., these texts caused many people within our Christian tradition to be reluctant to speak out and to take action against Hitler in Nazi Germany and against other oppressive rulers. These texts also cause some Christians even today to be reluctant to become actively involved as Christians in our political processes.

I do not wish to imply that Paul and the writer of 1 Peter did not mean what they said when they urged their fellow Christian believers to obey the civil laws of the Roman system so that they would not come to the attention of the governmental authorities. They certainly advised their hearers to respect the power of the Roman rulers. They could not have anticipated, however, that centuries later under quite different political conditions in nominally Christian lands many Christians would be influenced so heavily by Romans 13:1–7 and 1 Peter 2:13–17 that they would not oppose the policies and practices of tyrannical political leaders of their countries.

Let us look more closely at a few of the features of what Paul wrote in Romans 12–14. In 12:2 he said that his fellow believers should not permit themselves to be molded and shaped by this present age, which was obviously the Roman and Hellenistic culture in which they lived. Instead, they should be transformed by the new mindset that they have in their relationship with Jesus Christ as Lord. Like the Jesus of history, Paul urged his followers (12:14–21) to bless those who were persecuting them, to overcome evil by being good.

In Romans 13:1 Paul wrote that his fellow believers in Rome should respect the superior power of the Roman authorities. "Respect the superior power of" is a better translation of the Greek verb *hypotassesthō* here and in the "wife-husband" texts in Colossians, Ephesians, and 1 Peter than is the "be subject to" translation that we usually see. "Respect the superior power of" the slave owner is also the sense of the advice given to slaves in Titus 2:9. The translation "be subject to" suggests that you have neither the right nor the ability to question the power and authority of the other person. "Respect the power of" on the other hand, implies that you are wise not to try, at least at the present time, to challenge a power that is physically far greater than your own.

In the Romans 13:1–7 text that has been used so consistently to show that Paul advocated submission to Roman civil authorities, Paul clearly stated that the Roman civil authorities exercised derived authority, not absolute authority. As specifically as he could, given the political circumstances in which he lived, Paul indicated that followers of Jesus should never permit the Roman rulers to exercise the absolute control over them that should be the prerogative only of God and of Jesus the Risen Christ their Lord. Several times in 13: 1–7 Paul emphasized that the governing authorities are servants and servers of people and that they are under the authority of God, inferior to God in every way. Their task is to maintain order and stability in society so that people will be able to worship God and serve Jesus Christ, God's Son, as Lord. Therefore, what Paul wrote in 13:1–7 does not support the concept of the "divine right of kings," and the people of the church should never have permitted "Christian" rulers and their zealous followers to have used this Romans 13:1–7 text in support of that pernicious concept. Rulers and their enthusiastic assistants are not above the law of their lands, and they are certainly not "God" over us.[48]

Neil Elliott finds in Romans 13:1-7 an additional "glimpse into the Pauline hidden transcript." Elliott suggests that "Paul's phrases (in Romans 13:1–7) encouraging submission are remarkably ambivalent," that "in a Roman official's ear, Paul's language would have seemed to offer a peculiarly grudging compliance, rather than the grateful contentment of the properly civilized." For Elliott, Paul in Romans 13 was actually writing "a defiance of the empire's ideological insolence, by which it sought to legitimize a brutal rapacity."[49]

In Romans 13:11–14 Paul assured his fellow believers that "salvation is near." He wrote that "the night has nearly come to its end" and that "the dawning of the new day is very near." Perhaps in this context Paul was not thinking so much in terms of the end of time and of space as experienced within this expanding universe as he was about salvation from the long night of Roman rule that was oppressive, especially in its life-threatening form that Paul and his friends experienced at the hands of the zealous advocates of Roman Civil Religion. As he wrote in 14:11, quoting from Isaiah 45:23, "Every knee shall bend to God, and every tongue shall confess the Lord as God," perhaps he was implying "not to Caesar" in the first clause and "not Caesar" in the second. This was Paul's hope as he developed it further in Philippians 2:6–11, perhaps not so much as an other-worldly concept as it was for here in this world of time and space. Seen in this light, Romans 13:1-7 is good practical advice from Paul to his fellow believers who gathered in the house churches in Rome. It was good practical advice intended by Paul to save Christian lives until God would act through whatever means God would use to remove the oppressors and to accomplish God's will. As we shall see in chapter V below, the writer of 1 Peter at a later date almost certainly had the same goal of protecting the lives of Christians when that writer wrote 1 Peter 2:13–17 and 3:13.

Anti-Roman cryptograms that we might identify in the other sections of Paul's letter to the Romans are subtle, as was appropriate when we realize that he was sending this document, so to speak, to a place right in "the lion's mouth." Paul may have had promoters of Roman Civil Religion in mind when in Romans 1:18–32 he condemned those who exchanged the glory of the immortal God for their own image of a mortal man (Caesar) that they carried with them. From Paul's perspective, who more obviously than they worshiped and served the creature (Caesar) rather than the Creator? Very carefully, however, Paul placed all of this in a larger context, reaching back to the time of the creation of the world and including images of birds and of animals and reptiles as well as the image of a mortal man. In Romans 8 also Paul placed himself and his fellow believers in the context of the entire creation when he wrote that not only those persons who belong to Jesus Christ, but the entire creation (or at least the known, inhabited world) longs for redemption, to be set free from "its bondage to decay and obtain the glorious liberty of the children of God" (Romans 8:21). If Paul and his fellow believers were to submit to the "ungodliness and wickedness of those who by their impure actions suppress the truth" (Romans 1:18), they would die and decay with them. If, however, they submit only to the righteousness of God that is revealed through faith, they will have the glorious liberty of the children of God. Paul also in Romans 8 carefully placed the rulers and powers who were oppressing him and his fellow believers into a larger context of factors such as death, life, angels, height and depth that will not be able to separate them from the love of God, in order to protect his fellow believers by concealing his message of hope and of liberation for his intended readers from the understanding of their oppressors.

Finally, in Romans 16:20, Paul expressed his fervent hope that "*en tachei* (very soon) the God of peace will crush *ton satanan* under your feet." This fascinating statement was probably intended to be an allusion to the so-called "first expression of the gospel" in Genesis 3:15.[50] It can be interpreted as an expectation by Paul that the final eschaton with the concomitant elimination of all evil in the cosmos was imminent. It can also be seen as a brilliant anti-Roman cryptogram, an expression of Paul's fervent hope and expectation that very soon God, by whatever mysterious ways God might provide, would crush the power of Rome, of Caesar, and of the promoters of Roman Civil Religion who were threatening the lives of Paul and of other early Christian leaders.[51] The early Christians in the house-church communities in the city of Rome were located geographically in a place in which this fall from power of Roman authority would literally be "at their feet." Because Paul had protected this hidden transcript from detection by Roman authorities by his ostentatious "Respect the power of the governing authorities" statements in Romans 12–14, he could boldly make the fervent pronouncement in 16:20 that "Very soon the God of peace will crush Satan under your feet," a proclamation of hope and liberation that would be very encouraging to his intended readers.

Colossians—Delivered from the Dominion of Darkness

If there are anti-Roman cryptograms in this Pauline document, they are located in the statement in Colossians 1:13 that the Father has rescued us from the dominion of darkness and has established us instead in the kingdom of the Father's Son, and in the claims in 1:15–17, 2:9–10, and 2:15 of the superiority of Jesus Christ as Lord over all who sit on thrones and exercise lordship and majesty and authority on the earth. The writer of Colossians asserted that the Father, by raising the Son from the dead, had already placed the followers of Jesus in the safety of the kingdom of the Father's Son by making them alive together with Christ (2:12–13). The Pauline writer believed this, even though obviously the ruling kingdom of darkness centered in Rome still exerted its authority and power unabated. The ruling kingdom of darkness could still take the physical lives of the followers of Jesus, but could not harm them ultimately, since in the resurrection Christ had triumphed over those who exercised power in that kingdom.

The writer of Colossians believed that as the Son of God the Father and as Lord of all Jesus as the Risen Christ has power that is infinitely greater than any and all earthly power. After all, the writer said, it was in the realm of Christ the Son of God that all things in the celestial regions and on the earth—everything that can be seen and everything that cannot be seen—were created (1:15–20). Christ is the focal point of every governing power and authority. These powers and authorities must submit to Christ, the writer said, not only because their kingdoms were developed within Christ's previously existing realm, but also because Christ had triumphed over them and had taken from them their weapons and their power by appearing alive after they had thought that they had killed him.

The writer of the epistle[52] to the Colossians must have been referring, cryptically, to Roman powers and authorities in 2:15 and perhaps also in 1:16. Certainly it was Roman power and weapons that had been used to kill the Jesus of history. The swords brandished by those who held Jesus captive and the whips that tore flesh from his back were weapons chosen by Roman principalities. Scourging and crucifixion were utilized by Roman powers, the ones whom this writer described as "the rulers of this world." The writer of Colossians emphasized the belief that the Risen Christ had triumphed over the Romans (2:15) by appearing alive after the Romans, who were proud of their efficient use of the means of death, had thought that they had killed him. Only when we consider the governing powers and authorities mentioned in Colossians 1:13, 15–17 and 2:9–10, 15 to be exclusively references to angelic-demonic powers of evil are we unable to see that, in part at least, the writer of

Colossians was expressing triumph over the awesome but still earthly and limited power of the Roman State.[53]

The interpretation that the writer of Colossians had only angelic-demonic powers in mind is probably caused by familiarity with the somewhat parallel text in Ephesians 6:12–20. The more cautious writer of Ephesians 6:12-20 may have endeavored to protect the cryptogram there from detection by the Roman oppressors by stating that the struggle of the followers of Jesus Christ was not against human beings comprised of flesh and blood, but against wicked spiritual forces in celestial regions, as we shall see in the next section.

The writer of the epistle to the Colossians asserts that God raised Jesus from the dead to be the Christ of faith (2:9–12). God has made the followers of Jesus Christ alive together with Christ (2:13). Therefore, the followers of Jesus Christ are with the winner, the supreme champion, who is seated at the right hand of God (3:1). Certainly this is a message of hope and liberation, especially when we remember the political situation in which the early followers of Jesus lived, a situation in which suffering because of Roman oppression was an ever present reality, as the references to Paul's sufferings (1:24) and prison chains (4:3, 10, 18) clearly indicate.

Ephesians—Stand Firm Against the Wiles of the Devil

As indicated in the previous section, the writer of the epistle to the Ephesians was more cautious in protecting hidden transcripts of anti-Roman cryptograms in that document from detection by the advocates of Roman Civil Religion than the writer of Colossians had been, or if Ephesians was written by the same person as Colossians that person became more cautious when writing the document that later was designated as "to the Ephesians." Such caution was indeed prudent, especially since Ephesians includes many more instances of anti-Roman cryptograms than does Colossians.

As is well known, the epistle to the Ephesians is in many ways a redaction of the epistle to the Colossians, or a commentary on it. It is not surprising, therefore, that some of the hidden transcripts of anti-Roman cryptograms in Colossians are given further elaboration in Ephesians. The claim is reaffirmed in Ephesians 1:16–23 that God the Father has raised Jesus Christ from the dead and established Christ in power at the Father's right hand, far above all powers on the earth. The earthly powers are described in 2:1–3 as focused in what is called the ruler (or prince) of the power (or authority) of the air, the spirit that is active at the present time among the people who are disobedient to God, expressions used in literature such as the *Ascension of Isaiah* 11, 23, the *Slavic Enoch* 31, and the *Testament of Benjamin* 3:4 to apply to various manifestations of evil. Those who follow in the ways of that ruler are said to be by nature the children of wrath, subject to the wrath of God (Ephesians 2:3; 5:6). They walk in darkness (5:8), they harvest the unfruitful works of darkness (5:11), and they are asleep, dead (5:14). The followers of Jesus Christ in Ephesus, on the other hand, are said to have the light of Jesus Christ (5:8, 14). They are urged to provide no place or opportunity for the diabolical one (devil) to gain control over them (4:27). They are instructed to arm themselves against the wiles (stratagems or strategies) of the diabolical one (the devil) by equipping themselves with the armor of God, all of the defensive shields known at that time to protect a person from the flaming darts of an evil adversary (6:10–20). In addition, the writer urges the followers of Jesus Christ in Ephesus (or wherever they may be) to realize that they are in a struggle to the death against spiritual forces of evil in the celestial regions.

Whether the writer of the epistle to the Ephesians wanted the first readers of that document to visualize their adversary as a demigod with more power than a mortal but less than the power of God, or as the Caesar whose representatives had killed Peter, James, Paul, and countless other leaders among the followers of Jesus, or as both, the modern reader will have to decide. I suspect that although the power of the oppressors then and now may seem to those who are oppressed to be literally coming from above, from the air and from the sky, that kind of terminology was used in these texts, and in many other texts written by oppressed Christians, Jews, and others of that time, partially at least in order to provide a protective coat for the cryptogram. This protective cover enabled the oppressed to say, if accosted by the oppressors, that the oppressed were not talking about people on the earth, but about spiritual beings in a transcendent realm. Nevertheless, the oppressed people would understand. They would receive the message of hope. They would be strengthened to work and to wait for the day of liberation.

This raises the more important question for our time, for our proclamation of the gospel in our religious setting. Shall we interpret these biblical texts solely as references to Satan, the Devil, the Evil Demigod who opposes God and will finally, at the end of time, be totally crushed by the victorious Christ, or shall we interpret these texts also as cryptic references to the oppressors on earth at that time, as texts written to provide support, hope, and encouragement to oppressed early followers of Jesus who believed that God was active in Jesus Christ against known oppressors here on the earth? Which interpretation is more likely to be helpful to people today? Which interpretation will be more helpful in encouraging Christians and other people today to stand up against oppression in their own and in other lands? Each reader will have to decide, but I find that I and most of the people with whom I work are better able to contend against evil that is identified in its human form, in people who are also mortal and have "feet of clay," than against evil that is thought to be coming from some transcendent, supernatural force.

In addition, theologically, interpretations that identify the human sources of evil preserve our monotheistic faith. Dualistic perceptions of God and Satan are not conducive to our faith in God. Evil is indeed pervasive, now as it was during antiquity. Attributing evil to Satan perceived as a demi-god makes it difficult for us to oppose it. Attributing evil to Satan perceived as a fellow mortal human being or groups of human beings makes it feasible for us to resist it. Paul and the later Pauline writers may indeed have used the terminology that they chose because from their own experiences they felt the pervasive presence of evil and they did not have the political power that we today can muster against it.

Let us stand firm, therefore, against the wiles of the devil, as the writer of Ephesians admonished early followers of Jesus. Let us identify the devil and the devils not only in the supernatural sense, but also here within this universe, on this planet earth. Let us oppose the devil and the devils here, as the Jesus of history, the Paul of history, and the writers of the other documents that became the Newer Testament opposed the devil and the devils here on the earth during their time. Traditionally, we as Christians have put the emphasis on the supernatural aspects of evil in the interpretation of these texts. After the horrendous events of the previous century, we should put more emphasis on the human aspects of evil, as indeed most of us are. Recognition of the role of the hidden transcripts of anti-Roman cryptograms within the Newer Testament texts helps us to put more attention on the human aspects of evil alluded to in these texts.

2 Thessalonians—The Activity of Satan, the Evil One

There can be no doubt that the persons to whom this document was addressed were suffering severe persecution and oppression (1:4-7). As a result of this persecution, there were serious incidences of apostasy (*apostasia*) within the fellowship of the followers of Jesus Christ to whom this document was sent.[54] Perhaps some of the difficulties in interpreting 2 Thessalonians 2 can be reduced if we conclude that this chapter includes *vaticinia ex eventu*, predictions of apostasy that is already occurring at the time of the writing (2:3), of lawlessness that is rampant, and of fear of someone who is ruling haughtily as if the person were actually God sitting in the "temple of God" (2:4). Purportedly, the writer is the Apostle Paul, and supposedly the time of the writing is approximately the middle of the first century C.E. Actually, the situation that is described as future in 2 Thessalonians 2 is already underway at the time of the writing. The most likely time of the writing is at least forty years after the writing of 1 Thessalonians, during the final seven years of the reign of Domitian (90–96 C.E.), and the most likely destination intended for the writing is somewhere within the Roman province of Asia, probably in Ephesus, during the severe persecution of Christians there.[55]

The language of 2 Thessalonians 2 is in many ways reminiscent, of course, of the Book of Daniel and of the Apocalypse, which is not at all surprising, since the condition of most of the followers of Jesus within the Roman province of Asia during the period of 90–96 C.E. was similar in many respects to that of the Jews under the rule of Antiochus Epiphanes, and it is likely that the book of Revelation was written at approximately the same time as 2 Thessalonians. Perhaps the "man of lawlessness," the "son of perdition," the one who proclaims himself to be God (ruling as though he were God in the "temple of God")[56] is best understood to be a caricature of Domitian, perceived as an instrument of Satan, demanding worship of himself that should be reserved for God alone. We know from non-biblical sources that Domitian had demanded to be addressed as "Lord and God."[57] According to the writer of 2 Thessalonians 2, this "man of lawlessness" had not yet come to the areas in which the recipients of this document and its writer lived, but was expected by the writer to be coming there, where the Lord Jesus would then appear in order to destroy him utterly and bring redemption to the oppressed followers of Jesus.

To recapitulate, the Christian apostasy addressed in 2 Thessalonians 2 was caused by someone said to be "the lawless one," and "the one who causes utter devastation," who always opposes God and even dares to proclaim himself as God (2:3–4). The coming of this lawless one is an activity of Satan, the evil one, and it involves what appears to be unlimited power, as well as deceptive signs and wonders (2:9). This activity of Satan, the evil lawless one, is manifested in the cruelties imposed on the readers of the document as well as on the writer by wicked and evil men who do not have faith in God (3:2–3). God, through the Lord Jesus, restrains the lawless one now until he is removed from the middle of the stage of world power. The Lord Jesus will destroy the lawless one with the breath of the Lord's mouth and wipe away all evidence of his existence at the time when the Lord appears visibly on the earth (2:7–8). The Lord Jesus will strengthen and guard the faithful from the evil one and from the wicked and evil people through whom Satan, the lawless one, operates (3:2–3).[58]

It is tragic that so many Christian commentators, influenced by what they consider to be historically accurate reporting in the Acts of Apostles literary drama and by the viciously defamatory anti-Jewish 1 Thessalonians 2:13–16 interpolation into Paul's letter, have assumed that the severe persecution and oppression mentioned in 2 Thessalonians was caused primarily by Jews.[59] There is little or no internal evidence within 2 Thessalonians that would suggest a Jewish source for the persecution and oppression. Paul himself would not have labeled any religious Jew "the lawless one," the designation given to the chief culprit in 2 Thessalonians. In the context of a Christian community in Ephesus late in the first century C.E., the lawless one who causes utter devastation, who always opposes God and even dares to proclaim himself to be God, whose coming is said to be an activity of Satan, the evil one, and whose presence involves what appears to be unlimited power, as well as deceptive signs and wonders, is not Jewish but Roman. From the perspective of persecuted and oppressed followers of Jesus Christ of that time and place, the Roman State, the Roman Caesar, and zealous advocates of Roman Civil Religion were manifestations of the activity of Satan, the evil one, evil personified. No Jewish religious leader proclaimed himself to be God, as the lawless one is said in 2 Thessalonians 2:3–4 to have done, but those who promoted the Roman Imperial Cult made that claim for Caesar. They are the ones who are opposed so vehemently in 2 Thessalonians.

1 Timothy—Delivered to Satan; Avoiding the Devil

The reference to delivering Hymenaeus and Alexander over to "Satan" in 1 Timothy 1:20 in order that they may learn not to have contempt for God should be compared to the similar statement in 1 Corinthians 5:5. The word "Satan" in both instances could refer to Roman authority, but probably does not. As indicated in the section on 1 Corinthians above, it would have been foolish to have used the word "Satan" in this kind of a situation, for to do so would be to expose an important cryptogram to possible identification by those who were oppressing the early followers of Jesus. If Paul and others within his tradition had handed certain recalcitrant persons over to Roman authorities for discipline, they would most likely have said exactly that. It is not likely, however, that they had this kind of a relationship with Roman authorities. The expression "delivered to Satan" probably simply meant excommunication, separation from the fellowship of the religious community. A person "delivered over to Satan" would not have access to God within the religious community and, consequently, would not be able to show contempt for God within that religious community.

The references to the judgment (condemnation) of the devil *(tou diabolou)*, the snare of the devil, and straying after Satan in 3:6–7, and 5:14–15, however, are probably hidden transcripts that referred to Roman authorities. An arrogant church leader, especially one who had become a follower of Jesus only recently (3:6), could easily come to the attention of the Roman authorities and thereby endanger the entire religious community. Those who represented Rome and Roman power during the time when 1 Timothy was written probably sensed that their power was diminished whenever anyone within the Empire joined the Christian community, a community in which Jesus Christ rather than Caesar was boldly professed to be Lord, King, Ruler of the Universe. A bishop among the Christians must, therefore, be so highly regarded that in the conduct of his life the bishop would not fall into the hands of Roman authorities.

A young widow who remained unmarried could in her vulnerable condition, particularly in that culture, also come to the attention of Roman authorities and thus endanger the developing Christian community. The writer of 1 Timothy 5:14 may have quite naturally referred to Roman authorities as "the enemy," and then immediately protected the cryptogram just expressed by using the word "Satan" with its transcendent, supernatural connotations as a synonym.

2 Timothy—Rescued from the Lion's Mouth

The expression "snare of the devil," used in 1 Timothy 3:7 as noted above, is repeated in 2 Timothy 2:26. In both instances it may be a cryptic reference to Roman authorities who would, as 2 Timothy 2:26 indicates, wherever possible capture a servant of the Lord Jesus and make the servant of the Lord Jesus do the will of their Lord Caesar.

Few, if any expressions in the Pauline literature are more likely to have been intended as a hidden transcript, an anti-Roman cryptogram, than the words "rescued from the lion's mouth" in 2 Timothy 4:17. Paul is said to have been abandoned by all of his fellow believers when he faced the Roman trial. The Lord Jesus is said to have remained with Paul and to have given him the strength to proclaim the gospel to those who were seeking to kill him. Through the intervention of the Lord Jesus, Paul is said to have been rescued, therefore, from the lion's mouth, although now (4:6) he is about to be sacrificed. Being taken into the lion's mouth is an obvious metaphor for a horrible and violent death. That it referred to a horrible and violent death at the hands of the Romans and of the Roman State is highly probable, not only in this text but also in other Christian texts from roughly the same period.[60] We see this, for example, in 1 Peter 5:8–9, "Resist your adversary, the devil who prowls round like a roaring lion, seeking someone to devour," and in Revelation 13:3 in which the (Roman) beast rising out of the sea is said to have a mouth like that of a lion.

This use of the dreadful symbol of a lion opening its mouth to roar and to attack its victims is a vivid metaphor for the way in which many early Christians perceived Domitian and other Caesars, the Roman State, and particularly the zealous advocates of Roman Civil Religion who stalked Paul and other Christian leaders and then pounced on them. It implies that within this present world there was no escape from the rapacious Roman "king of the jungle."

The anti-Roman cryptograms provided some protection as hidden transcripts of the message of hope and liberation, but offered no guarantees of relief. If the Roman lion was determined to make the kill, Paul and other early followers of Jesus would die. Nevertheless, Paul and the other Pauline writers had a strong hope that soon Christ would prevail over Caesar. Jesus the Risen Christ (not Caesar) was truly Lord. Even though the forces of Caesar had killed Jesus, God had raised him from death to life as the victorious Christ. Even though Roman forces could kill Paul and other followers of Jesus, God would raise also Paul and other early Christians from death to life with Christ.[61] Our survey of the Pauline literature for anti-Roman cryptograms ends, therefore, on this note.

Conclusions

The designation of Jesus as Risen Christ and Lord by Paul and by the Pauline writers was both religious and political. As a religious designation, it defined the early Christian movement as separate from Jewish perceptions. As a political designation, it placed Christians into conflict with Roman claims that Caesar was Lord. Paul and the Pauline writers were not able to avoid the authority of the Roman State in the political realm, and they accepted it so long as that authority did not claim to be ultimate, but they would not accept it in the religious realm.

The use by Paul and by the Pauline writers of cryptograms that involved words such as "Satan," "the devil," "the tempter," "the dominion of darkness," "wild beasts," and "the lion's mouth" indicates that Paul and the Pauline writers were interested in liberation from the political oppression of the Roman State. They were interested in seeing Jesus Christ acclaimed as Lord here on the earth, as well as in eternal life in which Jesus Christ would be acclaimed as Lord forever. In other words, like the Jesus of history, Paul and the Pauline writers had "this-worldly" as well as "other-worldly" concerns. This is consistent with the two basic theses of this book and with criterion 3 as designated on page 18 above.

Finally, many of the words used in the letters of Paul and in the epistles composed by the Pauline writers to refer cryptically to Caesar and Roman power, especially the words "Satan," "the devil," "the tempter," and "wild beasts," are identical with words that may have been used in anti-Roman cryptograms, hidden transcripts, by the Jesus of history and, as we shall see in chapter III below, were used in anti-Roman cryptograms by the writers of the Synoptic Gospels.

III. Anti-Roman Cryptograms in the Synoptic Gospels

Within the past few decades, particularly while I was writing the final chapter on "Conclusions, Implications, and Future Agenda for a Mature Christianity in the Twenty-first Century" of *Mature Christianity in the 21ˢᵗ Century: The Recognition and Repudiation of the Anti-Jewish Polemic of the New Testament*[1] and while teaching January Interim courses on "The Messianic Age" and "The Evil One" at Texas Lutheran University, I have become increasingly aware that detailed analysis of the anti-Jewish polemic of the Newer Testament and of the anti-Roman polemic of the Newer Testament reveals much about the lack of power of the Jewish people and of the magnitude of the power of the Roman State vis-à-vis the power of the early followers of Jesus during the years 50–150 C.E.

The inclusion of vicious, defamatory, vitriolic polemic against Jews and Jewish groups in documents that would eventually be included within the Newer Testament canon is ample evidence of the relative lack of power of Jews during this period. It indicates that Jews, particularly after the destruction of the second temple, were not able to respond to early followers of Jesus who now considered Jesus to be their Lord and Savior other than to attempt to recover their own children who during the earliest years in the development of the Christian movement had joined communities of followers of Jesus. In this process, they issued words of condemnation of these followers of Jesus and eventually excluded most of the most aggressive among them from active participation in synagogue study and worship. Even this apparently occurred only when these followers of Jesus insisted on proclaiming in the synagogues that Jesus Christ raised from the dead, rather than Adonai, is Lord.

On the other hand, the limitation of anti-Roman polemic in what was to become Newer Testament documents to subtle hidden transcripts, cryptograms that in most instances only alert and informed hearers and readers will recognize testifies unambiguously to the awesome power of the Roman State and of anyone within the power structure of the Roman State who wished to exert that power over the lives of followers of Jesus who would not submit to the absolute claims of the advocates of Roman Civil Religion.

We have also become increasingly aware during the past few decades that most of the documents that were eventually incorporated into what became the Newer Testament were the products of three communities of faith among followers of Jesus, three communities of faith that developed for many years somewhat separately from one another. The first of these three communities to have written documents in the Greek language that would provide a core collection for the Newer Testament canon was what we can call the Pauline community, a scattered network of house-church congregations mainly in the Roman provinces of Asia, Macedonia, and Achaia. The second of these communities to have written Newer Testament documents in Greek was the so-called Markan community.[2] The Markan community apparently had its origins and earliest development in Galilee. During the period of the Jewish revolt against Roman oppression in Galilee and Judea that began in 66 C.E., it is likely that most of the members of the Markan community fled as refugees of war to the north out of the area that was in revolt, and, if Howard Clark Kee is correct in his *Community of the New Age: Studies in Mark's Gospel*[3] into the villages and rural areas of southern Syria, particularly in the areas of Caesarea Philippi,[4] Tyre, and Sidon.[5] As the Roman military forces approached and reoccupied Galilee, these Jewish background and Gentile background persons for whom Jesus was now perceived as the Christ, the Son of God, left their homes and the terraced hillsides in which they had gained their livelihood in subsistence agriculture and simple making, trading, and selling of crafts and fled from the area that had rebelled against Roman rule. They saw no reason to lose their lives in a Jewish nationalistic cause. Nevertheless, they went initially to areas in southern Syria and in the Decapolis that were all relatively close to Galilee. At first, they may have intended to return to Galilee as soon as possible. Also, if as indicated in Mark 16:7 they believed that Jesus as the Risen Christ would appear in Galilee, they would want to be close enough so that they could rush back to Galilee to see him. If Jesus as the Risen Christ appeared, they would have no fear of the Roman military forces.

The scenario depicted above provides an explanation for the relatively simple style of "The Gospel of Jesus Christ."[6] It also explains the reason for the inaccurate documentation of the source for the quotation regarding John the Baptizer as that documentation occurs in the earliest manuscripts that are available to us. Refugees of war have no opportunity to check the sources for accuracy when they are quoting them from their own memories.

One of the primary reasons for the composition of this first Gospel as an expression of the faith of the members of the Markan community may have been that the leaders of the group realized after only a few weeks or months that with the Roman troops firmly entrenched in Galilee there was no future for the members of the community back in Galilee. Very likely there were large numbers of Jews who also had fled from Galilee as the Roman task force approached, so that the areas to the north and east of Galilee were literally saturated with refugees from the war. If the members of the Markan community were to survive, they would have to split into smaller groups and settle in large cities in which they could use their crafts-making skills and ability as day laborers to eke out a living. By having a written expression of their faith and making a copy for each of the larger groups into which they would split, they might be able to survive economically as well as to retain their faith and to build upon it.

It is probable that one large group migrated to Antioch, where they continued and intensified their verbal conflicts with Pharisees, many of whom were also refugees from the war, competing for the same sparse resources as were the members of the Markan community. Others probably moved westward to Ephesus, and still others all the way to Rome, the largest city in the known world. During the ensuing two decades, the copies of "The Gospel of Jesus Christ" that were taken to Antioch and to Ephesus were improved and redacted to meet the changing needs of the members of this extended community of faith. Major redactions and new compositions resulted in what eventually came to be known as "The Gospel According to Matthew" and "The Gospel According to Luke," completing the Synoptic Gospels tradition.

Smaller and more parochial than either the Pauline or the Synoptic Gospels communities was the Johannine community. This community, which revealed so much of the story of its own development in what later was called The Gospel According to John and in 1 John, 2 John, and 3 John, originated in Judea in the Lower Jordan River Valley east of the Jordan River near Jericho, and eventually included a significant number of people from Samaria. Apparently it developed somewhat separately from the Markan community. Experiencing many internal divisions and hardships, most of the members of this community also migrated, like most of the Markan community, to the north and eventually to the west. Perhaps many of its members lived for a period of time in the southern part of the kingdom of Herod Agrippa II, in the region of Gaulanitis and Batanaea. Later, many of its members migrated to Syria, and others to the province of Asia, to the seven cities mentioned in Revelation 1:11–3:22.[7]

Within chapter II above, we evaluated texts from the documents of the Pauline community that may have included subtle hidden transcripts of anti-Roman cryptograms. In chapter IV below, we shall look for similar texts in the writings of the Johannine community. Here in chapter III, we shall examine texts within the documents produced by the Markan community and its successors that may have been intended in part also as subtle cryptograms, anti-Roman messages of hope and liberation for those whom we might call "mainline" Christians.

For the convenience of the reader, the material in this chapter is developed in four sections. It begins with an analysis of possible anti-Roman cryptograms that are incorporated into A. "The Gospel of Jesus Christ" (Mark) and continued in Matthew and/or in Luke. This is followed by shorter studies of possible anti-Roman cryptograms in B. Matthew and Luke, C. Matthew only, and D. Luke only.

In "the Gospel of Jesus Christ" (Mark) and Continued in Matthew and/or in Luke

The three major types of texts within the Synoptic Gospels that may contain subtle anti-Roman cryptograms are all introduced within Mark 1:12–45. All three types of texts have origins within the teachings and activity of the Jesus of history, and reference to the first two of these three types is given in chapter I above, "Anti-Roman Cryptograms of the Jesus of History." These three types of texts are considered here in the sequence in which they are introduced in Mark 1, i.e., in the Temptation of Jesus accounts introduced in Mark 1:12–13, in the Proclamation of the Kingdom of God texts introduced in Mark 1:14–15, and in the Exorcism Stories and in Other Healing Stories introduced in Mark 1:21–45.

In the Temptation of Jesus Accounts

There are actually three separate but related temptation of Jesus accounts in the Synoptic Gospels. The first and most obvious is the well-known temptation of Jesus in the wilderness account of Mark 1:12–13, Matthew 4:1–11, and Luke 4:1–13 at the beginning of Jesus' public ministry. The second occurs in Mark 8:31-33 and in Matthew 16:21–23 when Peter is said to have tried to dissuade Jesus from going to Jerusalem, and the third in Mark 14:32–42, Matthew 26:36–46, and Luke 22:39–46 in Gethsemane. All three may have been based on conversations between the Jesus of history and his closest friends in which Jesus may have referred to the temptation that he faced within his mind throughout his public life. This temptation involved the suggestions made by various people, such as pragmatic Herodians,[8] Simon Peter at certain times,[9] and perhaps Judas Iscariot near the end of Jesus' life,[10] that Jesus could live much longer and help his fellow oppressed Jews in Galilee and Judea much more if he were to cooperate with the Roman oppressors and urge his fellow Jews to cooperate with them than by encouraging his people to believe that soon Adonai rather than Caesar would be their "Lord" and "Boss" in a most tangible way.

Within a situation of violence in which one's nation is occupied by oppressive foreign powers, such as occurred for example when much of Europe was under the control of Nazi Germany during World War II, peace-loving persons are tempted to cooperate with the oppressors not only in order to survive, to try to live through the ordeal, but also in order to foster an illusion of peaceful acceptance of the occupation in order to attempt to reduce conflict. If the Jesus of history was essentially a peace-loving person, he may indeed have been tempted during his entire adult life to cooperate as much as he could with the oppressive Romans and with those among his fellow Jews who cooperated with them in an attempt to reduce conflict in the land. The larger the number of people who listened to Jesus and attached themselves in one way or another to him the greater, in a sense, was his temptation. Oppressors need the cooperation of decisive and effective leaders among the oppressed and are willing to reward those who are willing to work with them. The rewards to be offered will always be commensurate with the effectiveness of the leader among the oppressed to maintain control over large numbers of the oppressed people. It is obviously an exaggeration to say that if Jesus had been willing to submit unconditionally to the authority of Caesar and of Caesar's minions that the Romans would have given to Jesus significant power within Galilee and Judea, but they would have rewarded him with money and the amounts of money might have been increased significantly if Jesus had continued to cooperate and could continue to maintain a "positive" influence over large numbers of his fellow oppressed Jews in this process.

While the temptation of Jesus accounts within the Synoptic traditions may have their primary origin in conversations between the Jesus of history and some of his closest friends, the accounts as we have them in the Synoptic Gospels are all expressions of the faith of the writers and members of the Markan community and of their successors and should be perceived as such. We should be aware that in many ways the temptation of the Jesus of history to cooperate with the Roman occupation forces was also the temptation of the members of the Markan community prior to, during, and after the Jewish rebellion against Roman power in Galilee and Judea from 66–72 C.E. Had the members of the Markan community been willing to cooperate fully with the Romans, the community could have been appropriately rewarded by the Romans and the leaders of the community might have realized significant enhancement in their efforts to spread their message and to expand their community within the vast Roman Empire. In the long term, power over that empire might be given to them, as indeed it was to be given during the fourth century C.E., but at a heavy price to be paid.

Several significant observations should be made as we begin our analysis of the temptation of Jesus in the wilderness account in Mark 1:12–13, Matthew 4:1–11, and Luke 4:1–13.

First, these accounts were expressed in a story form that was not intended to be interpreted literally, except by those who were outside the faith tradition of those who composed them. The informed hearer or reader within the faith tradition did not think that Jesus had been physically led by the Spirit of God into the wilderness in order that Jesus might be tempted by Satan, nor that Satan physically had led Jesus around "by the nose," so to speak, from the wilderness to the pinnacle of the temple and to a very high mountain. The informed member of the faith tradition did not think that Satan physically had set Jesus on the pinnacle of the temple the way an adult might set a small child on a ledge, or that there is any mountain within the Roman Empire from which all of the provinces of that Empire can be seen, even on the clearest of days. In addition, the Lukan writer modified the sequence of the incidents of the Matthean story not only in order to have the series end in Jerusalem, as is often noted, but also to indicate that the story should not be interpreted literally.

Second, the Matthean and Lukan accounts should be seen to be the first and most important commentaries on the Mark 1:12–13 account, as well as interesting expansions of it. Mark 1:12–13 was obviously too packed full of interpretive possibilities simply to be repeated unchanged by the Matthean and Lukan redactors. Its succinctness called out for elaboration in expanded story form.

Third, these temptation accounts are all saturated with symbolism, symbolism that would have been apparent to the informed reader or hearer within the faith tradition of the early church. We should focus our attention, therefore, on the symbolism within the accounts, not on a superficial, "face value only" reading of them.

Some of the symbolism that is used in the temptation of Jesus accounts depicts Jesus' experiences as recapitulations of the earlier experiences of the people of Israel. Unfortunately, this has led to interpretations of these texts that are disparaging to the Jewish tradition, because Jesus is presented as successful in areas in which Israel had failed, especially in resisting all temptations. This symbolism is seen in the references to Jesus being driven or led by the Spirit of God, in the symbolism of life in the wilderness, of the presence of wild beasts, and of the forty days of Jesus' experience corresponding to the forty years of the pre-Israelites' experience in the desert.

The symbolism of the hidden transcripts of subtle anti-Roman cryptogram in these accounts has not been readily apparent during the past sixteen centuries. Nevertheless, informed hearers and readers, alerted to the symbolism of double meanings that conceals references to Caesar, Roman power, and oppressive Roman political and military presence behind words such as "Satan," "the diabolical one," "the tempter," and "wild beasts," can recognize the anti-Roman cryptogram in these accounts. The anti-Roman symbolism is similar to that which we have seen in the letters of Paul and in other Pauline literature in chapter II above. The message is that the Jesus of history resisted the temptation to cooperate with the Roman oppressors and idolatrously to serve Caesar as his "Lord." According to these accounts, God supported and strengthened the Jesus of history as he resisted this strong temptation to idolatry. His followers are to resist similar temptations to idolatry in the hope and expectation that God will also support and strengthen them. We too must resist and oppose the idolatry inherent in the claims and actions of those who are overly zealous advocates of our own civil religion and of the civil religions of other people now and in the future.

In order to see more clearly the "hidden transcripts" of subtle anti-Roman cryptogram in these temptation accounts, let us look at the final, climactic episode of the Matthew 4:1–11 story and at the second temptation in the Luke 4:1–13 account. When we ask, "Through whom did 'Satan' exercise power over all of the kingdoms of the world known to Jesus and to his followers, and who was the principal agent of 'Satan' with glory and splendor in them?" the only adequate answer is "Caesar!" Caesar claimed the supreme power and glory and splendor in all of these kingdoms. Only Caesar and Caesar's representatives could share that power and glory and splendor with Jesus, the followers of Jesus, and anyone else who would cooperate fully with them within that vast realm. Caesar and Caesar's representatives could give these things to those who would submit unconditionally to them and serve them as their "Lord" and "Boss."[11] The message for Jesus' followers was that just as Jesus had resisted this temptation to idolatry, so also must his followers resist that temptation. Like Jesus, they must worship only the Lord their God and only the Lord their God must they serve. If this path led to crucifixion for them at the hands of the Roman oppressors, they believed that God would raise them also, like Jesus, from the dead into a situation in which Roman power would have no authority over them.

It may be implicit in these accounts that Jesus and the writers of the Synoptic Gospels considered all Roman overtures to them to be temptations by "Satan" that must steadfastly be resisted and rejected. Furthermore, they considered the Romans to be "wild beasts," mindless and ravenous. If Jesus and his followers resisted them, God would send benevolent angels to minister to them, as they had ministered to Jesus, perhaps in the form of mythical messengers from heaven, or possibly in the form of kind and gentle persons such as the mother-in-law of Peter, who according to Mark 1:31 had served and ministered to Jesus and to his followers.[12]

To conclude this section on the temptation of Jesus accounts, let us look briefly at Mark 8:31–33 and Matthew 16:21–23 in which Peter is said to have tried to dissuade Jesus from going to Jerusalem, and at the Mark 14:32–42, Matthew 26:36–46, and Luke 22:39–46 accounts of Jesus in Gethsemane. Peter is said to be "Satan…not on the side of God but of evil people" when he tries to prevent Jesus from going to Jerusalem to share his message of hope and liberation there. As a result, Jesus orders Peter to go to the rear, out of Jesus' sight, away from Jesus' disciples. If Jesus had been convinced by Peter not to go to Jerusalem, it would have been a triumph for Satan and for the Romans through whom Satan worked, because then Jesus' message of hope and liberation would not have been proclaimed at the center of Jewish religious and political activity. The evil demonic forces would have prevailed. "Satan" would have won. The Jews would have remained in bondage to the Romans on the earth and to Satan in the spiritual realm. Jesus' mission would have been stopped in its tracks on the road to Jerusalem.

Again Jesus is said to have been tempted in Gethsemane on the night in which he was betrayed, tempted to flee for his life, to stop his proclamation and his demonstration of his message of hope in Adonai and of liberation from Satan and from Roman oppression. Jesus resisted this temptation, even at the point of death, according to the Gethsemane accounts. Had Jesus fled for his life, he would have been a coward. Satan would have prevailed in the spiritual realm and Satan's minions, the Romans, would have prevailed in the physical world. Jesus' message of hope would have been silenced because of his fear of Satan and of the Romans. Jesus would never have become Savior and Lord.

The followers of Jesus are expected, like Jesus in Gethsemane, to be awake and alert, engaged in prayer, willing to die rather than to be silenced by fear of Satan and of Satan's Roman agents. Anything less would be a denial of Jesus and of their faith. In the face of every temptation offered by the Roman kingdoms of this world, the kingdom of God in which Jesus, not Caesar, is Lord must be proclaimed. The Romans can kill their bodies, as they killed the bodies of Jesus, Peter, Paul, and others, but God will raise them from the dead to new and unending life with Christ.

In the Proclamation of the Kingdom of God

The succinct temptation of Jesus account in Mark 1:12–13 is followed by the equally terse words of 1:14–15, "And after John had been delivered over, Jesus came into Galilee, proclaiming the gospel of God and saying, 'The time has been fulfilled and the kingdom of God has come near; repent and believe in the gospel.'" In many respects, the entire Synoptic tradition is an expansion of what is introduced in these two verses.

Nineteen centuries later when there are few political systems that can still be called "kingdoms," and when the remaining kings and queens and royal families have little more than ceremonial functions to perform, it is difficult for most people to perceive what was intended within the Synoptic tradition by the terminology "the proclamation of the kingdom of God." Sermons within the Christian tradition often give the impression that this terminology refers almost entirely to heaven and to the life to come, or perhaps in some instances to the church. Neither of these designations, however, is adequate. The Jesus of history was not talking about the Christian church as it was to evolve during the succeeding nineteen centuries, and Jesus and the Synoptic traditions were probably not nearly so interested in heaven and "other-worldly" concepts as the Christian church was later to become.[13]

Our understanding of the texts in which "the kingdom of God" is an important symbol will be enhanced if we realize that references to the coming of "the kingdom of God" within the Synoptic traditions were originally primarily political, expressions of a desire for a radical change from the then-current political situation of oppression by the Romans. When "the kingdom of God" would come, there would be a political situation in which Jesus' followers would be free here on the earth to live their lives with only God through Jesus the Christ as their Lord having absolute power over them. The terminology within Matthew of "the kingdom of heaven" is a careful way of making the expression sound less political, probably partially in an attempt to try to protect Christians from additional political persecution by Roman authorities. Even though many of us have been told since the time that we were little children that political issues must be kept separate from our expressions of religion, within the Synoptic traditions that separation was not maintained. In the Synoptic tradition, "kingdom" terminology is in most instances primarily political terminology. The references to the proclamation of the kingdom of God within the Synoptic tradition are primarily messages of hope and liberation. They are subtle polemic against the political oppressors of that time, Roman authorities and Caesar, in Galilee, Judea, and throughout the Roman Empire wherever followers of Jesus lived.

One of the most helpful studies in which the concept of "the kingdom of God" in the Synoptic tradition is interpreted as a symbol with political implications is George Wesley Buchanan's *Jesus: The King and His Kingdom*.[14] Buchanan reminds us that the Kaddish, developed by Jews during the period between 20 B.C.E. and 70 C.E., expressed a passionate longing for their own kingdom on the earth that would replace the kingdom ruled by the Romans. In Buchanan's opinion,

> The titles attributed to Jesus were those appropriate for a king. The kingdom he was trying to obtain was the kind of kingdom all other kings rule. It was mythologically called the Kingdom of God or the Kingdom of Heaven, but Jews of New Testament times knew that this kingdom would come into being only when the Romans were expelled from Palestine and their own king sat on the throne, ruling from Jerusalem. (41)

Buchanan examines various parables within the Synoptic tradition to demonstrate the longing felt by the Jews in Galilee and Judea and by Jesus and his followers for a kingdom that would be their own, soon, during their own lifetimes, and here on this earth, without the Roman presence that was at that time preventing it.

While we may not go as far as Buchanan goes in depicting Jesus as one who was organizing a highly committed following of trained leaders, including tax collectors and other liberal businessmen, and planning to gain political control over Galilee and Judea, his insights make it easier for us to understand the symbolism of the kingdom concept within the Synoptic tradition. They help us to see that the call to repentance in Mark 1:15 and in similar texts elsewhere within the Synoptic tradition involved not merely repentance from sins directed against other human beings on a personal level as characterized in the latter commandments of the Decalogue, but repentance from the sin of permitting the Roman officials and the Roman military to have the authority over one's life that only God should have. "Repent" in Mark 1:15 and similar texts certainly meant, "Do not sin against God!" "Remember the First Commandment of the Decalogue, 'You shall have no other gods before me!'" It meant in practical terms, "Do not cooperate with the Roman authorities, except for the necessary payment of taxes and duties under duress." It meant, "Let them take your outer garment if necessary to save your life, and do not strike back when they hit you, but do not let them become God for you." "Be prepared for the time soon when only God will be ruling over you."

The writer of the Markan account subtly brought the oppressive political situation to mind by beginning Mark 1:14 with the words, "And after John had been delivered over," a reminder of Roman oppression expressed through the surrogate of Caesar in Galilee, Herod Antipas. Actually, of course, those for whom Mark's account was written would have no need of being reminded of Roman oppression. They were experiencing it all of the time.

Since we have already looked in some detail at a few of the parables of the kingdom in the section "Jesus' Teaching: The Kingdom of Adonai, Not of Caesar" within chapter I above, and since we shall be referring briefly again to the "kingdom of God" in the section on the "Lord's Prayer" later in this chapter, we shall not attempt here to analyze further additional texts within the Synoptic tradition that refer to proclamation of the kingdom of God. Instead, we shall move on to a consideration of hidden transcripts of anti-Roman cryptograms in exorcism stories and in other healing stories within the Synoptic Gospels.

In Exorcism Stories and Other Healings Stories

The third type of texts within the Synoptic Gospels that may contain subtle anti-Roman cryptograms is the type that is comprised of exorcism stories and other healing stories. These also are introduced in Mark 1, specifically in 1:21–28, 29–31, 32–34, 35–39, and 40–45. This is seen clearly, for example, by Richard A. Horsley, who writes that "Like the exorcisms, Jesus' healings were not simply isolated acts of individual mercy, but part of a larger program of social as well as personal healing."[15] With an awareness of the ways in which followers of Jesus in Galilee would have perceived the healings performed by Jesus of the woman who had been hemorrhaging for twelve years and bringing back to life the twelve year old daughter of Jairus as depicted in Mark 5:21–43, they would have understood that "When Jesus brings the seemingly dead twelve-year-old girl back to life just at the time she has come of age to produce children, he is mediating new life to Israel in general. In these and other episodes Jesus is healing the illnesses brought on by Roman imperialism."[16]

It is likely that the Jesus of history performed many what we today call "faith healings" as he went from place to place urging his fellow Jews to believe and trust in Adonai. There must have been many people in Galilee and Judea who at that time were so discouraged and depressed that they did not even try to get up and walk anymore. They had very little to live for, and the physical therapy that is accessible to us in our society was not available to them. Jesus must have helped many others to have better sight and insight, to hear where formerly they could not hear, and to be restored to health in other ways. Also, he certainly must have helped others who had been disabled by various psychoses and who were popularly thought to have been "demon possessed." Therefore, we should not be surprised to find that after Jesus had been seized, tortured, and crucified by the Romans the Jesus traditions as they developed within various groups of his followers included a variety of exorcism stories and other healing stories.

Within the exorcism stories and other healings stories in the Synoptic Gospels, we notice that those who are said to be possessed by demons recognize Jesus as "the Holy One of God" and as "Son of the Most High God" immediately, long before even the closest followers of Jesus recognize him by such high Christological titles. We notice also that when Jesus exercises his power over these demons the people who witness these events or hear about them are amazed at his awesome authority and, as a consequence, his fame spreads rapidly throughout the land. It is also implied in Mark 3:22–27, Matthew 12:24–29, and Luke 11:15–22 that according to popular expectation only the ruler of the demons, or someone who is stronger than the ruler of the demons, i.e., God, has the authority to cast demons out of the body of a person. All of this suggests that within the Synoptic Gospels a person who is said to be possessed by demons is thought to be strongly influenced by someone who has tremendous power and acumen, someone who is greatly feared by the people of the land, someone who ordinarily cannot be opposed. All of this points in the political setting of that time almost inevitably to an association of some kind between demon possession and Roman power. This in turn leads us to the awareness that in the subtle hidden transcripts of the Synoptic Gospels a person who rejected that person's own Jewish or early Christian religious tradition and cooperated fully with the hated and feared Roman authorities was considered to be severely psychotic, or in the terminology of that period to be "possessed by demons." In the words of Richard A. Horsley, "As presented in the Gospel of Mark, Jesus' exorcisms are similarly understood not only as an expulsion of alien forces that had taken possession of particular people, but as the defeat of the more general demonic forces working through the Romans who had taken possession of the people's lives."[17]

We find, for example, that in Luke 22:3 it is written that "Satan" (elsewhere the prince of demons) had entered into Judas Iscariot and as a result he arranged to deliver Jesus over into the hands of those who wanted to kill him, thereby cooperating fully with them. In the same chapter, in Luke 22:31, Jesus is represented as saying to Peter, "Simon, Simon, Satan urgently has desired to have you and others with you in order to sift you like wheat," again subtly implying full cooperation with the hated and feared Roman political and military authorities and with Caiaphas and his group.

To cite another example, in Luke 8:2 Mary Magdalene is described as one from whom seven demons had gone out, and in one of the additions to Mark, in Mark 16:9, it is said that Mary Magdalene was the one from whom Jesus had cast out seven demons. In the cryptic language of the early Christian tradition, this may have implied that she had been raped and enslaved by Roman soldiers and that seven of those "demons" had literally been "in" her sexually until Jesus had cast them out by rescuing her from them.[18] It is not surprising, therefore, that it was said that the demons recognized Jesus to be "the Holy One of God," that the Jewish people were said to have been amazed, and that Jesus' fame had spread so rapidly throughout all of the surrounding region. This also helps to explain why those who loved Jesus the most feared so much for his personal safety. If Jesus had somehow rescued Mary Magdalene from seven Roman soldiers who had been "using" her body for their own prurient purposes (possibly one each night of the week), the lives of both Jesus and of Mary Magdalene would have been greatly endangered, even if keeping a Jewish woman in bondage for sexual use was against Roman military regulations at that time.

Let us look more closely at the most complex exorcism story within the Synoptic traditions, the story about Jesus and the Gerasene demoniac in Mark 5:1–20 and its parallels in Matthew 8:28–34 and Luke 8:26–39. Let us see what evidence there may be that this story may at one time have been intended to be among other things a subtle hidden transcript, an anti-Roman cryptogram with an important message of hope and liberation for oppressed early followers of Jesus.

The story in Mark 5:1–20 about Jesus and his dynamic interaction with the man in the country of the Gerasenes who had been possessed by an unclean spirit—more specifically by an entire "Legion" of unclean spirits—continues to intrigue us as we read it and hear it today. It is obviously intended to be a miracle story, an exorcism story, proclaiming Jesus' marvelous power over the forces represented in the story as a "Legion" of unclean spirits. To put the story into perspective, perhaps we can say that the primary purpose of the story as it is related within the Markan tradition is to proclaim that just as Jesus as Lord had mercy on a man who had been under the control of the "Legion" of vicious unclean spirits in the story, so also Jesus as Lord will have mercy on those who are under the control of vicious unclean spirits as they read or hear the story. This use in Mark 5:9 and 15 of the Greek transliteration of the Latin loan word *legio* placed into the account a reminder of the presence in the area around the Sea of Galilee of a Roman unit of several thousand men, thereby associating the unclean spirit of the demon-possessed man with the Roman military presence. If the use of the word "Legion" brings the Roman military to *our* minds, it must have brought the Roman military presence to the minds of those who heard this account during the first century when the Roman military presence was a reality that constantly confronted the Jews and followers of Jesus in the area of the Sea of Galilee and of the entire eastern Mediterranean area.[19] Almost certainly, the use of the word "Legion" here and in the parallel in Luke 8:26–39 was a cryptic way to communicate that the reason this man was so thoroughly deranged was that he was cooperating totally with the Roman military forces. By cooperating totally with the Romans, he was "living among the dead." As Donald Juel put it[20] "The name **Legion** conjures up imagery of particular significance to a subject people. 'Legion' is a Latin word, not Greek, and it can only be intended to offer some comment about the link between Roman soldiers and demons."

By aligning himself with the demonic forces of Rome, the deranged man was "too powerful for the Jews to subdue." Completely separated from his own religious tradition, he was "crying out wildly and bruising himself with stones." Apart from God and totally under the control of these Satanic influences he was "naked," and "out of his right mind" until Jesus with the power of God made it possible for the "Legion" of demons to depart from the man and enter into the "pigs," in which form they could be tangibly destroyed.

The commercial production of hogs, pigs, swine in the area east of the Sea of Galilee, an area that had been an integral portion of the kingdom of Solomon, must have been especially abominable to the Jews of the first century C.E. For there to have been a herd of two thousand or more of them, as this story suggests, implied a massive takeover of the area by the Roman "swine."

According to R. H. Charles[21] the black wild boar depicted in 1 Enoch 89:10–27 represents Esau and the swine in that account represent the Edomites, descendants of Esau. In the same account, the wolves are the Egyptians, and it should be noted that the wolves were drowned in the sea. In the cryptograms of the Rabbinic Literature, the words "Esau" and "Edom" represent Rome.[22] Thus, as Charles suggests,[23] Jews associated Edom (Rome) with pigs, the animals that they detested the most. In Revelation 13:1–10, the Roman Empire is said to be like a beast rising out of the sea. Many of its troops came "out of the sea" at Caesarea and entered the "holy land." It would be appropriate, therefore, that they be drowned, like the Egyptians of old, in the sea. The way to accomplish this in the early Jewish-background Christian tradition was by the use of exorcism miracle stories, of which Mark 5:1–20 is the prime example.

Comparison with somewhat similar exorcism miracle stories in the New Testament Apocrypha *Acts of Peter*[24] and in Philostratus, *Life of Apollonius* iv. 20,[25] each of which will be summarized below, together with attention given to the social, political, and religious situation of those involved in the development of the Markan tradition, provides additional evidence for the likelihood that at least the Mark 5:9–17 portion of the account was originally intended to be a well constructed hidden transcript, an effective anti-Roman cryptogram, a prime example of the kind of protest possible for the Markan community at the time the Markan Gospel was written. Mark 5:9–17 would have been, for the storyteller and for the hearers at certain stages in the early development of the story, a relatively safe way to assert the Lordship of Jesus as the Christ over the

Roman Legion of unclean "pigs" who had crucified the Jesus of history and who continued to threaten the lives of followers of Jesus in the lands in which they lived. In this story the Markan writer-storyteller was able to use the common vehicle of an exorcism miracle account within which to include this cryptogram. In this way the Markan writer-storyteller was able to say that Jesus had symbolically and would soon actually cause those vicious, unclean Roman "pigs" to rush headlong westward over a cliff to be drowned in that great Western Sea over which they had come.

The Markan writer was influenced by the Daniel traditions in many respects.[26] Just as Jews living two centuries earlier under the oppressive power of the Seleucids developed an extensive cryptogram within the Daniel traditions as a means of encouraging each other to endure,[27] the teller and writer of the exorcism miracle story later to be known as Mark 5:1–20 encouraged early followers of Jesus to survive persecution by the Romans by assuring the followers of Jesus that Jesus their Lord had decisive power over the "Legion" of unclean Roman spirits who hounded them. In this way, the Markan storyteller was able to conceal from those who were outside the Markan community of faith, but to reveal to those who were in it, warnings against the Roman State and its representatives and acclamations of eventual victory over them.

The two non-canonical accounts of exorcisms mentioned above will now be summarized here as additional examples of similar hidden transcripts. First, in the New Testament Apocrypha *Acts of Peter*, section 11, it is written that Peter turned to the crowd of people who stood near him and saw in the crowd a young man who was half laughing, in whom there was a most wicked demon. When Peter commanded the man to show himself openly, the man ran into the courtyard of the house, shouted, and threw himself against the wall. In the name of Jesus Christ as Lord, Peter ordered the wicked demon to come out of the man, to do him no more harm, and to show itself to all who were standing there. The wicked demon then left the man, grasped a large marble statue that was in the courtyard of the house, and kicked it to pieces. The statue that was destroyed in this way is identified as a statue of Caesar. When Senator Marcellus saw what had occurred, he beat his forehead and said to Peter, "A great crime has been committed; if Caesar hears of this through some busybody, he will punish us severely." Peter responded to Marcellus by suggesting that if Marcellus is truly repentant and believes in Christ with his whole heart Marcellus should take some running water, pray to the Lord, sprinkle the water in the name of the Lord over the broken pieces of the statue, and it will be restored as it had been before the demon had attacked it. Marcellus did exactly as Peter had directed, and the statue was restored.[28] It was restored because of fear of reprisal by Caesar's agents. If it could be destroyed once in the name of Jesus, however, could it not be broken into pieces again, and could not Caesar and Caesar's power be destroyed as well?

Second, in Philostratus, *Life of Apollonius* iv. 20, it is written that as the philosopher Apollonius of Tyana was discussing the question of libations, a notoriously evil young man burst out into loud and coarse laughter, drowning out the voice of the philosopher. Apollonius recognized that it was not the young man who had insulted him, but a demon that drove the young man on without his knowledge of what was happening to him. As Apollonius gazed at the young man, the demon within the young man began to cry out in fear and rage and to swear that it would leave the young man alone and never again take possession of any man. Apollonius then addressed the demon sternly and ordered it to come out of the young man and to show by a visible sign that it had done so. The demon said that it would throw down a statue, one of the images in the king's portico where the scene occurred.[29] When the statue began to move and then fell down, the people who were there were greatly amazed. The young man rubbed his eyes as if he had just awakened. Returning to his natural self, the young man accepted the austerity of the philosophers and modeled his life on the life of Apollonius.

In the story about Apollonius, the opposition of the philosopher to the power of the ruler and the criticism of the worship practices sanctioned by the ruler are expressed cryptically in an exorcism story that is similar in many ways to the account in Mark 5:1–20. Both accounts are expressions of hope and liberation developed by followers of a respected leader.

For followers of Jesus and perhaps also for philosophers such as Philostratus, it was prudent to be on record publicly as teaching respect for Roman law, urging that the emperor be honored and that the required taxes be paid, as is amply illustrated within the Newer Testament documents. Apparently it was most inadvisable to write anything directly against the oppressive Roman State. When persecution was severe, as it must have been when segments such as Revelation 16:17–19:5 were written, those who were heavily oppressed used the code name Babylon to represent what was for them the wicked city of Rome.

Resentment by most Jews over the ongoing occupation of their land by the Roman military forces was obviously intense. The extensive military rebellions of 66–72 and 132–135 C.E. are well-documented evidence of this Jewish resentment. In the cryptograms of the Rabbinic Literature, the code words "Esau" and "Edom" were used for Rome and for Roman power, as indicated above, as can be seen in comments on Isaiah 43:9 in *Abodah Zarah* 2 of the Babylonian Talmud. For followers of Jesus whose leader had been seized, tortured, and publicly crucified by Roman political and military forces, there must have been many private expressions of resentment, fear, and hatred of Roman personnel. Public expressions of resentment and inclusions of such resentment within written documents would have been limited, however, to subterfuges such as hidden transcripts, cryptograms. Within such cryptograms, if they were well crafted, it was possible even to express triumph over the Roman forces, although the use of such cryptograms was not without risk of detection by the oppressors. Use of words such as "Legion" and "a herd of pigs" considered above in Mark 5:1–20 involved such a risk. Nevertheless, within an exorcism miracle story mingled among other exorcism miracle stories such a risk was apparently considered to be affordable. Perhaps the Matthean redactors of Mark 5:1–20 did not use the portion of Mark that included the word "Legion" in order to reduce that risk somewhat. Possibly the Matthean redactors considered the account to be less important than it was for the Markan writer and chose to give it less emphasis.

One more challenging and fascinating text within the Synoptic tradition will be considered here, a text in which there are no apparent code words as such utilized, no use of words such as Satan, the Devil, the Evil One, the "Render to Caesar" text in Mark 12:13–17, Matthew 22:15–22, and Luke 20:20–26. Christopher Bryan uses the "Render to Caesar" words as the primary title of his extensive book, *Render to Caesar: Jesus, the Early Church, and the Roman Superpower,* and writes with regard to the "Render to Caesar" text in Mark 12:13–17 and parallels, that "Only a fool would claim to be sure about the meaning of a passage that has puzzled exegetes for centuries."[30] Nevertheless, William R. Herzog II in "Onstage and Offstage with Jesus of Nazareth: Public Transcripts, Hidden Transcripts, and Gospel Texts," in *Hidden Transcripts and the Arts of Resistance: Applying the Work of James C. Scott to Jesus and Paul,*[31] using insights provided by James C. Scott, builds what to me is a compelling case for seeing the "Render to Caesar" texts as hidden transcripts. Herzog points out that the Roman denarius "was no ordinary Roman coin," that "its ubiquity throughout the empire made it a familiar symbol of Caesar's presence and power" (54). The denarius that Caesar had authorized and utilized as public currency was stamped with Caesar's "image and likeness." It "can be given back to Caesar because it came from Caesar." Moreover, "it must be given back because it is blasphemous and idolatrous" (58). Jesus' statement was, in Herzog's words, a disguised, ambiguous and coded way of maintaining the hidden transcript of resistance while leaving a public transcript that is in no way actionable." Jesus responded in a way in which he was able "to balance seeming deference to the powers that be with a coded message of resistance," an encouragement to "those who had 'ears to hear'" (58). As Warren Carter puts it,[32] for disciples of Jesus "'in the know,' payment is an act of disguised nonviolent dissent that anticipates Rome's downfall and expresses their alternative loyalty while also safeguarding their lives." Therefore, we may conclude that, even though there were no code words in the "Render to Caesar" text, a very subtle message was given, a message of contempt for Caesar and for all that Caesar represented.

Having examined some of the texts in Mark that are repeated in Matthew and in Luke that may have been intended and may have served effectively as anti-Roman cryptograms, let us turn to possible anti-Roman cryptograms in Matthew and Luke that are not present within Mark. We shall limit our attention to possible anti-Roman cryptograms in the well-known "Lord's Prayer."[33]

In the "Lord's Prayer" in Matthew and in Luke

In the context of our study of texts in Newer Testament documents that may at one time have been intended as subtle anti-Roman cryptograms, it becomes apparent that the "Lord's Prayer" of Matthew 6:9–13 and Luke 11:2–4 during its formative period was a prayer of oppressed people and still includes many elements that during its formative life situation were cryptogrammic. As Richard A. Horsley notes in "Jesus and Empire," *In the Shadow of Empire" Reclaiming the Bible as a History of Faithful Resistance,*[34] "The Lord's Prayer is a prayer for the kingdom, which focuses on the people's economic needs of sufficient food and a (mutual) cancellation of debts (Luke 11:2–4), the two principal dangers that constantly threaten peasant life because of demands for taxes, tribute, and tithes."

During the time when this prayer was being developed, we can see now that "Save us (Rescue us) from the evil one" meant to many early followers of Jesus, in part at least, "Rescue us from the Roman Emperor and from the evil brought upon us by his representatives who have crucified Jesus and have killed Peter, Paul, James, and many others among our leaders." At that time, "The evil one" was not merely a supernatural oppressor. "The evil one" was also the supernatural oppressor's agents, instruments, and minions in human institutions. "The evil one" was someone here on earth who could hurt you and who often did hurt you and your loved ones. Even if most early followers of Jesus thought about "the evil one" as the cosmic adversary of God and of Jesus, for many of them "the evil one" was also Caesar and any zealous advocate of Roman Civil Religion who chose to use the awesome and uncontested Roman power against them. We lose much of the meaning that the Lord's Prayer had during its formative period when we translate the Greek *apo tou ponerou* ("from the evil one") with the much more general "from evil" that is so widely used.

"Rescue us from the evil one" is connected by the word "but" to another petition, "Do not bring us into a situation of temptation." We should see, therefore, a close connection between these two pleas in this prayer of the oppressed. In its formative life situation, "Do not bring us into a situation of temptation" probably meant "Give us the strength to resist the temptation to submit unconditionally to the authority of Caesar as demanded by advocates of Roman Civil Religion. Give us the strength to endure torture and death rather than to deny you and Jesus as our Lord in this way!" Centuries later, this petition also would be individualized and generalized and applied to many kinds of temptations involving harmful sexual activities and selfish monetary gain by Christian people, most of whom had forgotten the corporate nature of the prayer and the life situation in which it was formulated.

"Forgive us our sins, as we have forgiven those who have sinned against us" in the context of its formative period may have meant, to some early followers of Jesus at least, "Forgive us our sins as we have forgiven those among us who sinned against us by submitting to Roman power as ultimate in order to save their lives." We know from other sources that apostasy under duress caused many problems within the early church during periods of severe persecution. The specifics regarding this petition, like the specifics of the others, were largely lost as time passed. This petition too was generalized and applied to many kinds of sinful actions, not only corporate but individual as well.

"Give to us each day the bread that will sustain us until the end" may, in part at least, have been a prayer of the oppressed early Christians for the courage and sustenance needed so that they could resist the temptation to submit to Caesar as their Lord. The Romans generally did not object at all when people had other religious allegiances in addition to the Roman Cult. There is ample archeological evidence of the popularity of the Mithra Cult among Roman military personnel, among persons who certainly were required also to pledge their allegiance to Caesar. Most early Christians, however, were similar to the Jews in that they rejected multiple expressions of religious allegiance.

"May your will be done on earth as it is done in heaven" may have been, in part at least, a prayer that God's will, not Caesar's will, be done among them. Early Christians believed that God's will was being done in heaven. Their desire that God's will rather than Caesar's will be done also on the earth must have been very strong, especially when they were subjected to pressures to submit to the will of Caesar by Roman political leaders who could use Roman power to accomplish whatever they wished. This petition has sustained and guided the church, at least when the church was at its best, throughout its history. Our use of this petition sustains and guides us also today. It reminds us that Christianity, like Jewish faith and life, must be at least as "this-worldly" as it is "other-worldly" in its concerns.

"May your kingdom come!" was certainly the fervent and poignant prayer of generations of oppressed early Christians that the kingdom of God with Jesus the Risen Christ as Lord might come on earth soon to replace the present kingdom of Caesar as Lord that prevailed over them. This basic petition, which in many ways is the most comprehensive and important of all of the petitions within the Lord's Prayer, must have been packed full of meaning for oppressed early Christians. They believed that the Risen Christ would appear in some way, and that through the coming of the Christ God would remove the cruel Romans from their position of power, since no human force within the Mediterranean world seemed to be capable of overthrowing them. Using language that was both religious and political, they expressed their religious and political hope. In the context of the Matthean and Lukan traditions, this was not simply a longing for heaven in the life to come. The petition that follows this, which we have just considered above, calls for God's will to be done on the earth, an indication that they were longing for freedom here and now when they prayed, "May your kingdom come!"

"May your name be hallowed!" was certainly, in part at least, a prayer of oppressed early Christians that God's name and no longer Caesar's name be hallowed on the earth, especially since it had been in Caesar's name that Jesus, Peter, Paul, James, and so many others whom they loved had been tortured and killed. "Father in heaven" must have been contrasted in the minds of many within the early church with Caesar on the earth. Finally, as during the second and third centuries and later various doxologies were added to the Matthean and Lukan expressions of the Lord's Prayer, we should see that it is to God rather than to Caesar that the oppressed asked that "the kingdom and the power and the glory be given forever," since in the life situation in which they lived Caesar was the one who claimed the kingdom and the power and the glory and deserved none of these.

We need not think that every Christian who prayed this prayer during the process of its development had every nuance of contrast between God and Caesar in mind that has been suggested here. Nevertheless, any interpretation of the Lord's Prayer that does not include an awareness that during its formative period this was a prayer of oppressed people and that it included an elaborate hidden transcript, an anti-Roman cryptogram, is inadequate.

The context in which we pray the Lord's Prayer today differs considerably, of course, from the context in which it was formulated. We shall find that the Lord's Prayer will be more meaningful to us even in our quite different life situation, however, if we are aware that, among other things, it was at one time a hidden transcript, a complex anti-Roman cryptogram expressing a message of hope and liberation for oppressed early Christians.

We turn now to brief comments about possible anti-Roman cryptograms in the stories about Herod the Great and other rulers as representatives of Roman power in Matthew and in the lists of Roman rulers and in the references to the Roman census in Luke.

In the Stories About Herod the Great and Other Rulers As Representatives of Roman Power in Matthew

The narratives about the birth of Jesus and the infancy experiences of Jesus that are included in Matthew 1:18–2:23 were obviously intended to show clearly that the events that occurred during Jesus' life, even when he was being conceived and while he was still an infant, were fulfillments of specific prophecies written in the Israelite Scriptures. They were also intended to show that Jesus, even as a child, was a manifestation of "God among us," a ruler who would govern Israel, a person whose life experiences recapitulated the life experiences of Israel prior to his time.

These narratives, however, also include the secondary themes of the cruelty of Herod the Great and of his son Herod Archelaus, who were representatives of Roman power in the land of Israel at the time of Jesus' birth, and of the belief that God thwarted the evil designs of these representatives of Roman power and will ultimately prevail over them. Although Caesar and Roman power are not directly mentioned in these narratives, the early Christians who heard or read them would have known that it was Caesar and Roman power that had made it possible for Herod the Great and his son to be the cruel rulers that they were. It was not necessary to label Herod the Great and Herod Archelaus as "Satan" or as "evil," since their actions as rulers were well known. Therefore, these narratives served well in their secondary sense as anti-Roman cryptograms. By making these representatives of Roman power appear to be stupid and ineffective in spite of the great power that they held, these narratives were messages of hope and liberation for Christians who later had to live under the authority of similarly cruel representatives of Roman power. The message for their time was that if God could guide the magi from the east and protect Joseph, Mary, and the baby Jesus from the Roman oppressors, then God could also guide them and protect them from the Romans who were oppressing them.

In the References to the Lists of Roman Rulers
and to the Roman Census in Luke

Because the inspired writer of Luke and of Acts included the names of so many persons who ruled over the Roman Empire and over various provinces within it and because this writer mentioned events such as a Roman census, some twentieth century interpreters have concluded that the Lukan writer, more than those who composed the other Gospel accounts, functioned as a historian. The Lukan writer obviously was scholarly, and clearly was more familiar with the Septuagint than were the other writers of Gospel accounts and more capable of copying the style of the Septuagint than were the others. The Lukan writer apparently used the names of Roman rulers primarily to provide a historical backdrop for the two Lukan dramas and utilized the Roman census to provide a reason in the Lukan drama for Joseph and Mary to have to travel to Bethlehem at the time of Jesus' birth.

As we become more aware of the skills and subtleties employed by the inspired Lukan writer, we see that by providing this historical backdrop the Lukan writer was also highlighting Roman oppression. Most of the rulers listed were known to have been very oppressive of the poor people of the eastern provinces. What would be more oppressive than to force a poor pregnant woman to have to travel a great distance on foot or riding a donkey during the final days of her pregnancy and then to have to experience labor and childbirth far from home among the unsanitary conditions of animal feeding and manure?

There are other indications also. When we look at the content of the songs that the Lukan writer provided for Mary, for Zechariah, for the angel Gabriel, and for the chorus of angels, we see that each of these songs contains motifs of political oppression and desire for liberation. For example, Mary declares that the Lord God her Savior has put down the mighty from their thrones. Who was more powerful during the first century than Caesar Augustus, Tiberius Caesar, Quirinius the Roman legate in Syria, and the other political and religious leaders mentioned in Luke 1:5, 2:1–2, and 3:1–2? Who were the rich whom Mary sings that they have been sent empty away? Were they not those who cooperated fully with the Roman rulers? Having deposed the Roman rulers, the Lord God has exalted those of low degree and has filled the hungry with good things, according to Mary's song. According to Zechariah's song, the Lord God of Israel has redeemed the Lord's people, has raised up a horn of salvation for them, has saved them from their enemies, from the hand of all who hate them, so that they will be able to serve the Lord without fear.

To the shepherds in the fields the angel Gabriel announces that Jesus will reign over the house of Jacob forever, and that Jesus' kingdom will have no end. Finally, the chorus of angels proclaims to the shepherds that the baby, the

Christ, the Savior, will bring peace on earth to those with whom God is pleased. The peace that the angels announce is to be enjoyed here on earth, just as peace is enjoyed in heaven. Consistent with this, the Lukan writer picked a text for Jesus in his hometown of Nazareth in the Luke 4:16–30 drama in which release to captives and setting free those who are oppressed on the earth figure prominently.

Although Rome and the Roman Empire are never mentioned specifically by name in these texts, the rulers who are mentioned were Roman or appointed by the Romans. These texts, which also of course serve many other purposes, are subtle cryptograms, anti-Roman messages of hope and liberation that the oppressed would clearly understand. Here also, in the portions of the Synoptic Gospels that are attributed to Luke only, the primary interest is in freedom from suffering and in peace on the earth here and now.

Richard A. Horsley sees this clearly. He points out that the Luke 2 account "illustrates the ridiculous and counterproductive hardships that the Roman emperor was forcing upon the struggling people." In this account "Jesus is proclaimed as the Messiah who will lead Israel against the oppressive empire." In addition, the baby Jesus "is also proclaimed as 'Savior.'" For the Romans, however, "'Savior' was a title for Caesar, who had supposedly brought 'Peace and Security' to the world." In Luke 2 "Jesus is born as the alternative savior, the savior of the people, in opposition to Caesar, whose 'security' was oppressive to the people." As a "response to the coming of Jesus, his mother Mary, like Zechariah and Simeon, sang militant victory songs in anticipation that God 'has brought down the powerful from their thrones, and lifted up the lowly.'"(Luke 1:46-55; 2:67-79; 2:29-32)[35]

Conclusions

In the temptation of Jesus stories in the Synoptic Gospels we have seen that the Jesus of history is depicted as having resisted all temptations to idolatry, including the temptation to cooperate fully with the Roman oppressors and idolatrously to serve Caesar as his Lord. In the texts in the Synoptic Gospels in which "the kingdom of God" is an important symbol, it is apparent that references to the coming of the kingdom of God in these texts were originally primarily political. They expressed a desire for a radical change from the then-current political situation of oppression by the Romans. The exorcism miracle story of Mark 5:1–20, a strange story of Jesus' power over a "Legion" of demons that were released into "a herd of pigs," expressed triumph over the Roman military forces and the return of a possessed man to calm and peace. The various petitions in the Lord's Prayer can appropriately be seen as expressions of hope that soon God's will rather than Caesar's may be done on the earth. The narratives about the birth and infancy experiences of Jesus included in Matthew 1:18–2:23 express cryptically the belief that God has thwarted the evil designs of the principal representatives of Roman power in Jerusalem and will ultimately prevail over them. Finally, the Lukan writer skillfully used dramatic stories and songs to proclaim freedom from suffering imposed by the powerful Roman rulers and the enjoyment of peace on the earth here and now.

Our analysis of subtle anti-Roman cryptograms within the Synoptic Gospels indicates that, like the Jesus of history, Paul, and the Pauline writers, those who developed and recorded the Synoptic traditions had "this-worldly" as well as "other-worldly" concerns. They used the words "Satan," "the devil," "the tempter," and "wild beasts" in reference to Caesar and Roman power in ways that are similar to the usages in the letters of Paul and in the epistles of the Pauline writers. This is consistent with criteria 1, 2, 3, 4, 6, 8, and 9, as designated on pages 17-20 above.

IV. Anti-Roman Cryptograms in John and in the Johannine Epistles

In this study of hidden transcripts of anti-Roman cryptograms in the Newer Testament documents, we turn our attention now to attempt to identify hidden transcripts, coded messages of hope and liberation, in both the Gospel According to John and in the Johannine Epistles. The Johannine Epistles clearly are a product of the same early Christian community that produced the Fourth Gospel. In vocabulary and in literary style, the Johannine Epistles are more closely allied to the Fourth Gospel than to any other segments of the Newer Testament literature.

When we compare the Pauline communities, the Synoptic communities, and the Johannine communities, based on what we can know about these three communities from our study of the Newer Testament documents produced by writers within these three communities for the people of these three communities, we see some very significant differences.

One major difference that can be identified is that the writers of the Gospel According to John were heavily pre-occupied with vicious anti-Jewish polemic, more than were the writers of the Synoptic Gospels and much more than were Paul and the other writers of the Pauline Epistles. They were "throwing stones" at the Jews, who were nearer at hand, rather than at the Romans, who by comparison were farther away. Later, as their anti-Jewish polemic subsided when their contacts with Jews decreased, the Johannine writers became preoccupied with intra-Christian polemic, with attempts to demonstrate their superiority over what they considered to be crypto-Christians, over Jewish-Christians, over the "mainline" Christians of the Synoptic traditions, and over various groups of gnostic Christians.[1] These preoccupations took much of their time and energy, as can be seen especially in 1 John.

A second major difference, closely related to the first, is that the Johannine writers, much more than the writers in the other two communities, thought of "Satan," "the devil," and "the evil one" primarily as a semi-divine, spiritual being who had been a factor for at least as long as human beings had been on the scene.

A third major difference between the writers and people of the Johannine community and those of the Pauline and Synoptic communities is that the writers and people represented in the Johannine writings were probably relatively insignificant in numbers and in influence at the time of the writing of these Johannine works. Being small in numbers and influence, they may rarely have come to the attention of the Romans. If the Romans knew them only as a small and insignificant group, the Romans would have relatively little reason to oppress and harass them. The members of the communities represented in these Johannine writings may have lived in relatively isolated areas in the Jordan River Valley at first. Later, as Klaus Wengst suggests,[2] they may have migrated to the sparsely populated regions of Gaulanitis and Batanaea northeast of the Sea of Galilee in which there were only a few followers of Jesus, so few that they would not appear to be a threat to anyone.[3]

Still later, segments of or most of the Johannine community apparently moved again north and west into the seven cities in the province of Asia where there were significant numbers of followers of Jesus from the Pauline and Synoptic communities. There, during the period of 90–96 C.E., they may for the first time have encountered prolonged, intense oppression and persecution from zealous advocates of Roman Civil Religion in that area and experienced the death by martyrdom of a substantial percentage of their numbers.

Finally, a fourth major difference between the Johannine writers and people and the Pauline and Synoptic writers and people, a difference closely related to the third difference considered above, is that while the Fourth Gospel and the Johannine Epistles were being written the Johannine people may have been relatively less oppressed and less concerned about the Roman State than were the writers and people of the Pauline and Synoptic communities. They may have felt less oppressed and less concerned about the Roman State than other early followers of Jesus for the same reasons that some Christians today are less critical of their governments, and more "patriotic" in a superficial flag-waving sense than are other Christians. Some Christians are primarily interested in what may be called "spiritual" matters, seeming to have little concern for people who are suffering injustice, unless they are within their own small cultural group. These Christians are less inclined to speak out against oppressive governments than are Christian people who are concerned about removing injustice here and now as well as anticipating life in "the world to come."

Unlike the writers and people of the Synoptic communities, the writers and people for whom these Johannine works were written did not talk and write about the kingdom of God that they hoped and prayed would soon come to replace the present evil kingdom centered in Rome. They were more interested in "eternal life" (John 3:16) than were the larger groups of Pauline and Synoptic Christians. This interest in "eternal life" is apparent not only in the Fourth Gospel and in the Johannine Epistles, but also in the work of a segment of the Johannine community that did later experience severe Roman oppression, the book of Revelation, which we shall examine in chapter V.

As an indication of the differences between the Synoptic Gospels and the Gospel According to John, it is important and helpful to note here the additional and closely related factor that the writers of the Gospel According to John did not use the types of texts that contain anti-Roman cryptograms in the Synoptic Gospels. These types of texts simply do not exist in John, as the following brief summary indicates.

There are no temptation of Jesus texts in the Fourth Gospel. The Johannine Jesus is not tempted, not at the beginning of his public activity, not later by Simon Peter, not in Gethsemane on the night in which he was betrayed. The Johannine Jesus is basically a divine figure, not a human figure subject to the temptations that characterize human nature. Consequently, unlike the Synoptic Gospels, there are no temptation of Jesus texts in the Fourth Gospel that could be used in expressing anti-Roman cryptograms. There are also no parables about the kingdom of God in John. The Johannine Jesus proclaims himself as the focal point of salvation in the great "I am" texts; the Johannine Jesus does not provide parables about the coming of God's rule on the earth. There is no contrast between the kingdom of Caesar and the kingdom of God in John. There is no expectation that the kingdom of God will replace the kingdom of Caesar. With no parables about the coming kingdom of God, there are no texts of this genre that could be used in expressing subtle anti-Roman cryptograms.

There are no exorcism stories in John. The Johannine Jesus is repeatedly accused of having a demon by "the Jews," but the Johannine Jesus does not exorcize demons from people, even though we might expect that the powerful Johannine Jesus would be doing this wherever he went. With no exorcism stories, there is no exorcism vehicle in which to conceal anti-Roman cryptograms.

There *are* stories about healings other than exorcism healings in John. These stories are used in portraying serious conflicts with "the Jews," but they are not used in John as they are in the Synoptic Gospels to convey anti-Roman cryptograms.

The "Lord's Prayer" is not used in John. Its "kingdom of God" emphasis is not a factor in John. Therefore, the "Lord's Prayer" cannot be a vehicle in John in which to express anti-Roman cryptograms.

There are no stories about Herod the Great and other rulers as cruel representatives of Roman power in John. The execution of John the Baptizer in prison by order of Herod Antipas is not a part of the Johannine record. It is merely stated in John 3:24 that at the time cited John had not yet been put into prison. Even the most direct representative of Roman power in the land of Israel, Pontius Pilate, is depicted as attempting to be just and compassionate in the Fourth Gospel (John 18:28–40; 19:4–16). Therefore, there are no stories about consistently cruel representatives of Roman power in John that could be used in expressing anti-Roman cryptograms.

There are no lists of Roman rulers and there is no mention in John of the Roman census such as we have in Luke. In the Fourth Gospel, Mary is not said to have been forced to travel great distances on foot or on a donkey near the culmination of her pregnancy. She is not said in John to have had to give birth to the Savior amid the dust of the feeding stalls and manure of animals. Therefore, there are no such accounts that could be used in expressing subtle anti-Roman cryptograms in the Fourth Gospel.

While we should not develop an argument from silence based on the absence of texts in John that are used in the Synoptic Gospels to express anti-Roman cryptograms, the non-use of these six types of texts in John is significant. Perhaps it is related to the absence of the types of anti-Roman cryptograms in John that are in the Synoptic Gospels even in those instances in which the Fourth Gospel uses some of the same words that are used in the Synoptic Gospels and in the Pauline writings to convey subtle hidden transcripts of anti-Roman cryptograms.

When words such as "the evil one" and "the devil" are used in the Fourth Gospel and in 1 John, their usage is generally more "spiritual" and "other-worldly" and less "this-worldly" than when the same words are used in the Synoptic Gospels and in the Pauline writings. They are not entirely "other-worldly," however. There is also a "this-worldly" emphasis. When there is a "this-worldly" emphasis in the use of these words in the Fourth Gospel, the usage is viciously anti-Jewish, not subtly anti-Roman. "Satan" is said to be at work in this world in the person of Judas Iscariot, a Jew who delivers Jesus over to the "goons" employed by the Jewish chief priest, and "the devil" is said to be the father of "the Jews."

In the Gospel According to John and in 1 John, "Satan," "the evil one," "the devil," and "the ruler of this world" are in most instances used in the mythical, spiritual sense of a semi-divine opponent of God, the sense that later became dominant throughout most of the Church. For example, in 1 John 3:12 it is said that "we should not be like Cain, who was influenced by the evil one and murdered his brother." It is said in 1 John 3:8 that "the devil has sinned from the beginning."

In John 8:38 and 44, however, the devil is said to be the father of "the Jews." Specifically, "the Jews" are addressed directly in this Johannine drama and are said to be

descendants of *your* father, the Devil, and you wish to do whatever *your* father desires. The Devil has been a killer of people from the beginning, and has not taken the path of truth, because there is no truth in the Devil. When the Devil speaks the opposite of truth, the Devil speaks the Devil's own language, because the Devil is the primary liar and the father of all lies" (8:44)[4]

In this text, "the devil" is said to be involved in this world, but not, however, through oppressive Roman rulers or their agents. The "devil" is said to be involved in the activities of "the Jews." Therefore, as stated above, this text and the other texts in John that are similar to it are not subtle anti-Roman polemic, but are vicious, blatant, defamatory anti-Jewish polemic. These are not primarily cryptograms.

Judas Iscariot is said in John 6:70 to be a devil, because Judas—like "the Jews" in John 8:38, 44 and elsewhere in the Fourth Gospel in vicious anti-Jewish polemic—is said to be under the influence of the devil, who has existed from the beginning of human existence and probably even longer. This is the devil who had already, according to John 13:2, put it into the heart of Judas Iscariot to betray Jesus. After Judas had taken the morsel of bread from the Johannine Jesus, "Satan" is said in John 13:27 to have entered into him. In the Fourth Gospel and in 1 John, it is this mystical, spiritual, pre-existent "Satan-devil," who is "the ruler of this world." The Romans are clearly designated as the Romans in John 11:48. There are no code words for them there. They are said to have the power to come and to destroy the Jewish temple and the Jewish nation, which they, of course, had already done by the time that John 11:48 was written.

Nevertheless, in references such as the Johannine Jesus being "in the world" (John 1:9–10), that "the ruler of this world" is being cast out (John 12:31-32), and that "the ruler of this world" is coming (John 14:30) there may, indeed, be complex hidden transcripts, very subtle anti-Roman cryptograms in the Fourth Gospel.

Warren Carter[5] perceptively asks whether the Fourth Gospel as "the 'spiritual' or 'mystical' Gospel" is "so utterly untouched by the imperial world, as most contemporary scholarship assumes, that it knows nothing of a sociopolitical world of domination and resistance?" He suggests that "Perhaps the initial placement in the Gospel of the story of the temple scene, Jesus' rupturing of the domination world with a challenge that exposes one of its means of exploiting peasants, signifies from the outset of the narrative the Gospel's engagement with and resistance to the imperial world."

The World of Darkness

In the Prologue to the Fourth Gospel, as well as within the Fourth Gospel itself and in 1 John 1:5–7; 2:8–11, 15–17; 3:1; 4:2–5, 9; 5:4–5,19, there is sharp contrast depicted between the light of God and the darkness that is in the world. It is written that the *Logos*, the Word of God, was "the Light of God for the illumination of all people." The *Logos*, the Light of God, "shines in the darkness, and the darkness has not diminished it" (John 1:4–5). John the Baptizer "came in order that he might tell everyone about the Light. The *Logos* of God "was the True Light, the Light of God that illuminates all people. This True Light was coming into the World. The *Logos* (Word) of God was present in the world, and the world came into being by means of the Word of God, and yet the world did not understand the Word of God" (John 1:8–10).

We read in John 3:16–17 that "God has loved the world so much that God has given God's unique, special Son, in order that everyone who believes in him may not perish, but may have life eternally. For God did not send God's Son into the world in order that the Son might condemn the world, but in order that the world might be saved through him."

The "world of darkness" in the Fourth Gospel is obviously a broad concept, not limited to the Roman Empire, but certainly inclusive of it. We see more clearly that it not only includes the Roman Empire, but is focused on it in John 12:31–32, "Now is the time for the judgment of this world. Now is the time when the Satanic Roman ruler of this world shall be cast out of this land. And if I am lifted up from this land by the representatives of that Satanic Roman ruler to die on a Roman cross, I shall pull along, attract all people to myself."

In John 14:30, within the "Farewell Discourses," the Johannine Jesus says, "No longer shall I speak with you very much, for the ruler of this world, the Satanic representative of Caesar, is coming, and the ruler of this world does not have any position in my plan for life."[6]

For the writers of the Fourth Gospel, the ruler of the "world of darkness" may indeed have been able to kill the Johannine Jesus, but that ruler is not included in their Jesus' plan for life.

Did that ruler of this world, that Satanic representative of Caesar, Pontius Pilate, actually have the power to condemn the Johannine Jesus to death on the cross? In the theological understanding of the writers of the Gospel According to John, the power of Satan, of Pilate, of Caesar, and of the world was limited; the Ultimate Power was and is in God. The Johannine Jesus, as the only-begotten Divine One, was in charge and in control of everything, even when he had made Pilate cause him to die on the cross as the Lamb of God taking away the sin of the world, to finish the task for which he had come into the world.

No Power Unless Given from Above

The two conversations between Jesus and Pilate constructed by the Johannine writers (John 18:33–38 and 19:9–11) depict Pilate as *claiming* to have the power and authority to set Jesus free or to condemn Jesus to death on the cross, but actually as frustrated, confused,[7] and wondering "What is truth?" The final words of the Johannine Jesus to Pilate are that "You would not have authority over me of any kind if it had not been given to you from above."

The skill of the Johannine writers in formulating words and phrases that have double meanings is easily seen here. In the words "no power unless given to you from above," the words "from above" could be thought of as a reference to "Caesar," who was clearly in authority over Pilate, or to "God," who was ultimately in authority over Pilate and is ultimately in authority over all of us. Just as "the world" in the Johannine writings can have the meaning either of the entire universe or of the Roman Empire, so also "from above" can have the meaning of either "Caesar" or "God," or of both. Thus, these elements of the Johannine writings meet the criterion of hidden transcripts of words and of phrases with more than one meaning.

Conclusions

The six types of texts identified in chapter III above as containing anti-Roman cryptograms in the Synoptic Gospels were not used in the Gospel According to John. Words that in the Synoptic Gospels were used in expressing anti-Roman cryptograms are used in the Gospel According to John in a somewhat different way. They are used to describe the semi-divine adversary of God believed to have been pre-existent already at the time of the inception of human life and active during the first century as the father of "the Jews" and as the one who influenced Judas Iscariot to betray Jesus. They are not used to present anti-Roman cryptograms.

The kinds of anti-Roman cryptograms that are used in the Synoptic Gospels are largely absent from the Fourth Gospel and from the Johannine Epistles because the people of the communities that produced these documents were preoccupied with viciously anti-Jewish polemic and with intra-Christian polemic. Further, they thought of "Satan," "the devil," and "the evil one" primarily as a semi-divine, spiritual being, they were probably a relatively small and insignificant group in number that rarely came to the attention of the Romans, and they did not feel so oppressed because their orientation was primarily in terms of eternal life.

On the other hand, they used the characteristic Johannine dualism of contrasting the factors of light and darkness to designate in hidden transcripts the Roman world as "the world of darkness" and to state that Pilate, the representative of Rome in Jerusalem, had "no power" whatsoever unless it would be given to him from God. Therefore, their anti-Roman cryptograms, though different in most instances from the anti-Roman cryptograms elsewhere in the Newer Testament documents, can be seen as anti-Roman cryptograms nevertheless. They have very subtle, hidden transcripts that are consistent with criterion 2 on page 18 above.

V. Anti-Roman Cryptograms in Revelation, 1 Peter, and Acts: Three Vastly Differing Responses to Severe Roman Oppression

Violence is the factor that links together the three documents that we shall examine in this chapter. Revelation, 1 Peter, and Acts of Apostles[1] are all responses to violence. Revelation can best be understood as written to provide encouragement to Christians who were suffering the loss by martyrdom of many of their loved ones. These early Christians were themselves facing the immediate prospect of the violence of arrest, torture, and death by representatives of the Roman State, and they were strongly urged in this document to accept martyrdom willingly rather than to compromise their faith in Jesus the Risen Christ as their Lord.

1 Peter was written to provide practical advice and guidance to scattered groups of early Christians who had fled to the interior areas of Asia Minor to avoid the violence that was occurring, most likely the same violence experienced by the people for whom Revelation was written.[2]

Acts, which, along with Revelation, includes more emphasis on violence than any other document within the New Testament,[3] apparently—among other things—included an attempt to reduce the killing of Christians by depicting Christians as loyal to the Roman State. Jews, rather than Christians, are shown to be agitators. Jews, rather than Romans, are always trying to kill Paul, Peter, and other early Christian leaders. In this process, the writer of Acts actually perpetrated another injurious act, a deliberate distortion of history intended to produce what was considered to be a good cause, i.e., to try to save Christian lives.[4] The writer of Acts added greatly to the distortion of history that had been begun already within the Synoptic Gospels and John. This distortion of history involved removing the blame for the suffering and death of Jesus and many of his followers from the Romans, who were the oppressors, to the Jews who were the victims of that oppression. In view of subsequent events in Jewish history, this distortion of history was the most violent act of all.[5]

The geographical location in which most of the violence against the early Christians at this particular time (90–96 C.E.) occurred, causing the vastly differing responses of these three documents, is indicated within the three documents. The most specific references are in Revelation. The intense suffering that gave occasion to the writing of Revelation was occurring among groups of Christians in the seven cities of Ephesus, Smyrna, Pergamum, Thyatira, Sardis, Philadelphia, and Laodicea. All of these cities were in the Roman province of Asia on the eastern shore of the Aegean Sea, as the "letters" to the seven churches in Revelation 1:11–3:22 clearly indicate.

The "aliens and exiles" to whom 1 Peter was addressed were scattered in the interior areas to the north and east of these seven cities, in the Roman provinces of Pontus, Galatia, Cappadocia, and Bithynia, and in the eastern portions of the province of Asia. This implies that the persons addressed in this document had fled into the interior areas from Ephesus and other cities near the coast.

The location of this violence in Ephesus and in its surrounding areas is supported also by the author of Acts, the most subtle of the three writers of these documents. The writer of Acts placed Paul in Ephesus for two years (Acts 19:10) and then still longer (Acts 19:22; 20:18, 31) and, with some exaggeration, wrote into the Acts drama that "all those who were dwelling in the province of Asia were able to hear the word of the Lord, both Jews and Greeks" (Acts 19:10). In trying to protect the lives of Christians in this geographical area, the writer of Acts could not openly depict a struggle between Paul and zealous advocates of the Roman Imperial Cult in Ephesus. Therefore, the Lukan writer utilized something that was known and available, the prominence of the temple of Artemis in Ephesus (like the Roman census in Luke 2:1–5), and used it to conceal a reference to conflict also with the Roman Imperial Cult.[6] Alert early Christians would probably think about conflict with advocates of the Roman Imperial Cult also when they read about conflict with devotees of the great goddess Artemis, without any potentially damaging written evidence in their literature that they were disparaging the Imperial Cult and its leaders.

It is possible also that in this subtle way, by formulating a dramatic story, the writer of the Acts drama was able to utilize an anti-Roman cryptogram of Paul himself from 1 Corinthians 15:32, "I fought with the wild beasts in Ephesus." The writer of Acts, as well as many of the persons for whom it was written, would have known that Emperor Domitian had arranged for the construction of a huge temple in Ephesus in which he would be venerated during his lifetime as *dominus et deus* ("LORD and GOD").[7] They would have known also, especially because many of them may have lived in this area, that the western part of the Roman province of Asia was increasingly becoming a region of Roman "patriotism," of strong vocal allegiance to Domitian, expressed in the form of the Roman Imperial Cult. As Helmut Koester puts it,

"Western Asia Minor, with its quickly-growing Christian communities, would have provided the best conditions for a development in which the uncertain political situation of Christianity could deteriorate into a direct confrontation with the Roman state."[8]

The probable time when most of this violence occurred has already been indicated in the previous paragraphs. Many critical biblical scholars think that all three of these documents were written during the last seven years of the reign of Emperor Domitian, that is, between 90–96 C.E., when Domitian was demanding that he be addressed as LORD and GOD. In the cities of the Roman province of Asia zealous advocates of the Roman Imperial Cult enthusiastically responded to this demand and used the power of the Roman State to seize, torture, and kill those who stubbornly refused to express their allegiance to the Empire in this fashion. As a result, the writers of these three documents perceived Domitian to be the horrible beast rising out of the sea with a mouth like a lion's mouth (Revelation 13:1–10), who goes around like a roaring lion, seeking someone to devour (1 Peter 5:8–9), and sends fierce wolves who speak perverse things, not sparing the flock (Acts 20:29–30). It should be noted that it is to those who were the elders of the church at Ephesus that the writer of the Acts drama has Paul address these words about what will happen after his departure (Acts 20:17–18). This is a strong indication that the writer of Acts may have lived in the area in or near Ephesus.

It is possible, therefore, to reconstruct with considerable assurance of accuracy the scenario in which most of this violence and these three differing responses to this violence occurred. As we reconstruct this scenario, we increase our understanding of these three documents and of an important stage in the development of the early Christian Church. We shall limit our consideration to the three "communities of faith" for whom the letters of Paul, the Synoptic Gospels, and the Johannine works were written.

During the decades following the death of Paul, many of the people among whom Paul had proclaimed Jesus to be raised from the dead as Lord and Christ continued to meet in house-churches in various areas, most of which were within the Roman provinces of Macedonia, Achaia, and Asia. They had learned from what had been done to Paul by zealous advocates of the Roman Imperial Cult that they would survive best if they maintained a low profile, sharing their joyous message of salvation in Christ for the most part in private rather than public settings. They had learned from Paul and from others how to honor the Emperor without having to submit to him as *dominus* and *deus*. That is, they were careful to obey the Roman regulations, but to have as little contact as possible with the kind of people who had killed Paul. They understood the hidden transcripts of anti-Roman cryptograms that Paul had used, both in his letters and in his conversations with them, and these messages of hope and liberation helped them to sustain their faith in God Transcendent and in Jesus Christ as God Active in this world and to believe that there would be an end to Roman oppression. These spoken and written anti-Roman cryptograms helped the members of these Pauline communities to endure many of the injustices of their society and to tolerate the arrogance of those who promoted the Roman Imperial Cult.

Since most of the people in these Pauline communities were natives of the cities and towns in which they lived, they were on the whole relatively stable, well established, and indigenous in their areas. As a result, they were able to continue their lives and to maintain their Christian faith during the turbulent period of severe oppression and violence in the province of Asia during the latter years of Domitian's reign. Although there may have been serious incidences of apostasy among them during the most severe persecution, if the life situation addressed in 2 Thessalonians was also from that time and place, the majority of them must have survived that ordeal with their faith and their lives intact. At any rate, the writers of 1 Peter and of Acts appear to have been familiar with some of the seven basic letters of Paul that were preserved by the members of these Pauline communities and that later were incorporated into the Newer Testament canon.

At some point during the Jewish revolt that ended with the fall of Jerusalem in 70 C.E. and of Masada three years later, it is likely that members of the Markan community scattered into various areas, taking copies of their expression of faith, "The Gospel of Jesus Christ" (Mark), with them. The evil age of Roman rule had obviously not come to an end during the Jewish revolt, and the members of the Markan community could not continue to be refugees for long periods of time. In order to survive, they had to find ways of making a living. It is probable that many of them moved northward into Antioch and other cities and towns of Syria, where writers among them eventually redacted a copy of "The Gospel of Jesus Christ" into what a century later would be called the Gospel According to Matthew. This expanded and updated document helped them to teach and to transmit their new and developing religious tradition to their children and to other new adherents to their community of faith.

Other segments of the Markan community apparently migrated farther, generally to the north and west, across Asia Minor, Greece, and even to Rome. Many settled in the provinces of Asia, Macedonia, and Achaia, where they met and interacted with members of the Pauline communities, and added considerably to the numbers of followers of Jesus in these areas.

Perhaps they learned from the members of the Pauline communities how to honor the Emperor without having to submit to him as their *dominus* and their *deus*, for they were now living in areas in which the Imperial Cult was much more active than it was in Syria and in Galilee. Their own Markan tradition, stemming in many ways from the Jesus of history himself, provided for them the important guideline of "Render unto Caesar the things that are Caesar's, and unto God the things that are God's" and they used the spoken and written anti-Roman cryptograms from their own tradition to maintain their hope during the times when oppression became severe. As fairly recent migrants to these areas, the Markan followers of Jesus were more vulnerable to oppression than were the members of the Pauline communities. As a result, when the lives of these Markan followers of Jesus were threatened by the various trials (1 Peter 1:6) and tests of fire (1 Peter 1:7), by evil, reviling, and other abuses brought upon them by those who were zealous for what is "not right" (1 Peter 3:9–17), many of them who had been living in Ephesus and in other cities in the province of Asia near the Aegean Sea where the oppression was most severe fled into the interior regions to the north and east, to the provinces of Pontus, Galatia, Cappadocia, other areas in Asia, and Bithynia that are mentioned in 1 Peter 1:1 .

In these regions in the interior of Asia Minor to the north end east of Ephesus, oppression was probably much less severe, partly because there were fewer followers of Jesus in the more remote rural and small town areas, and partly because the Roman Imperial Cult was less active in those regions. As a response to the violence being experienced in the province of Asia, someone who was familiar with both the Pauline and Synoptic traditions used materials from those traditions to write the document that we call 1 Peter. This was done in order to provide assurances to those who would read and hear this message that they were a chosen people and good practical advice and guidance for these frightened and vulnerable "aliens and exiles."

Someone else, almost certainly the same person who a few years earlier had produced the thorough redaction and rewriting of "The Gospel of Jesus Christ" (Mark) that later was to be called "The Gospel According to Luke," composed a sequel to that Gospel, the Acts literary drama, as a quite different kind of response from Revelation and 1 Peter to the severe oppression being experienced by members of the Synoptic Gospels community who were living in Ephesus and in the surrounding areas. In Acts, this writer added considerably to the distortion of history that had already been in process within the tradition of all Four Gospels, the distortion of history by removing the blame for instigating the death of Jesus and of prominent followers of Jesus from the Romans and placing it upon the Jews. The purpose of this distortion of history in Acts was to attempt to reduce Roman persecution of followers of Jesus by depicting the Romans as just and fair[9] while portraying the Jews as cruel and vindictive.[10] Most likely, the author of Acts could assume that a copy of it would fall into the hands of zealous advocates of the Imperial Cult, which could be expected to happen in Ephesus during the reign of Domitian, so that they would see that the followers of Jesus had a tradition of friendly relationships with Roman rulers[11] and of respect for them. Therefore, Christians should be permitted to live in peace and safety. If oppressive policies were considered necessary to maintain the stability of the Roman State, they should be directed at what this writer considered to be cruel and vindictive Jews, not at the Christians.

Perhaps this response to Roman violence by the writer of Acts was at least partially successful. Perhaps the oppression of Christians was reduced in Ephesus and elsewhere in the province of Asia and held to a lower level throughout the Roman Empire for the following two centuries as a result of this distortion of history. At any rate, the cost of this subterfuge was enormous. Who can measure the suffering caused in subsequent centuries and continuing still today to the lives of Jews by this distortion of history? Who can measure the pejorative effect on the lives of Christians that this distortion of history has caused by establishing within Christians the mindset that the lives of Christians are valuable, but the lives of Jews and of others who are not Christians are worthless?

In order to complete this scenario, we must look also at what was happening to the members of the Johannine community. From what we have seen in chapter IV above, the people for whom the Gospel According to John and the Johannine Epistles were written probably had relatively little experience in dealing with Roman oppression. Perhaps they had lived in remote areas and were few in number and had not come to the attention of the Romans. As a small and divided group they had posed no threat to those who controlled the lands in which they had lived. Their natural enemies were "the Jews," the World, and "Satan" perceived as a pre-existent demigod. Their opponents, as they perceived it, were Jewish-Christians, Gnostic Christians, and "Mainline" Christians of the Synoptic traditions, not the Romans. As a result, they had poorly developed guidelines for dealing with Roman oppression.

Therefore, when some of the Johannine followers of Jesus, like many of the followers of Jesus of the Synoptic Gospels tradition, migrated to the north and west during the decades following the fall of Jerusalem and settled in areas such as Ephesus and other cities in the province of Asia in which the Roman Imperial Cult was active, they were not prepared for what happened to them. Like a tree that has never experienced strong winds, they were not prepared to stand against the storm. Like a person who does not have an effective immune system, they were easily overcome by this new threat to their health. As a small group, recent arrivals in the area, with a rigid doctrinal position and few contacts with the more numerous and better established members of the Pauline and Synoptic communities who could have taught them how to cope with those who promoted the Roman Imperial Cult, they were easy victims of Roman persecution. A large percentage of their members experienced martyrdom, especially in the cities of Ephesus, Smyrna, Pergamum, Thyatira, and Philadelphia, according to Revelation 1:11–3:22, and were gathered, they believed, around the throne of God in heaven, their garments washed clean by the "blood of the Lamb." Their response to Roman oppression, therefore, was not to provide practical advice on how to survive Roman oppression, nor to add to the distortion of history by continuing the process of transferring the blame for Jesus' death from the Romans to the Jews, as the writers of 1 Peter and Acts were doing, but largely to give up on this world and to "escape" into "new heavens and a new earth."

Some writer among them, not fully skilled in the koiné Greek language that they were using in Greek-speaking lands, employed the literary vehicle of apocalyptic vision as the most appropriate response to the violence that seemed to be everywhere. This writer evaluated the faith and life of members of these segments of the Johannine community, and perhaps of Synoptic and Pauline Christians as well, who lived in the seven cities of Ephesus, Smyrna, Pergamum, Thyatira, Sardis, Philadelphia, and Laodicea just east of the Aegean Sea. The ways in which followers of Jesus in these cities were coping with Roman oppression was judged, and Domitian and the leaders of the Roman Imperial Cult were condemned. This condemnation of Roman oppressors was expressed in only thinly veiled cryptograms, an indication that the writer was almost, but not quite, giving up on the present and on all hope for survival. That cryptograms, hidden transcripts, were used, however, is evidence that the writer and the people for whom Revelation was written were still hoping that the oppression would subside and some of them might survive.

In the opinion of some commentators, Revelation should not without reservation be designated as apocalyptic because it is not pseudepigraphical and its visions are not located in some fictitious place. Its visions are not said to have been revealed to Enoch, to Elijah, Ezra, Abraham, Noah, Adam, Seth, or any other ancient Israelite figure. The author is "John," presumably one of the youngest of the twelve disciples of Jesus, who as a sort of elder disciple-statesman[12] saw these visions while exiled or otherwise resident on the island of Patmos in the Aegean Sea off the coast of the Roman province of Asia. We should be aware, however, that the book of Revelation is *Christian* apocalyptic literature, not Israelite apocalyptic literature. Therefore, the author chose a Christian, not an Israelite, pseudonym.

It is likely that the disciple John had died, perhaps a decade or more prior to the time of the writing of this document, and was remembered as a respected leader who had known the Jesus of history. As such, he was one of the "oldest" Christian notables whose name could be used as a recipient of apocalyptic visions in this new document that was modeled rather closely on the pattern of portions of the books of Daniel, Ezekiel, Isaiah, and Zechariah, and has some similarities to *4 Ezra* and *2 Baruch*. Given the thinly transparent disparaging references to Rome as "the wicked harlot seated upon many waters ... and on seven hills...and drunk with the blood of the martyrs of Jesus" in Revelation 17, the author would be foolish indeed to reveal his true identity and location. If this document fell into the hands of the leaders of the Roman Imperial Cult during the reign of Domitian, they would dispatch a contingent of Roman military to the nearby island of Patmos, which was already under their control, to pick up this impudent old man and bring him back to Ephesus where he could be tortured end executed. The author and first readers of this document may have found some satisfaction during their suffering at the prospect of their oppressors searching in vain for an old man named "John" on an island on which there were probably no followers of Jesus at all. Oppressed people who speak out against their oppressors in their writings do not use their own names as the authors of their documents. They use the names of dead heroes of their past. They know that their oppressors cannot kill these dead heroes again.

Therefore, we can assume that the author of Revelation was not the disciple John and the author was not on the island of Patmos. The author knew the situation in the province of Asia very well and probably wrote at a location somewhere in that area, perhaps in Ephesus.

In a somewhat similar manner, the author of 1 Peter, who risked a reference to Domitian and the Roman State in the statement in 1 Peter 5:8 that "your enemy, the devil, goes around like a roaring lion, seeking someone to devour" and who in 1 Peter 5:15 referred to Rome as "Babylon," utilized a pseudonym, among other reasons, to make it impossible for the Roman oppressors to identify the one who was giving hope to the oppressed. "Peter," as the principal spokesman for the Twelve within the Synoptic Gospels tradition, was a logical choice for this pseudonym. Like "John" in Revelation, "Peter" was one of the "oldest" Christian notables, a respected figure in the new Christian faith tradition. In addition, it was probably known to the intended audience of this document that Peter had been martyred several decades earlier. To use his name as the author of this message of hope was a way to give substance to the Christian claim that God raised martyrs from the dead and thereby to ridicule the efforts of the oppressive Romans. It was a way in which the early Christians could say that their martyrs could not be silenced by the Romans, no matter how much the Romans tortured and killed them. In this sense, it was not the Peter of history but the martyred Peter raised by God from the dead who was the specified author of this document, and also later of the subsequent document that we call 2 Peter.

The particular pseudonym chosen in most if not all instances reveals something about the community in which the actual author functioned. Therefore, the pseudonym "Peter" suggests that the actual author was most likely a member of a Synoptic Gospels community. Use of the admonition to respect the power of the Emperor and of his vassal princes that Paul had employed in Romans 13:1–7, the references to baptism in 1 Peter 3:21-22, and basically the same "household rules" that are utilized in Colossians 3:18–4:1 and Ephesians 5:22–6:9 are all evidence that the author and the community in which the author functioned had interaction with the Pauline traditions also. There is little evidence of contact with or use of the Johannine traditions. All of this supports what is said in the scenario section above.

The author of the Acts drama was almost certainly also the author of the thorough redaction of "The Gospel of Jesus Christ" (Mark) that later came to be known as "The Gospel According to Luke." This author spoke directly in the first person singular in Luke 1:1–4 and in Acts 1:1. In accordance with the style of the "gospel" genre, however, this writer focused the writing on the person whose life is acclaimed as "good news" in the Gospel According to Luke and did as little as possible to draw the attention of the reader to himself or herself, except to write with consummate skill and inspired creativity. The same can be said for the work of this writer in the composition of the sequel to the Gospel According to Luke that is Acts of Apostles. If the playwright of Acts put himself or herself into this drama, perhaps it was only as "the man of Macedonia" of Acts 16:9 who is said to have appeared to Paul in a vision during the night to appeal to him to come over into Macedonia and "Help us!" If there is any substance to this identification, it might indicate that the author of Luke–Acts was a native of the Roman province of Macedonia who became interested in the Jewish sacred Scriptures and thoroughly skilled in them and who eventually became a highly partisan follower of Jesus who composed what would become approximately one fourth of the Newer Testament. This author was obviously a major direct contributor to the Synoptic Gospels tradition and may have been living in the province of Asia during the latter years of the reign of Domitian. At any rate, the author would have been familiar with the violence directed against Christians there and may have determined to continue to do whatever possible through literary composition to reduce the violence that zealous advocates of Roman Civil Religion perpetrated against Christians. This author was also, in my opinion, familiar with many of the basic seven letters of Paul that later were included in the Newer Testament canon, and used material from them freely and creatively as information resources in composing the Acts 9 and 12:25–28:31 portions of this drama.

We have identified violence against early followers of Jesus by zealous advocates of Roman Civil Religion within the cities of the Roman province of Asia during the last seven years of the reign of Emperor Domitian as the principal factor that precipitated the composition of Revelation, 1 Peter, and Acts, three vastly differing responses to that violence. We have also attempted to reconstruct some of the details of the scenario that led to the composition of these documents and to make a few comments about the authors of these works. Let us now focus on the hidden transcripts, the subtle anti-Roman cryptograms that were written into these three documents.

Revelation—The Great Harlot, Babylon the Great, the Beast Rising from the Sea, the Beast That Rose from the Land, the Devil Himself

Even the title of the document, "The Apocalypse of Jesus Christ," expressed in its first three words in the Greek text, suggests that its author's intention was to reveal something to some persons (the servants of Jesus Christ) that was hidden from others. Only to John are the visions given, and they are intended for those who have the correct ear to hear and the ability to guard and keep what is written in the document (1:1–3). The message is expressed in the form of visions, coded language, hidden transcripts from beginning to end.

The symbolism of the Apocalypse is incredibly complex. The entire document can be considered to be one multi-faceted cryptogram, with many analogies intertwined with the others. Most people who read Revelation today and interpret it within its historical context recognize within it quite readily an extensive, multiplex cryptogram for Rome and Roman power.[13] This is seen in the great red dragon who is also the Devil and Satan (Revelation 12), the beast with ten horns and seven heads rising out of the sea (13–16), the wicked harlot Babylon "drunk with the blood of the saints and with the blood of the martyrs of Jesus" (17:6), "seated on seven hills" (17:9) and on "many waters" (17:1), the "great city that has sovereignty over the kings of the land" in which the followers of Jesus live (17:18).

The author of the Apocalypse obviously utilized the Daniel 7 symbolism of four horrible and destructive beasts rising from the sea in the vision of the monstrous beast with a mouth like a lion, feet like a bear, and the appearance of a leopard coming up from the sea (13:1–10). For this author, the beast from the sea that was allowed by God to make war on the saints and to conquer them, this beast that had authority over every tribe and people and tongue and nation, was an elaborate hidden transcript for Rome, the Roman Empire, its emperors, and its military forces. For the author of the Apocalypse, Rome and the exercise of Roman power over the saints of the Lord Jesus Christ were as evil and destructive as Babylonia, Media, Persia, and Greece had been and worse.

Adela Yarbro Collins[14] fully agrees that not only modern critical readers, but also "Any reader in the Mediterranean world in John's time, when reading the words, 'And authority was given it over every tribe and people and tongue and nation, and all who dwell on earth will worship it' (13:7–8), would think of Rome. Other allusions, such as the mention of seven mountains in 17:9, are equally transparent." In her opinion, however, the allusions to Rome are so transparent that the document is not a cryptogram. Since, in her words, "the public identity of Christians in Asia Minor in John's time was precarious," the "explicit, extreme, even abusive anti–Romanism of the book of Revelation could have made their status only more threatened." She states that the symbolic language of the document was used, not to keep the criticism of Rome secret from outsiders, but because of the "intrinsic evocative power" of the language. For her, the "literary attack on Rome is the most basic element of social radicalism in the Apocalypse."

The language of the document does have intrinsic evocative power, and it is likely that the many explicit anti-Roman statements in it may have resulted in increased persecution of followers of Jesus in the seven cities of the province of Asia. Also, if we measure and evaluate the *quality* of cryptograms in terms of how well they communicate messages of hope and liberation selectively to those who are severely oppressed, while hiding those same messages from the oppressors, the extensive, multi-faceted anti-Roman cryptogram of which most of Revelation is comprised is not a good quality cryptogram. The much more subtle cryptograms used by the African-American slaves, the Apostle Paul and the writers of the Pauline epistles, the writers of the Synoptic Gospels, and perhaps by the Jesus of history, as depicted in the Introduction and chapters I–III above, are of much higher quality than is the almost completely transparent cryptogram of the Apocalypse. Having personally studied these various types of cryptograms with some intensity for many years, I am much more attracted to those that are subtle in their symbolism than I am to the extensive, easily detected cryptogram in "The Apocalypse of Jesus Christ." The subtle cryptograms are more interesting. The subtle cryptograms are more effective. They save more lives. They do a better job of maintaining hope among the oppressed.

Nevertheless, even though the allusions to Rome and to the Romans in the Apocalypse are so diaphanous, the book of Revelation must still be classified as a cryptogram. Rome and the Romans are never explicitly mentioned in the document.[15] Rome and the Romans are always referred to symbolically as "the Great Harlot," "Babylon the Great," "The Beast Rising From the Sea," "The Beast That Rose From the Land," and "The Devil Himself." In addition, the hidden transcript in the Apocalypse has its own unique character and features.

Unlike the cryptograms in the Daniel traditions, which covered the time span of four great world empires during a period of more than four centuries, the cryptogram in the Apocalypse is focused on one world empire, the Roman, and on a period of about one century. There are other significantly different features of the cryptogram in Revelation. The most significant new factor in the symbolism of the cryptogram in Revelation, when compared to the symbolism of the cryptograms of the Daniel traditions, is that in the Apocalypse the beast, the great red dragon, is portrayed also as the Devil and as Satan, the deceiver of the entire world and the one who brings accusations against the people of God (Revelation 12) and produces demonic spirits (16:14). We see this significant new factor of the Devil, Satan, the deceiver, the accuser, the one who engenders demons and demonic spirits in one form or another in many different Newer Testament documents,[16] but never elsewhere as transparently as in the Apocalypse. In the Apocalypse, as elsewhere in the Newer Testament, this factor is in two forms.

In its "other-worldly" form, the scene begins in heaven. Michael, the patron-angel of the Jews in Daniel 10:13–21 and 12:1, and angels allied with Michael are engaged in war against the dragon and the angels who are cooperating with the dragon. In Revelation 12:7–17, the dragon, also called the ancient serpent, the Devil, and Satan, along with the angels who fought on the side of the dragon, is defeated and thrown down to the earth. In its "other-worldly" form, the scene also ends, at least for a long time, when an angel comes down from heaven, seizes the dragon, that ancient serpent who is the Devil and Satan, and binds this demigod in the bottomless pit for a thousand years (20:1–6). The final scene (20:7–10) has Satan loosed from the bottomless pit and, supported by Satan's minions, marching over the broad earth to surround the saints in the beloved city. The saints are rescued, however, by divine intervention, and the Devil is thrown into the lake of fire and sulfur to be tormented day and night forever.

In its "this-worldly" form, the realm of human experience, the dragon who is the Devil and Satan is a symbol for Rome, the Roman Empire, and its emperors. Influenced by the demigod, these humans make war against those who keep the commandments of God and proclaim Jesus as Lord (12:17). In its "this-worldly" form, the dragon and the beast, the Devil and Satan who are Rome and the Roman emperors in the cryptogram, are acclaimed by their zealous followers as "Lord." They utter haughty and blasphemous words against God and are so powerful that no human forces can fight against them (13:1–18). The oppressed early followers of Jesus who hear this message are alerted to the anti-Roman cryptogram within the Apocalypse just as they had also been alerted to it in the Synoptic Gospels with the cryptic words, "If anyone has an ear, let that person hear!" (13:9).

For the oppressed early followers of Jesus addressed in the Apocalypse, the multi-faceted anti-Roman cryptogram was the central core of the apocalyptic genre of the document. People did not express themselves in apocalyptic during the period in question just because they liked this literary form or to amuse themselves. They used this means of expression because they were severely oppressed. The message of hope and liberation revealed to them in the cryptogram helped them to endure the severe oppression.

The oppressed early followers of Jesus for whom Revelation was written knew exactly who their oppressors were. Their oppressors were not Jews.[17] They are not Jewish Christians, nor Gnostic Christians, nor any other kind of Christians whose perceptions of God, of Jesus as the Christ, of the world, and of themselves differed in various ways from the perceptions of the Johannine Christians. Their oppressors were the Romans, more specifically the Roman State, its Emperor Domitian who directly or indirectly was claiming the title of "LORD and GOD" for himself, and the zealous advocates of the Roman Imperial Cult who used the invincible power of the Roman State mercilessly against the oppressed. As Elisabeth Schüssler Fiorenza suggests, the dehumanizing powers of Rome and of its vassals within the Imperial Religion had become so destructive that to the writer of Revelation any compromise with them would be an affirmation of those who destroy the earth.[18]

These oppressed early Christians considered Rome, the Roman Emperor, and the promoters of the Roman Imperial Cult collectively to be the great harlot who is seated upon many waters (of the Mediterranean Sea), the one with whom the kings of the lands around those waters have committed sexual immorality. To these oppressed early followers of Jesus, it seemed that all who dwell on the earth except themselves had become intoxicated with the wine of this great harlot and were immoral with her (Revelation 17:1–2). This harlot, Babylon the great, like Babylon the destroyer of Jerusalem, mother of all harlots and of everything that is detestable on the earth, is seated, they said, not modestly like Jerusalem and other cities of that time on one or two hills, but immodestly is sprawled over seven (17:9). Her promiscuity is so obsessive that the merchants of the entire world have become rich by providing and transporting the gifts that she receives for her sexual favors (18:3). She is said to be making a horrid spectacle of herself, a woman repulsively drunk from devouring the lifeblood of the saints and martyrs of Jesus (17:6).

Because it was well known during the last decade of the first century C.E. that Babylon, like the other great world powers (Egypt, Assyria, Persia, and Greece)—in spite of their tremendous might—had fallen completely and utterly into ruin, the use of the code word "Babylon" was much more effective in a message of hope and liberation than use of the actual word "Rome" would have been in the Apocalypse. Those to whom the book of Revelation was addressed had no reason at all to fear Babylon; they had every reason to fear Rome.

Babylon, rather than Egypt, Assyria, Persia, or Greece, was chosen to represent Rome in the Apocalypse because it had been Babylon rather than any of the others that had totally destroyed the nation of God's people, leveled the beautiful temple of Solomon, and removed the leaders of the people of God from their land. What Babylon had done at the beginning of the sixth century B.C.E. Rome had done near the end of the first century C.E. Like Babylon, Rome had destroyed the nation of God's people, leveled its temple, and scattered God's people. Compared to Rome, as Richard L. Jeske puts it, "No more sinister enemy of God's people could be envisioned than that ancient Mesopotamian empire...."[19] After 70 C.E. both Jews and Christians made this association, as we can see in *2 Baruch* 67:7, *Sibylline Oracles* 5:143, 159, 1 Peter 5:13, as well as in Revelation 14:8; 16:19; 17:5; 18:2, 10, 21.

Just as the desolation of Jerusalem after the siege and fall of that city is described in the Book of Lamentations and elsewhere in the Israelite biblical tradition, so also the desolation of Babylon (Rome) is depicted in Revelation 18:22–24. No longer will the ordinary sounds of life (music, industry, marriage) be heard in the city. No lamp will be lit. The blood of those who were good and those who were evil will flow together in its streets. All its inhabitants will be dead. The symbolic act of the mighty angel throwing the huge stone into the sea initiates the destruction of the city (18:21).

Along with the city of Rome itself, judgment comes also to those who mourn over it, especially the kings who cooperated fully with it, the merchants who had become wealthy from the sale of commodities intended for it, and the ship owners who transported these goods (18:9–19). The author of the Apocalypse probably was thinking primarily here about "citizens of the cities of western Asia Minor who had amassed great wealth from commerce and the transportation of goods," to use Adela Yarbro Collins' terminology.[20] Collins summarizes the reasons for the judgment against Rome and its supporters in Revelation 18 succinctly as follows: (1) the idolatrous and blasphemous worship offered and encouraged by Rome, especially the emperor cult; (2) the violence perpetrated by Rome, especially against Jews and Christians; (3) Rome's blasphemous self-glorification; and (4) Roman wealth.

Collins' first and primary reason for the judgment against Rome in the Apocalypse is expressed graphically in terms of the wicked harlot analogy. This analogy is not new in the Apocalypse. Cities and nations are designated as harlots frequently within the Israelite prophetic tradition. For example, Jerusalem is called a harlot in Isaiah 1:21, Tyre in Isaiah 23:16–18, Israel and Judah in Jeremiah 3:6–10, Jerusalem in Ezekiel 16:15–21, Samaria and Jerusalem in Ezekiel 23:1–49, and Nineveh in Nahum 3:1–19. Within the Israelite prophetic tradition, a city or nation is a harlot if it is engaged in the worship of anyone and anything other than Adonai. Because of the covenant relationship of the people of God, both Jewish and Christian, with their Lord God, worship of anyone else is like illicit sex. As Gerhard Krodel states it, according to the writer of the Apocalypse, Rome "played the harlot with its vassal kings and made the dwellers on earth drunk with the wine of her fornication, leading them into the fascinating and intoxicating stupor of the emperor cult."[21]

The woman sitting on the scarlet beast that was full of blasphemous names was holding in her hand a golden cup that was full of abominations and the impure genital discharges of her illicit sexual actions. While we cannot be certain of all that this description of the woman was intended to signify, it is probable that the author intended the hearers to imagine that the woman would drink the contents of the cup (17:4). As G.B. Caird says, the writer succeeds in making "an otherwise splendid figure appear utterly repulsive," and by that is meant not just the woman but Rome itself. Perhaps as Caird puts it, "She makes others drunk on the wine of her fornication and herself drunk on the blood of God's people."[22] By bringing in the idea of the woman (Rome) becoming repulsively drunk by devouring the lifeblood of the saints and martyrs of Jesus (17:6), the writer focuses on the violence that representatives of Rome and the Roman Imperial Cult perpetrated on the early Christians of the Johannine communities. The woman symbolizes Rome's blasphemous self-glorification and Rome's wealth. Nevertheless, she will become desolate and naked (17:16), even though now she rules over the kings of the earth (17:18).

The analogy in which the city of Rome is depicted as a wicked woman rather than as a cruel man may be considered inappropriate and unfortunate, since it was for the most part male emperors, provincial governors, military leaders and personnel, not women, who were severely oppressing the early followers of Jesus for whom this document was written. Perhaps the female analogy was chosen for two principal reasons, one grammatical and the other based on human experiences. In terms of grammar, the Greek words *polis* (city, city-state) and *komé* (village, small town) are both feminine nouns, and in terms of human experiences there are many possibilities. Perhaps a male writer had some kind of curiosity or even fascination regarding the figure of a female prostitute. The harlot may represent artificiality, painted beauty, pretense rather than love. It is important to note that the writer artfully contrasted the wicked harlot with the glorious queen of heaven, the symbol of the Church of God (12:1), and with the "Bride" of Christ of Revelation 21:2, 9.[23] It is likely that a woman bereft of her splendor was considered to be a more tragic figure than a man in similar circumstances.

Even today, cities and city-states are often referred to as feminine, as having sons and daughters and providing "maternal" nurture for them, as well as being barren and desolate in a "feminine" sense when the economy of their area becomes blighted and their children move away to make their living elsewhere.

Rome and Roman power are also depicted as a horrible, ravenous beast rising out of the sea, with ten horns and seven heads, with ten diadems on its horns and blasphemous names on its heads. Reminiscent of the beast analogies of the Daniel traditions, it is like a leopard, and like a bear, and like a lion, all known for their rapacity. All people worship the beast that rises from the sea, except those whose names are written in the book of life of the Lamb who was slain (13:1–10).

The beast that rises from the sea is probably an allusion to the Jewish tradition that on the fifth day of creation God formed two mythical creatures, the female Leviathan to inhabit the abysses of the sea and the male Behemoth to roam upon the earth (*1 Enoch* 60:7–24: *2 Esdras* 6:49–52; *2 Baruch* 29:4). The beast that rises from the sea "represents the Roman imperial power which, for the province of Asia, annually came up out of the sea, with the arrival of the proconsul at Ephesus."[24] The seashore here may be "the Mediterranean Sea with Rome geographically located on its opposite shore."[25] Therefore, the beast that rises from the sea is the Roman Empire. Its greatest threat to the Church is not its sword, but its pretensions of absolute power supported from within the Church, "which may lead Christians to take the wrong side when the final attack on the saints comes (v.7), and thus expose them to a more deadly sword."[26]

The second beast, related to the male Behemoth, which rose not from the sea but from the earth and utilizes the authority of the first beast to force the earth and its inhabitants to worship the first beast (13:11–18), represents the authority with which advocates of Roman Civil Religion who were native (having risen from the land) to the province of Asia forced those who lived in that province to participate in the Imperial Cult.[27] Only those who bowed down before the image of Caesar were given the mark of Caesar on their right hands or foreheads and were permitted to buy and sell in the land. "Citizens of the empire and especially the provinces expressed their loyalty toward Rome by prostrating before an imperial cultic statue and by burning incense in honor of the divine emperor."[28]

The total depravity of the representatives of the Roman Imperial Cult as the oppressors of this segment of the Johannine community is indicated by the references to the great red dragon, the ancient serpent who is called the Devil and Satan, the deceiver of the entire world who is said to have given power and authority to the beast (12:1–17; 13:2, 4; 20:2–10). Nothing could be more cruel and perverted than for this devilish, Satanic creature to seek to devour a most precious child just as it is being born, when it is most vulnerable.

The myth of the Great Mother was common in antiquity. At times she is portrayed as good, the bringer of life. In other instances she is terrible, associated with death. Sometimes in her the powers of life and of death can be seen. She may provide wisdom and inspiration, or she may deprive people of all reason, turning them into beasts.[29]

Revelation 12 is a variation of the specific Great Mother myth of the queen of heaven, bearer of the divine child. This myth, in many different forms, was known in Babylonia, Egypt, Greece, and Asia Minor during the first century C.E. The basic elements of this myth were (1) the goddess who is about to give birth to the divine child, (2) the great red dragon that stalks the queen mother in order to devour the divine child as he is being born, and (3) the motif of protection of the queen mother and divine child. This "queen of heaven" myth could be seen even in the Roman Imperial Cult, particularly in areas of Asia Minor in which Roma was worshiped as the queen of heaven, the mother of the gods. There was a temple dedicated to Roma in Smyrna. A coin from Pergamum depicts Roma with her son, the divine Roman emperor, the savior of the world, an incarnation of the sun-god Apollo.[30]

The author of the Apocalypse, however, presents the queen of heaven in terms of Jewish and Christian messianic expectations. In Revelation 12, the mother represents God's people (Israel and the Church) and the child is Jesus Christ. In the Apocalypse, God distracts the red dragon, rescues and exalts the divine child, and nourishes the mother in the wilderness. The divine child Jesus Christ is contrasted to the divine child Caesar. Christ, not Caesar, is the savior of the world.

The earth is depicted in Revelation 12:16 as being protective to the mother (the people of God). The earth, created by God for God's people, opens its mouth and swallows the floodwaters that flow from the mouth of the dragon. Satan, in the form of the red dragon, defeated in heaven (12:7–8), was thrown down to the earth (12:9). Therefore, for Satan to establish a throne on the earth in Rome, or many thrones in places such as Pergamum (2:15) and Smyrna where the Imperial Cult flourished, was an intrusion into the area that had been created by God for God's people.

Satan, as the repulsive spirit at work within the evil empire of Babylon (Rome), will not prevail on the earth, even though when the Apocalypse was written Satan and the Romans were celebrating their victories, as Barbara R. Rossing indicates. In her words, "Romans celebrated Victory, but more than that—they *worshipped* Victory. This is key to grasping the urgency of Revelation, for John wrote Revelation in opposition to the empire's entire ideology and worship of Victory."[31] The primary message of the book of Revelation is that just as the dragon was defeated in heaven, so also the evil empire will be defeated on the earth. This triumphant message of hope is heard again and again within the complex cryptogram. The refrain, "Fallen, fallen is Babylon the great!" is sung repeatedly and joyously (14:8; 16:19; 18:2–24). The city of Rome, the destroyer of Jerusalem, shall itself be destroyed. The vibrant sounds of life shall no longer be heard in it. The great wicked city shall be thrown down and shall be no more. None of God's people should remain in it, lest they be destroyed with it. The kingdom of this world (Rome and Roman power) proleptically has been replaced by the kingdom of God Transcendent and of Jesus Christ. Not Caesar, but Jesus Christ shall rule forever on the earth (11:15). Those who are destroying the earth shall themselves be destroyed (11:18). They shall be replaced by the saints who have been ransomed by the Lamb of God. The saints shall dwell in the "New Jerusalem," the Church, the Bride of the Lamb (21:7). The redeemed shall have a kingdom, and as priests of God they (not Caesar) shall reign on the earth (5:9–10).

It should be noted that even under the severe stress of Roman oppression, these early Christians were not totally "other-worldly." It was their hope that the Lord God would give power over the nations *on the earth* to those who conquer evil, who do not bow down before the image of Caesar but obey God's commands until the end of their lives (2:26). Jesus Christ, not Caesar, will be the ruler over the kings who are now loyal to Caesar *on the earth*. To Jesus Christ be glory and dominion for ever and ever *on the earth* (1:5–7). "Let the one who has ears to hear listen to what is written here" (2:7, 11, 17, 29; 3:6, 13, 22; 13:9). This reminder that the document is basically a hidden transcript, a cryptogram, a message of hope expressed in symbolic language, is very significant. Those who are up in power now shall be put down. Those who are down now, without power, shall be raised up and shall have power *on the earth*.

The language is thoroughly symbolic. All things, including Death and Hades, are to pass sway, not necessarily literally, but certainly symbolically. The present heaven and the present earth shall pass away, again not so much literally as symbolically. The "New Jerusalem" shall come down out of heaven from God, not literally but symbolically. These are all flashes of the magnificent vision, the vision of the end of this unjust world and seeing in its place a new, just world, as Fiorenza sees clearly in giving her 1991 volume, *Revelation*, the subtitle *Vision of a Just World*. As she says in it, "The series of messianic judgments in Revelation reaches its fulcrum in the vision of a qualitatively new and different world." We must not "construe Revelation as predictive description but instead must understand it as prophetic encouragement and persuasive exhortation." The new heaven and the new earth "stand in continuity with the former heaven and earth, but they form a qualitatively new and unified world." God will be present among God's people. Heaven "will move down to earth."[32] What has been done in heaven will be done *on the earth*.

In many respects, we might say that the "Lord's Prayer" of Matthew 6 and Luke 11 is paraphrased artistically and elaborately in the Apocalypse. Each of its seven petitions, as well as the doxology that was added later, is portrayed graphically in this document. Especially prominent is the prayer "May your Kingdom come!" and with it "May your will be done *on the earth* as it is in heaven."[33] Again, Fiorenza is insightful. "Unlike Paul," she says, the author of Revelation "does not envision that at the Last Day Christians 'shall be caught up' in the clouds to meet their Lord (1 Thess 4:17), nor does he hope, as Daniel did, that the righteous shall shine like stars in heaven (Dan 12:3f)." Instead, "the center of the theological vision and rhetorical movement of Revelation is the earth. This new earth differs from the earth as we know it, in that 'heaven will be on earth.'" Throughout the document, "Revelation's vision of salvation centers on the earth.... God's justice and judgment bring not only vindication of those persecuted and murdered but also engender total human well-being and salvation on earth." Symbolically, "the sea, the place of the beasts and the symbol of evil (13:1), no longer exists (21:1). The future intended world of God's salvation is not envisioned as an island but as encompassing all of creation." (109–110)[34]

We see, therefore, that like the letters of Paul, the epistles of the Pauline writers, the authors of the Synoptic Gospels, and perhaps the Jesus of history, the Apocalypse also is not as "other-worldly" as we had thought when we had interpreted parts of it too literally. We should not interpret the passing away of "the first heaven and the first earth" and the coming of "a new heaven and a new earth" (21:1) literally while perceiving expressions such as "Babylon," "the red dragon," "the wicked harlot," "the devil," and "Satan" symbolically.

The Apocalypse is indeed "a vision of a just world." The complex anti-Roman cryptogram of the book of Revelation carries the message of hope in the entire document. The polemic against the zealous advocates of the Roman

Imperial Cult and the message of hope are both near the surface of the texts of Revelation from its beginning to its end. In 1 Peter, to which we now turn, both are present also, but in 1 Peter the polemic against the representatives of the Roman Imperial Cult is carefully packaged and concealed in a hidden transcript.

1 Peter—Honor the Emperor, but Watch Out! That Devil Is Prowling Around Like a Roaring Lion, Seeking Someone to Devour

A casual reader of 1 Peter, or anyone who is not familiar with the code words employed in anti-Roman cryptograms in the literature of the early Christians, would probably conclude that one of the main emphases in 1 Peter is that Christians should be submissive to the government and to all who are in authority over them. Christians should do whatever is right, and if they suffer any injustice they should accept the injustice submissively, for this will impress those who are unjust and will be pleasing to God. According to this interpretation, this kind of advice may be considered valid and helpful for Christians and for any other religious people at any time. It suggests that if you want to get along and to live your private faith with as little hindrance as possible, go along with those who are in authority over you, and maintain a low political profile.[35]

A closer look, however, particularly in the context of severe Roman oppression in the province of Asia and in Rome itself[36] during the last years of the reign of Emperor Domitian, indicates that beneath the surface of 1 Peter, hidden from the view of Roman government officials who might gain access to it, there is a hidden transcript of hope, a subtle anti-Roman cryptogram. Even though those for whom this document was written may have to suffer various trials and are being abused now (1 Peter 1:6; 3:16; 4:4, 12) as they are suffering throughout the Roman world (5:9) and as the Jesus of history once had to suffer at the hands of the same cruel Roman authorities (4:13), the Resurrected Jesus Christ is at the right hand of power with God Transcendent, and all authorities and powers in heaven and on the earth are subject to the Risen Christ (3:22). To the Risen Christ (not to Caesar) be dominion for ever! (5:11). The Risen Christ is "a stone that causes powerful rulers to stumble, a rock that will block their path" (2:8).

Respect the power of the emperor (2:17), but be sober, be alert. Watch out for your adversary, that devil who is prowling around like a roaring lion, seeking someone to devour (5:8). Withstand him, firm in your faith (5:9), and God Transcendent will restore you, will strengthen you, make you strong again, rebuild your foundations (5:10).

If the author of 1 Peter intended to refer only to the concept of "the Devil," or "Satan," as a pre-existent fallen angel demigod when the author warned the hearers and readers of the document in 5:8 to "Watch out for your adversary, that devil who is prowling around like a roaring lion, seeking someone to devour," it was a very general statement and there is no hidden transcript in the document. That warning would be appropriate in any situation, and there would be no cryptogram, since there is no point in attempting to conceal anything from a demigod. A demigod can easily penetrate any coded language.

If, however, the author was conveying to the early Christian refugees who had fled to the interior areas of Asia Minor that even in the remote areas of that peninsula their adversary was active in a human form, there is an important cryptogram in the document. It is a cryptogram in which the author was saying that the adversary through whom "the devil" was at work was in human form, human but as rapacious as a lion. The "devil" here, who causes the suffering of Christians and of others throughout the Roman world (5:9), is also Emperor Domitian, the Roman State, and the zealous advocates of the Roman Imperial Cult.[37] This devil can be resisted, for this devil is comprised of mortal flesh and blood. This devil will soon be dead. Avoid this devil now, the faithful are told, for the Risen Christ will soon crush him and his power. Then he will no longer roar, nor devour anyone. As if to seal the cryptogram with a final message of assurance, the writer sends a greeting from the community of early followers of Jesus in Rome itself with the words, "The church that is in Babylon (Rome) greets you!"(5:13).

The advice in 1 Peter 2:13–17 to respect the power of the Roman emperor and of his regional governors and to honor the emperor, like its antecedent in Romans 13:1–7, served two purposes. First, it was intended to be taken at face value by the early Christians to whom the document was addressed and by any representatives of the Roman State who might gain access to the document. We can assume that the writer wanted the Christians who would read the document to live in accordance with all of the Roman rules and regulations that were intended to establish a stable society of law and order. To the extent to which the Roman emperor ruled honorably, honor should be given to him, for "the Lord's sake." When representatives of the Roman State gained access to the document and read 1 Peter 2:13–17, they would feel assured that the writer and the people for whom the document was written were basically loyal to the State. Certainly these people were not seditious. They should not be subjected to persecution.

Second, this advice, so clearly and unambiguously given, made it less risky for the writer to slip in the cryptogram in 1 Peter 5:8–14 advising the Christian readers to "watch out for their adversary, that devil who prowls around like a roaring lion, seeking victims to devour." The advice given in 1 Peter 2:13–17 made it relatively safe to slip in the assurance in the final verses of the document that "the God of all grace" will soon restore the scattered Christian refugees to their homes from which they had fled. To God (not to Caesar) shall there be dominion and power forever and ever (5:11). Those who have ears to hear will hear. Those who have no ears for this will be destroyed. Then there will be peace (5:14) for all who are in Christ.

    The beauty of 1 Peter is that its writer was able to transmit this message of hope and liberation without harm to the Jews and without a distortion of history. The same cannot be said for the writer of Acts to which we shall now turn.

Acts of Apostles—the Romans Are Fair and Just; Turn Away from That Satan–Devil and His Savage Wolves Who Are Tearing Up the Flock

If the writer of Acts had copies of the book of Revelation and of 1 Peter in hand[38] while contemplating the situation in the province of Asia during the latter years of the reign of Domitian, the writer probably considered Revelation and 1 Peter to be understandable but inadequate responses to the problem of Roman oppression. The writer of Acts probably decided that Revelation was negative and ill-advised, that it exposed all early followers of Jesus to further suffering since its thinly concealed anti-Roman cryptograms and unrealistic triumphalism over Roman power would risk angering Roman authorities even more than they already were. In the opinion of the writer of Acts, the document that we call 1 Peter would probably have been considered to be no more than a "band-aid" approach to the problem of Roman oppression, a treatment of some of the symptoms of the illness but not adequate in addressing the root causes of the problem. Something far more effective was needed, something that would cause advocates of the Roman Imperial Cult and Roman rulers in the province of Asia and elsewhere to look more favorably at the early followers of Jesus. If the writer of this vivid literary drama could show that the earliest followers of Jesus had enjoyed good relationships with the Roman authorities and that this erudite contemporary Christian writer considered the Romans to be as fair and just as the Romans themselves said that they were, perhaps the current Roman officials in the province of Asia and in Rome would be less inclined to harass, arrest, torture, and kill followers of Jesus. There was no way in which the writer of this literary drama could not go directly to Roman officials and attempt to persuade them to reduce their oppression. It would be far more effective to write something positive, in this instance, a high quality literary drama about actions of certain of the earliest leaders of the Christian "way," something that could conveniently "fall into the hands" of the Roman oppressors. The drama would also be designed for circulation and use among nascent Christians, to attempt to influence contemporary followers of Jesus to adjust their behavior to reduce conflict with Roman authorities.

Each of these two purposes was highly important. If the slaughter of followers of Jesus within the province of Asia would continue or increase, execution of followers of Jesus might be extended empire wide. Participation in this new way to live might then go into a free fall of decline, or even cease. Followers of this way might return to their traditional Jewish lifestyle, or, if they were Greeks, to their prevailing Greek heritage. The suffering and death of Jesus as the Son of God would then have been of no avail. Some action was needed that would alleviate the anxieties of the oppressors and strengthen the resolve of the oppressed.

The writer of Acts was well-equipped to compose such a document. This writer had already composed the most excellent of the Four Gospels, a thorough literary redaction of "The Gospel of Jesus Christ" (Mark) and of other material about Jesus that was available. This redaction included the composition of many highly effective, memorable scenes such as of the angel Gabriel appearing to the Virgin Mary, of Mary and Joseph traveling from Nazareth to Bethlehem just before Jesus was born, of no room in the inn, of Jesus being born among the dust and dirt of a feeding area for animals, and of angels announcing his birth to shepherds who were watching their flocks at night. It added accounts of Jesus as a youth in the temple and as a rejected prophet in his hometown, and of the Risen Christ talking with two incredulous disciples on the road to Emmaus. These skills of inspired creativity could be employed now in a kind of sequel to this author's "Gospel," a sequel comprised of similar memorable scenes that might relieve the pressures on the current followers of Jesus in the province of Asia, in Rome itself, and elsewhere throughout the Empire.

There was no "Mark" that could serve as a basis for a redaction, but there were oral and perhaps written traditions about activities of some of the disciples of Jesus after his death. In addition, there were letters that had been written by Paul and by others in Paul's name and perhaps a travelogue by Luke, the "beloved physician" companion of Paul, that could be utilized as source material. The personal experiences of the writer would also, of course, be incorporated into this drama in various ways. Perhaps the writer was not only "a man from Macedonia" (Acts 16:9), but also one of the few early Christians who was a Roman citizen, born with that citizenship, a person who had used that citizenship effectively in avoiding repression (Acts 16:37–39; 22:25–29;

23:27). Perhaps the writer even had friends among the "Asiarchs in Ephesus," who as rulers in the province of Asia were strong supporters of Rome and of the Roman State (Acts 19:31).

As a playwright writing with a specific purpose, in this instance to reduce pressure on contemporary Christians, the playwright had the license to present the material in whatever way the playwright considered to be most effective in fulfilling that purpose. If, for example, presenting Paul as a friend of the Asiarchs in Ephesus will reduce oppression of Christians in the province of Asia, then Paul will be presented in that way, even though Paul actually had been harassed, arrested, and killed by an earlier generation of people who were similar to these Asiarchs. If presenting the Jews as villains will reduce the oppression of Christians, then the Jews will be presented as villains in this literary drama. After all, the process of blaming the Jews rather than the Romans for the suffering and death of Jesus had been well under way already in all four of the Gospel accounts, and the writer of Acts was a person who had been a significant participant in that process. Certainly to this inspired writer the end justified the means. Something radical must be done to save Christian lives, and this playwright did what this playwright was fully equipped to do, produce a vivid, multifaceted literary drama.

The result of this playwright's efforts, as we have it in Acts, demonstrates that the Christian message was taken from Jerusalem to Rome and to the uttermost parts of the earth (Acts 1:8; 28:16–31). Jews who remained Jews, with Adonai as their primary manifestation of God Active in History, are presented as the villains in this literary drama. Christian leaders, for whom Jesus Christ raised from the dead was now "Lord," a more recent manifestation of God active in their history, are the heroes. Paul is presented as at first a villain and then a hero. He had been a particularly evil villain as "Saul" the Jew, but as a Christian he became a shining hero. From what Paul himself had written in Galatians 1:13–17, in 1 Corinthians 1:1, 9:1, 15:8, and in 2 Corinthians 12:1–12, the playwright fashioned a call story that the playwright liked so much that the playwright used it twice more in the same drama, with some modifications and further development.[39] Roman military and political authorities are depicted in Acts as friends of the heroes, as eminently fair and just in their difficult position of having to maintain "peace" between the Jewish villains and the Christian heroes. Therefore, the basic sketch of the Acts document is relatively simple.

There is historical information in this literary drama, but the primary purpose of the playwright was not to present historical data. The primary purpose of the playwright was to reduce Roman oppression of Christians and thereby to save Christian lives *in this world*. The damage that this document would do to Jewish lives *in this world* was apparently not a concern of this playwright, or this damage was considered to be part of the price that must be paid. After all, to this playwright the future of Israel was not in Judaism but in the Church.

I must respond briefly here to those who object that the writer of Acts and those who composed the Four Gospels could not have transferred so much of the guilt for the suffering and death of Jesus and of his followers from Romans to Jews, because many people would have remembered exactly what had happened and because the biblical writers were inspired by God. We must begin with the realization that not all of the Romans were guilty of causing the suffering and death of Jesus. Neither were all of the Jews innocent. There were a few Jews who had cooperated fully with Pontius Pilate and with the Roman occupation forces, and this was remembered by followers of Jesus. Jewish "goons" employed by the Jewish chief priest Caiaphas had seized Jesus in the Garden of Gethsemane and had delivered him over to the Romans who then under orders from Pilate tortured and crucified him. The Roman soldiers had tortured Jesus privately, out of sight of Jesus' followers; Jewish goons had taken Jesus directly away from his followers. That it was Jews employed by Caiaphas, a Jew, who had seized Jesus in Gethsemane was firmly implanted in the minds of Jesus' followers. This made it easy for later Christian writers to blame the Jews. They should not, however, have blamed *all* of the Jews for the suffering and death of Jesus, for that is a major and horribly serious distortion of history.

It should also be noted that a single individual does not accomplish a major distortion of history, and a major distortion of history does not occur overnight. Many people are involved over a lengthy period of time. In this instance, it had been more than sixty years between the death of Jesus and the composition of the Acts literary drama. In addition, we must realize that history can be distorted relatively easily when many people want it to be distorted. For this, we have only to look at some of the major distortions of history involved in the past and present portrayals of our own nation's history. Similar distortions have been made and are being made in the histories of other nations.

With regard to the other objection, that the biblical writers were inspired by God, I fully affirm their inspiration. Inspired persons, however, can and do distort history. They retain their biases, their prejudices, and their purposes. We need only to look at ourselves for ample evidence of this. God does not prevent these distortions today, and Acts and other biblical literature are evidence that God did not prevent distortions of history during the period in which the biblical documents were composed and accepted as sacred Scripture. We must be open, honest, and accountable with regard to our biblical traditions, for our own integrity and for the sake of our children and all future generations. We cannot change the past. We can, however, change the present and the future.

Most of all, our ultimate accountability is not to our biblical traditions. Neither is it to our religious and political institutions. Our ultimate accountability is to God.

Whether it was morally justifiable for the writer of Acts to transfer most of the guilt for the suffering and death of Jesus and his followers from Romans to Jews in order to attempt to reduce the oppression of early Christians by the Romans can and should be debated, both in the context of the situation during the last decade of the first century and in light of events since that time. We must also be responsible in our use of Acts as sacred Scripture for Christians today. We must repudiate in it what must be repudiated[40] and affirm in it that which can be affirmed. Among the portions that can be strongly affirmed in it are the messages of hope within the anti-Roman cryptograms that its author developed and included in the document.

Deep within Acts, the discerning reader who is alert to the nature of hidden transcripts and anti-Roman cryptograms can find these carefully concealed messages of hope. Some of the same code words that are employed in the Pauline literature and in the Synoptic Gospels are used in Acts. The playwright carefully concealed them by speaking openly and favorably of "the Romans" (Acts 10:1-48; 16:21; 25:16; 28:17-21), while at the same time within the cryptograms obliquely referring to the Romans as "lawless men"[41] who had crucified Jesus (2:23). According to this writer, God has made Jesus (not Caesar) "both Lord and Christ" (2:36) and "Lord of all" (10:36) and will make Jesus' enemies (the representatives of Caesar who had crucified him) a "stool under Jesus' feet" (2:35). The Romans who rule over the early Christians are cryptically called "this crooked generation" (2:40), a designation that was probably intended by the writer to refer also to Jews who remained Jews. Those "afflicted by unclean spirits" in 5:16 and in 8:7 may be Jews and Samaritans who had cooperated with the oppressive Romans. In a similar way, the "evil spirits" in 19:11–16 may suggest the condition of those who cooperated fully with the zealous advocates of the Roman Imperial Cult in the Roman province of Asia. The same people may be the "men speaking perversions of the truth" of 20:30 who make it easier for the "savage wolves" (20:29) of the Roman Imperial Cult to "tear up the flock."

One of the most daring and explicit anti-Roman cryptograms in Acts is included in the speech that the inspired playwright prepared for Peter to use in addressing Cornelius, the Roman centurion in Caesarea (10:38–39). Here Peter describes Jesus to a representative of Roman power as one who "went around doing good things and healing all who were being oppressed by the devil" and says that "we are witnesses of all of this" and that "they put an end to all of this by hanging Jesus on a cross of wood." The "devil" who had oppressed the Jews at that time was not merely some pre-existent semi-divine being who constantly opposed God. The "devil" who had oppressed the Jews at that time was Pontius Pilate, the Roman procurator in Jerusalem, and Caiaphas, the Jewish chief priest of the temple who had been appointed to that position by the Romans. The "devil" was the Roman military presence in Judea that at the command of Pilate had crucified Jesus. Jesus, on the other hand, had been "healing" his fellow oppressed Jews and giving to them hope that soon they would be free from the "devil" of Roman oppression in their midst. Much of that "healing" undoubtedly involved giving the people hope of liberation from Roman oppression.

Another cryptogram within Acts, nearly as daring as the one cited above, was prepared by the Lukan writer for the character Paul in this document to address to Herod Agrippa II (Acts 26:17–18). Here Paul's lines in this play call for him to speak about his work as "opening the eyes of the Gentiles, so that they may turn from darkness to light and from the power/authority of Satan to the power/authority of God." Only the code words of "the devil" and "Satan" keep these texts from being specific condemnations of Roman oppressors addressed to people of considerable power themselves within the Roman system. The Lukan playwright safeguarded the code words, however, by having Paul condemn a Jewish "false prophet named Bar-Jesus and Elymas" as a "son of the devil" in the demigod sense that prevails in the Fourth Gospel (13:6-12) and by having Peter ask Ananias, "Why has Satan filled your heart, to cause you to lie to the Holy Spirit?" (5:3) also in the sense of "Satan" as a pre-existent semi-divine being.

We see, therefore, that although anti-Roman cryptograms as coded messages of hope and liberation to oppressed early Christians were not major emphases in Acts, they were used. When they were used, they were of high quality, carefully crafted, encoded, and protected from easy detection.

Conclusions

The three documents considered here (Revelation, 1 Peter, and Acts), while vastly differing responses to the severe oppression of Christians by zealous advocates of the Roman Imperial Cult in the Roman province of Asia during the last seven years of the reign of Emperor Domitian, all contain significant anti-Roman cryptograms, hidden transcripts of hope and liberation for the oppressed. Concern for survival in this life pervades all three documents. Even though near the end of Revelation its writer anticipates the passing away of the present heaven and of the present earth, the new heaven and the new earth are perceived to be populated by people, good people who "eat fruit" and "reign for ever," two activities that characterize joy and prosperity in this world (Rev 22:1–5). The anti-Roman hidden transcripts that we have seen in these three documents are consistent with criteria 3, 5, and 7 on pages 18-19 above.

Having finished our examination of anti-Roman cryptograms in the three documents that most specifically were written in response to a period of severe Roman oppression, we turn to the four remaining documents that were eventually incorporated into the New Testament: Hebrews, James, Jude, and 2 Peter.

VI. Anti-Roman Cryptograms in the Remaining Newer Testament Documents: Hebrews, James, Jude, and 2 Peter

Since there is relatively little material in these four documents that may have been intended to be anti-Roman cryptograms bearing messages of hope to oppressed early Christians, this final chapter of our survey will be appropriately brief. The hidden transcripts of anti-Roman cryptograms that can be identified are primarily in Hebrews and in the Epistle of James, in each of which there is one reference to "the devil" that may incorporate an anti-Roman cryptogram in addition to the sense of the devil as a pre-existent demigod.

Hebrews—Destroying the Devil Who Has the Power of Death

Since "the devil" in Hebrews 2:14–15 is said to be "the one who has the power of death," and "one who has held many in bondage throughout their lives because of their fear of death," we should look at other references to power, to suffering, to bondage, and to death in this document to help us to understand the identity intended for "the devil" in this document.

According to Hebrews 1:8, God says to the Son, who is symbolized as an Israelite king being crowned, "May your throne, like the throne of God, be for ever and ever. May the scepter with which you rule always be straight and fair!" Everything, according to Hebrews 2:8, is to be placed in subjection under the feet of the Son. Nothing is left outside the control of the Son, even though at the present time "We do not yet see everything subjected to the Son." Fear of death still keeps many subject to lifelong bondage (2:15). The writer speaks about the present condition of the writer and of those who are close to the writer with the words, "We who have fled to find refuge" (6:18). The great heroes of faith cited in 11:4–32 are said in 11:33–38 to have endured horrendous torture. Jesus is said to have endured the cross (12:2), enduring severe hostility from sinful people (12:3). The readers of the document are urged to remember those who are imprisoned, as being imprisoned with them, those who are being treated badly, as being treated badly with them, being in the same body/community of faith (13:3). The readers of the document are called to go out to Jesus outside the fortification, bearing the same abuse that he suffered (13:13). Finally, in the postscript it is said that "our brother Timothy has been released" (13:23).

In the context of all of these references to power, suffering, imprisonment, and death, perhaps the writer of this document did intend the readers for whom it was composed to understand the "devil" to be the Roman State. Certainly it was the Roman State that late in the first century C.E. in the area in which almost all of the early Christians lived "had the power of death" and "held many in bondage throughout their lives because of their fear of death." The "devil" in these texts was not merely a demigod hurting the early Christians. The "devil" was active in history as the Roman State and more specifically as zealous advocates of Roman Civil Religion who were hurting them.

The strong desire that the Jesus of history, as well as many other Jews and later many Christians, expressed for the benevolent rule of God to replace the malevolent rule of the Romans may lie behind Hebrews 1:8 and its "May your throne, like the throne of God, be for ever and ever. May the scepter with which you rule always be straight and fair!" The same fervent desire may lie beneath the statement in 2:8 that everything is being placed in subjection under the feet of the Son, even though at the present time "We do not yet see everything subjected to the Son." It was indeed the fear of death that kept many Jews and early Christians subject to lifelong bondage within the areas controlled by the Romans (2:15).

It was not from the "devil" perceived only as a demigod that the writer and those for whom this document was originally intended "had fled to find refuge" (6:18). It was from the "devil" active in zealous advocates of Roman Civil Religion that they had fled, as is indicated in 1 Peter and perhaps also in James 1:1–2, 2:6–7, 4:4–7, and 5:5–7. Some early Christians known to the writer and to the intended readers of Hebrews had suffered horrendous torture similar to the torture suffered by the great heroes of faith cited in Hebrews 11:4–38. The sinful people whose hostility caused the Jesus of history to endure the cross (12:2-3) were representatives of the Roman State, figuratively speaking in league with the devil.

The people who are said in 13:3 to be imprisoned and being treated badly, who are of the same body/community of faith as are the writer and intended readers of this document, are not convicted drug dealers, arsonists, burglars, rapists, and murderers. They are early Christians who would not bend their knees before the image of Caesar as demanded by the zealous advocates of Roman Civil Religion. The readers of this document who are called in 13:13 to bear the same abuse that Jesus suffered outside the walls of Jerusalem are suffering abuse from the "devil" active in certain Romans, or super-patriotic supporters of the Romans. The statement in the postscript (13:13) that "Our brother Timothy has been released" must refer to release from the hands of these super-patriots. Therefore, "the devil who has the power of death" in Hebrews 2:14 probably was the Roman State, which appeared to the writer of this document to be a current manifestation of the demigod to whom all evil was attributed.

Incidentally, the familiarity that the writer of Hebrews shows to themes that are common in much of the Pauline literature, the Synoptic Gospels, and 1 Peter are indications that Hebrews may have been written near the end of the first century, but no later than the last year of the reign of Domitian (96 C.E.), since Clement of Rome quoted from this document at that date.

James—Stand Firm Against the Devil, and the Devil Will Flee from You

We note first of all some significant similarities between James and 1 Peter. We see these similarities not only in the frequently noted references in James 1:1 to the *diaspora* (1 Peter 1:1), in James 1:2, 12 to various trials (1 Peter 1:6; 3:16–17; 4:4, 12–16; 5:8–9), and in James 4:10 to bowing down in the presence of the Lord (1 Peter 5:6), but also in the idea of "resist the devil" in James 4:7 (1 Peter 5:8–9). Both James 4:7 and 1 Peter 5:8–9 use the same imperative verb form *antistēte* and the same noun *diabolos*. Therefore, if as we have seen in chapter V above it is likely that the author of 1 Peter intended that those for whom that document was written should realize that the "devil" to be resisted was the Roman State and the super-patriots, the writer of James may have intended also that those who would read James should realize that the "devil" that they should resist was manifested in the Roman State and its super-patriots and not merely the demigod.

Perhaps the diatribes against "the rich" that are so prominent in the Epistle of James are indications that its author also intended those for whom James was written to identify "the rich" with that "devil" that was the Roman State and its zealous advocates. "The rich" addressed in the diatribe of James 2:6–7 are said to be oppressing the early Christians, to be dragging them into court, and to be blaspheming the good name that was spoken when God's gifts came to them. Those who were super-patriotic supporters of the Romans were the rich of that time. They were the ones who dragged the early Christians into court. They were the ones who blasphemed the name of Jesus by demanding that the early Christians bow down before the image of Caesar. According to James 1:10 and 5:1–6, "the rich" will soon wither like wildflowers in the field and pass away. Soon the Roman State and its super-patriots will no longer oppress the early Christians. Those who have lived in luxury and pleasure on the earth, who have condemned and killed "the righteous one" (the Jesus of history), will soon be miserable and will fade away (5:1–6). This is the message of hope for the early Christians in this subtle cryptogram.

We see also that early Christians for whom the Epistle of James was intended may have been poor laborers who had mowed the fields of these rich super-patriotic supporters of the Romans and harvested their crops, only to be deprived of their wages (5:4). Perhaps it is the rich super-patriots who in these diatribes are the proud whom God opposes (4:6), who have "friendship with the world" (4:4). Perhaps the writer of James was warning those for whom the Epistle was intended to avoid at all costs the temptation to show honor and favor to these people (2:1–7) as a means of improving their own station in life.

We have tended to interpret the Epistle of James in our post-Constantinian context rather than in its own pre-Constantinian setting. We have also not adequately realized that in a diatribe not all of the persons addressed are necessarily included in the community to whom the document is being sent. Perhaps "the devil" in James 4:7 was originally not simply the demigod, but also the Roman State and the zealous advocates of the Roman Imperial Cult who, in the eyes of the early Christians, were in league with the devil perceived as a demigod.

Jude and 2 Peter—Lordship for Jesus Christ (Not for Caesar)

Only if zealous advocates of the Roman Imperial Cult had infiltrated some early communities of followers of Jesus, denying Jesus Christ as their Master and Lord (Jude 3–23 and 2 Pet 2:1–22) and "taking people in" with their false words are these two documents directed against the Roman State and its zealous super-patriots. From the content of what is said against the false prophets in Jude and in 2 Peter this does not appear to be likely. Nevertheless, there could be a subtle anti-Roman cryptogram in the implied contrast to the temporal kingdom of the Roman State in the reference to "the eternal kingdom of our Lord and Savior Jesus Christ" in 2 Peter 1:11 and in the reference to the dominion and authority of Jesus Christ in Jude 25.

Conclusions

It is likely that the writers of Hebrews and of James intended that their readers would interpret "the devil" in Hebrews 2:14–15 and in James 4:7 as references to the Roman State and its zealous super-patriots as manifestations of the demigod. They made this reference in order to encourage their readers to persevere in their Christian faith in spite of Roman oppression and to hope for relief from Roman economic, political, and religious oppression at an early date. These writers, like many other leaders in the nascent Church, were less "other-worldly" and more concerned about freedom from oppression in this life than we have usually supposed.

The Lordship of Jesus Christ is acclaimed in Jude and in 2 Peter. Indirectly, this acclamation is a repudiation of the Lordship of Caesar that was being stressed by the zealous participants in Roman Civil Religion at the time of the writing of Jude and of 2 Peter.

VII. Conclusions, Implications, and Future Agenda

The two basic theses of this book have been supported by our survey of the Newer Testament literature in this study. This study has indicated that the Jesus of history and his earliest and closest followers within the early church during the decades after he was crucified had a strong desire for freedom in this life, as well as a deep longing for eternal life with God beyond the limits of this world and its problems. We have seen this strong desire for freedom in this life, together with the deep longing for eternal life with God, within traditions that can be traced back with considerable certainty to the Jesus of history. We have seen them also within the writings of Paul and of others within the Pauline traditions. They are apparent also within other Newer Testament documents. This desire and this longing is consistent with the Jewish background of the early Christian tradition and links Jesus and his earliest and closest followers to other oppressed Jews historically, to African-Americans, to the campesinos of Latin America, to native South Africans, and to many others.

This study also has indicated that within the Newer Testament there are more anti-Roman hidden transcripts of hope for "freedom now," within this present life, than we have generally realized. These anti-Roman cryptograms are not limited to the book of Revelation, but can be detected with some assurance also within most of the other Newer Testament documents.

Although the full meanings intended by the writers of the Newer Testament documents cannot be discerned by interpreters of another time and place, it is likely that in most instances when the writers of Newer Testament documents referred to "the devil," "Satan," "the tempter," and synonyms of these words they intended their readers within the early Church to think not only in terms of a demigod, but also in terms of the Roman State, Caesar, and certain representatives of Caesar.

In this connection, it is helpful to note that as a result of this study we can conclude that it was the hope of the Jesus of history and many of his earliest followers not so much that the world would be destroyed before their generation would pass away as it was that soon they would be free from Roman oppression. When the Jewish revolt in Judea and in Galilee occurred approximately forty years after Jesus had been crucified, and when the revolt was brutally crushed by the Roman military forces, it became obvious to the early followers of Jesus that the world had not been destroyed, that Jesus had not reappeared on the earth to destroy the Romans, and that Roman oppression was continuing. The adjustment to their thinking that the early followers of Jesus made during the 70s and 80s of the first century C.E. was not so much an adjustment to the ongoing existence of the universe as it was to the continuation of oppression by the Romans. At that time their hope for "freedom now" from Roman oppression seemed to be increasingly unrealistic. It became more realistic for them to "make disciples in all nations" and to hope for "freedom after death." They believed that Jesus as the Risen Christ would provide that freedom, if not during their present lives, then certainly after death.

The conclusions reached in this study must be judged by each reader. Perhaps in some instances I have suggested that subtle hidden transcripts of anti-Roman cryptograms exist in places that were not intended by the writers of the Newer Testament documents. It is likely that I have missed some hidden transcripts of anti-Roman cryptograms that were intended by the writers. The readers of this study will make these judgments.

The use of subtle anti-Roman cryptograms as messages of hope and liberation for oppressed Jews and early Christians by the Jesus of history and by inspired writers of the Newer Testament documents has important implications for us today. Although our situation differs considerably from the situation of the Jesus of history and from the situation of the earliest followers of the Jesus of history, we who are Christians today should be guided in our faith and life by the Jesus of history and by the Newer Testament foundation documents. Therefore, we should not be oppressors of others, politically, socially, economically, or in any other way. We should courageously oppose those who are oppressive within our own nation and in every nation. We should strongly support those who are being oppressed today and who have been oppressed in the past. We should support them with our power and influence, with our resources, and with our lives. We should guard against the delusion that we are not responsible for the quality of life of others. We should not use the concepts of "the devil," "Satan," and "the tempter" to make it easier for us to avoid our responsibilities to God and to the other people of the world.

This study has indicated that "the kingdom of God" has a specific reference over against "the kingdom of this world," which at the time of the Jesus of history and of the developing Church was the Roman State and its power. The symbols of "the kingdom of God" in the Gospels According to Mark and Luke and of "the kingdom of heaven" in Matthew were probably not intended primarily to refer to some "other-worldly" mode of existence. For the most part, they were probably intended to refer to a situation of peace and freedom here on this earth, in the words of Luke 2:14 to "peace on the earth among people of God's good will."

Therefore, if we wish to be true to the Jesus of history and to the meanings of the Newer Testament documents as they were originally intended by the inspired writers, we should put somewhat more emphasis on "this-worldly" concerns and somewhat less emphasis on "other-worldly" concerns than our Christian systematic theologians and preachers of the past sixteen centuries have placed on them. For us in this post-9/11 time of global economic recession and recognition of the grave repercussions of global warming, this means that we should place less emphasis on competitive nationalism. Instead, we should be working to expand regional economic cooperation in the Middle East, in Africa, in the Americas, in Europe to include Russia, in Southern and in Eastern Asia, and in the East Indies and Australia, as a replacement for intense nationalism, physical walls, and war.[1]

The most important time for us is the present and the immediate future. We share our present and our immediate future with others in a way that is different from the manner in which we share our past. This means that constructive dialogue with other Christians, with Jews, with Muslims, with Hindus, with Buddhists, and with all others who with us are advocates of God and of oppressed people should be entered into with ever more joy and enthusiasm as we strive for peace on the earth.

Our present and future agenda, therefore, is to be what the Jesus of history and what most of the inspired writers of the Newer Testament documents were, that is, advocates for God and for oppressed people. We should actuate the messages of hope and liberation that this present study has sought to identify within the Newer Testament documents. We should do this in every way, alone and in conjunction with all others who share in this hope. To this we are called.

Notes

Introduction

1   Among the persons to whom I am most indebted for guidance and information regarding coded messages of hope and liberation in the songs of African-Americans prior to 1865 are O. Fred Cravens, who for many years was the pastor of Wesley Harper United Methodist Church in Seguin, Texas, and Kim and Reggie Harris of Philadelphia, Pennsylvania. Kim and Reggie Harris have produced an album and a tape, *Music and the Underground Railroad* (Philadelphia: Ascension, 1984). They present their reproductions of African-American slave songs associated with the Underground Railroad on college and university campuses and provide assembly programs and lesson plans for classroom activities throughout the country.

2   Early descriptions of the Underground Railroad include William Still, *The Underground Railroad* (Philadelphia: Porter, 1883), Wilbur H. Siebert, *The Underground Railroad: From Slavery to Freedom* (New York: Macmillan, 1898), and continue in more recent years with Henrietta Buckmaster, *Let My People Go: The Story of the Underground Railroad and the Growth of the Abolition Movement* (Boston: Beacon, 1959), Larry Gara, *The Liberty Line: The Legend of the Underground Railroad* (Lexington: University of Kentucky Press, 1967), and Charles L. Blockson, *The Underground Railroad in Pennsylvania* (Jacksonville, NC: Flame, 1981). Among the most important publications on the lives of individual African-American heroes are: Sarah Bradford, *Harriet Tubman: The Moses of Her People* (2d ed., 1886; reprint, New York: Corinth, 1961); Frederick Douglass, *Life and Times of Frederick Douglass* (Boston: DeWolfe, 1892; reissue, New York: Collier, 1962); Oswald Garrison Villard, *John Brown, 1800–1859: A Biography Fifty Years After* (Boston: Houghton Mifflin, 1910); Earl Conrad, *Harriet Tubman* (Washington, DC: Associated, 1943; reissue, New York: Erricksson, 1969); and Dorothy Sterling, *Lucretia Mott: Gentle Warrior* (Garden City, NY: Doubleday , 1964).

3   For analyses of the coded messages in the songs of the African-American slaves, see John Lovell, "The Social Implications of the Negro Spiritual," *Journal of Negro Education* 8 (1939) 636–643; Miles Mark Fisher, *Negro Slave Songs in the United States* (New York: Citadel, 1953); W.E.B. DuBois, *The Souls of Black Folk* (New York: Fawcett, 1961); Lindsay Patterson, ed., *The Negro in Music and Art* (New York: Publishers, 1967); Gilbert Osofsky, ed., *Puttin' On Ole Massa: The Slave Narratives of Henry Bibb, William Wells Brown, and Solomon Northup* (New York: Harper, 1969); Ruth Miller, *Blackamerican Literature: 1760-Present* (Beverly Hills, CA: Glencoe, 1971); J. Garfield Owens, *All God's Chillun: Meditations on Negro Spirituals* (Nashville: Abingdon, 1971); James H. Cone, *The Spirituals and the Blues* (New York: Seabury, 1972); and Christa K. Dixon, *Negro Spirituals: From Bible to Folksong* (Philadelphia: Fortress, 1976).

4   *Music and the Underground Railroad.* The codes used and identified in these quotations are printed in italics.

5   "John Brown's Trail" was one of many codes used for the Underground Railroad.

6   *All God's Chillun*, 25.

7   Translated by John Bowden (Philadelphia: Fortress, 1987). See also, among many others, Richard J. Cassidy, *Jesus, Politics, and Society: A Study of Luke's Gospel* (Maryknoll, NY: Orbis, 1978); Ernst Bammel and C. F. D. Moule, eds., *Jesus and the Politics of His Day* (Cambridge: Cambridge University Press, 1984); Richard A. Horsley and John S. Hanson, *Bandits, Prophets, and Messiahs* (Minneapolis: Winston, 1985); Calvin J. Roetzel, *The World That Shaped the New Testament* (Atlanta: John Knox, 1985); Douglas E. Oakman, *Jesus and the Economic Questions of His Day* (Lewiston, NY: Mellen, 1986); Luise Schottroff and Wolfgang Stegemann, *Jesus and the Hope of the Poor* (Maryknoll, NY: Orbis, 1986); John E. Stambaugh and David L. Balch, *The New Testament in Its Social Environment* (Philadelphia: Westminster, 1986); Michael Walsh, *The Triumph of the Meek* (San Francisco: Harper, 1986); Richard A. Horsley, *Jesus and the Spiral of Violence* (San Francisco: Harper, 1987); Norbert F. Lohfink, *Option for the Poor* (Berkeley: Bibal, 1987); Richard J. Cassidy, *Society and Politics in the Acts of the Apostles* (Maryknoll, NY: Orbis, 1987); Philip F. Esler, *Community and Gospel in Luke-Acts* (Cambridge: Cambridge University Press, 1987); Ivo Lesbaupin, *Blessed Are the Persecuted* (Maryknoll, NY: Orbis, 1987); Bart D. Ehrman, *Jesus: Apocalyptic Prophet of the New Millennium* (Oxford: Oxford University Press, 1999); Richard J. Cassidy, *Christians and Roman Rule in the New Testament: New Perspectives* (New York: Crossword, 2001); Richard A. Horsley, ed., *Hidden Transcripts and the Arts of Resistance* (Atlanta: Society of Biblical Literature, 2004); Christopher Bryan, *Render to Caesar: Jesus, the Early Church, and the Roman Superpower* (Oxford: Oxford University Press, 2005); Richard L. Rohrbaugh, *The New Testament in Cross-Cultural Perspective* (Eugene, OR: Wipf & Stock, 2006); Warren Carter, *The Roman Empire and the New Testament* (Nashville: Abingdon, 2006; John Dominic Crossan, *God and Empire: Jesus Against Rome, Then and Now* (NY: HarperCollins, 2007); Seyoon Kim, *Christ and Caesar: The Gospel and the Roman Empire in the Writings of Paul and Luke* (Grand Rapids: Eerdmans, 2008); and James W. Ermatinger, *Daily Life in the New Testament* (Westport, CN: Greenwood Press, 2008).

8   For a more detailed analysis of the Jesus of history and his message of hope and liberation, see chapter I below.

9   Jewish, as well as Christian, commentators on the Ezekiel texts have been fully aware of the political situation in which Ezekiel and those who compiled the Ezekiel traditions lived. S. Fisch, for example, in his *Ezekiel: Hebrew Text & English Translation with an Introduction and Commentary* (London: Soncino Press, 10th edition, 1985), xvi, 195–220, is aware of the hidden references to the cruel Egyptians and Babylonians within the Ezekiel traditions. We see similar observations in Walter Eichrodt, *Ezekiel: A Commentary* (Philadelphia: Westminster, 1970), 407–441. Lawrence Boadt, *Ezekiel's Oracles against Egypt: A Literary and Philological Study of Ezekiel 29–32* (Rome: Biblical Institute Press, 1980) 173–180, states that (Egypt) the seventh nation condemned in the oracles against the nations in the Ezekiel tradition as the most evil of the seven should receive the greatest punishment.

10   As André Lococque puts it in *The Book of Daniel* (Atlanta: John Knox, 1979) 10, as quoted from his introduction to the Book of Daniel in P. Grelot and A. Lacocque, *Daniel* (La Traduction Oecuménique de la Bible) Paris, 1975, "Seen within the context of its time, the Book of Daniel presents an original combination of two genres which Jewish literature favoured at that time: the didactic story (*agadah*) and the apocalypse."

11   *A Critical and Exegetical Commentary on the Book of Daniel* (NY: Scribner's 1927) 83.

12   According to Albert C. Sundberg, "On Testimonies," *Novum Testamentum* 3 (1959) 272–274, every one of Daniel's twelve chapters is cited in the Newer Testament, no other

Older Testament document has citations in the Newer Testament of every one of its chapters, and for the writer of Mark, Daniel was the most important document of what is for Christians the Older Testament.

13   James H. Charlesworth, ed., *The Old Testament Pseudepigrapha* 1 (Garden City, NY: Doubleday, 1983) 15–19.

14   In James H. Charlesworth, ed., *The Old Testament Pseudepigrapha* 2 (Garden City, NY: Doubleday, 1985) 43–44.

15   Elaine Pagels, "The Social History of Satan, the 'Intimate Enemy': A Preliminary Sketch," *Harvard Theological Review* 84:2 (1991) 105–128, proposes that the concept of Satan as the leader of an "evil empire," of "an army of hostile spirits who take pleasure in destroying human beings," developed among what she calls "dissident Jews," which included early followers of Jesus and perhaps, although she does not say this, the Jesus of history himself. Her article identifies some of the ways in which Satan appears in various extracanonical Jewish sources. She points out that this concept of Satan as the leader of an evil empire is not found in classical Jewish sources and is not a factor in traditional Judaism. She carries her analysis farther in "The Social History of Satan, Part II: Satan in the New Testament Gospels," *Journal of the American Academy of Religion* 62:1 (1994) 17–58.

16   It is also an extended allegory. It can be categorized as a vision with an interpretation, a characteristic of apocalyptic literature of its period. These are all rather general categories. The designation cryptogram and particularly anti-Roman cryptogram is more specific.

17   The Vision of the Forest, the Vine, the Fountain and the Cedar in *2 Baruch* 36–40 is another anti-Roman cryptogram within the Jewish Pseudepigrapha, but it is much less complex than the Eagle Vision of *4 Ezra* 11–12. The Vision in *2 Baruch* 36–40 is dated in the first or second decade of the second century C.E. by A. F. J. Klijn in Charlesworth, *The Old Testament Pseudepigrapha* I, 616–17. The figure of the Messiah of the Lord is very significant in the Vision in *2 Baruch* 36–40.

    The anti-Roman material in the Sibylline Oracles 8:37–193 is open and explicit. Therefore, it is not a cryptogram. In addition, its composition occurred a century after the writing of most of the documents that were incorporated into the specifically Christian Scriptures. John J. Collins in Charlesworth, *The Old Testament Pseudepigrapha* I, 416, suggests the period of 175–180 C.E.

18   In Aboda Zara 1 b of the Babylonian Talmud, the fourth kingdom depicted in Daniel 7:23 is also said to be Roman rather than Greek.

19   In his *Pax Romana*. The eagle as a symbol can be lofty and beautiful, as in the song, "And he will raise you up on eagle's wings," or it can be dreadful and horrible, as in this Eagle Vision of *4 Ezra* 11–12.

20   In his Introduction to the document in Charlesworth, *The Old Testament Pseudepigrapha* I, 520. It should be noted that, unlike the Daniel traditions, the composer of the Eagle Vision expected a Davidic-type Messiah. For a discussion of this, see John J. Collins, *The Apocalyptic Imagination: An Introduction to the Jewish Matrix of Christianity* (New York: Crossroad, 1984) 166.

21   James C. Scott, *Weapons of the Weak: Everyday Forms of Peasant Resistance* (New Haven: Yale University Press, 1985), and *Domination and the Arts of Resistance: Hidden Transcripts* (New Haven: Yale University Press, 1990).

22   Scott, *Domination and the Arts of Resistance*, 136–138.

23   "Onstage and Offstage with Jesus of Nazareth: Public Transcripts, Hidden Transcripts,

and Gospel Texts" *Hidden Transcripts and the Arts of Resistance: Applying the Work of James C. Scott to Jesus and to Paul* (edited by Richard A. Horsley, Atlanta: Society of Biblical Literature, 2004), 49.

24   Atlanta: Society of Biblical Literature, 2004. Within this collection, in addition to the essays by Horsley and Herzog, especially relevant are the contributions of Allen Dwight Callahan, Warren Carter, Neil Elliott, Susan M. (Elli) Elliott, Cynthia Briggs Kittredge, and Gerald West.

25   Minneapolis: Fortress, 2003.

26   Oxford: Oxford University Press, 2005.

27   Bryan, *Render to Caesar*, 34, 39–46

28   John Howard Yoder, *The Politics of Jesus: Behold the Man! Our Victorious Lamb*, 2nd ed. (Grand Rapids: Eerdmans, 1994).

29   Seyoon Kim, *Christ and Caesar: The Gospel and the Roman Empire in the Writings of Paul and Luke* (Grand Rapids: Eerdmans, 2008), unlike most of the other sources cited in this book, concludes that his "examinations of 1 Thessalonians, Philippians, Romans, and 1 Corinthians in interaction with some representative 'anti-imperial' interpreters have confirmed that in those epistles there is no warning about the imperial cult and no message subversive to the Roman Empire" 66. In Kim's opinion, "there is no anti-imperial intent to be ascertained in the Pauline Epistles. All attempts to interpret them as containing such an intent, as shown above, are imposing an anti-imperial reading on the epistles based merely on superficial parallelism of terms between Paul's gospel preaching and the Roman imperial ideology, while the texts themselves clearly use those terms to express other concerns. Several attempts have turned out to suffer from grave self-contradiction. Some have betrayed their arbitrariness or desperation by appealing to the device of 'coding,' that Paul coded his real anti-imperial message in politically innocuous language or in anti-Jewish polemic" 68. Also Denny Burk, "Is Paul's Gospel Counterimperial? Evaluating the Prospects of the 'Fresh Perspective' for Evangelical Theology," *Journal of the Evangelical Theological Society* 51/2 (June 2008) 309–337, argues that to "single out the emperor cult as Paul's target probably particularizes too much what Paul intended to be a universal opposition to every power or speculation raised up against the knowledge of God (2 Cor 10:5). This observation makes Paul's so-called 'coded' anti-imperial messages look all the more tendentious. Perhaps there was no 'code' at all, and maybe Paul used more generic terminology because he wanted to oppose all of the powers, not just Rome's empire narrowly conceived (e.g., Col 2:10, 15)" 326–327.

30   In *Binding the Strong Man: A Political Reading of Mark's Story of Jesus* (Maryknoll, NY: Orbis, 2008) 193.

31   Here also Ched Myers is perceptive, for example on page 191 of *Binding the Strong Man*.

I. Anti-Roman Cryptograms of the Jesus of History

1   For an excellent discussion of the problem of subjectivism in Jesus of history research, see John P. Meier, *A Marginal Jew: Rethinking the Historical Jesus* 1 (Garden City, NY: Doubleday, 1991) 1–6.

2   For descriptions of the "third quest," see among others N. T. Wright and Stephen Neill, *The Interpretation of the New Testament* 1861–1986 (New York: Oxford University Press, 1988) 379–403; Marcus J. Borg, "A Renaissance in Jesus Studies," *Theology Today*

45 (1988) 280–292; James H. Charlesworth, *Jesus Within Judaism* (Garden City, NY: Doubleday, 1988) 9–29, 187–207, 223–243; Marcus J. Borg, "Portraits of Jesus in Contemporary North American Scholarship," *Harvard Theological Review* 84:1 (1991) 1–22; and Walter F. Taylor, "New Quests for the Historical Jesus," *Trinity Seminary Review* 15 (1993) 69–83. Some of these writers prefer the designation "Jesus Research" to "third quest."

3   *A Marginal Jew*, 10.
4   Philadelphia: Fortress, 1985. Also, *The Historical Figure of Jesus.* (New York: Penguin, 1993).
5   Philadelphia: Westminster, 1982.
6   *In Memory of Her* (NY: Crossroad, 1983) 107.
7   Kansas City: Sheed & Ward, 1988.
8   *The Halakhah of Jesus of Nazareth According to the Gospel of Matthew* (Lanham, MD: The University Press of America, 1987) 248–250.
9   Swidler, *Yeshua*, 67.
10 San Francisco, Harper, 1991.
11 San Francisco: Harper, 1987.
12 Lewiston, NY: Mellen, 1984.
13 "Portraits of Jesus in Contemporary North American Scholarship," *Harvard Theological Review* 84: 1 (1991) 12. See also his *Meeting Jesus Again for the First Time* (San Francisco: Harper, 1994).
14 *Jesus*, x.
15 *Conflict*, 235–236.
16 *Jesus and the Spiral of Violence* (San Francisco: Harper, 1987); *Sociology and the Jesus Movement* (NY: Crossroad, 1989); *The Liberation of Christmas: The Infancy Narratives in Their Social Context* (NY: Crossroad, 1989); and with John S. Hanson, *Bandits, Prophets, and Messiahs: Popular Movements at the Time of Jesus* (Minneapolis: Winston, 1985).
17 *Jesus*, 322.
18 Garden City, NY: Doubleday, 1991.
19 See note 15 of the Introduction section above. By "dissident Jews" Pagel means Jews whose literary works were not accepted among the "Writings" by the rabbis at Jamnia and whose perspectives are not reflected in the Rabbinic Literature.
20 Macon, GA: Mercer University Press, 1983.
21 Philadelphia: Fortress, 1987.
22 Minneapolis: Fortress, 1992.
23 Minneapolis: Fortress, 2003.
24 *Jesus*, 324.
25 Wengst, *Pax Romana*, 55.
26 *Reclaiming the Jesus of History*, 63–88.
27 *Mature Christianity: The Recognition and Repudiation of the Anti-Jewish Polemic of the New Testament* (Susquehanna, PA: Susquehanna University Press, 1985), now available also in an expanded and revised edition with a Prologue and Introduction by Christopher M. Leighton as *Mature Christianity in the 21st Century: The Recognition and Repudiation of the Anti-Jewish Polemic of the New Testament* (New York: Crossroad, 1994). In this thorough analysis of the anti-Jewish material in the Newer Testament, I identify three types of anti-Jewish polemic. The first is christological. Christological anti-Jewish polemic is present on nearly every page of the Newer Testament and can be expressed in simple terms as: in the past Adonai was Lord, but now Jesus the Risen Christ is Lord! To put

it another way, for those who produced the Newer Testament documents Jesus is to God (Theos) almost what Adonai is to God (Elohim) within the Jewish Scriptures and in the Jewish religion. I argue that this christological essence of Christianity should be recognized and articulated with sensitivity within a mature Christianity. This Christology should be expressed by each new generation of Christians in new, dynamic ways. This Christological essence of Christianity distinguishes Christianity from Jewish life and culture and should not be repudiated. Nevertheless, in the articulation of this Christology we should put less emphasis on realized eschatology and more on futuristic eschatology, upon unfulfilled messianism, which draws us closer together with Jews, Muslims, and others.

The second is supersessionistic. Supersessionistic anti-Jewish polemic, while not so widespread as the Christological, to which it is related, is nevertheless present in most portions of the Newer Testament literature. Although this type of polemic may be expected within religious literature, particularly within religious literature that is developed during the formative period of a religious community, the supersessionistic anti-Jewish polemic of the Newer Testament begins what James Parkes and Jules Isaac called the Christian "Teaching of Contempt" for Jews, and as such it must be repudiated as unnecessary and as harmful to Jews as well as to us as Christians. We are the Church. We are not the "New Israel of God." Jews, as well as Christians, are "People of God." As mature Christians, we can repudiate the supersessionistic anti-Jewish polemic of the Newer Testament by more sensitive translations and interpretations and by decreasing or avoiding our use of such polemic.

The third type of anti-Jewish polemic in the Newer Testament—an outgrowth of the supersessionistic anti-Jewish polemic—is vicious, defamatory, name-calling anti-Jewish polemic. It is limited to an interpolation into one of Paul's letters (1 Thessalonians 2:13–16), portions of the controversy dialogues of the Synoptic Gospels, the passion accounts in all Four Gospels, the central core (chapters 5–12) of the Gospel According to John, and virtually all of Acts. In it Jews are called "Christ-killers," "offspring of the Devil," "hypocrites," etc. This vicious, defamatory, name-calling anti-Jewish polemic is not in any way essential to our Christian message nor to Christianity. It is negative and damaging to Jewish people and dehumanizing to us as Christians. It provided a religious incentive and validation for innumerable pogroms and for the Holocaust. It continues to supply fuel for attitudes and actions of anti-Judaism by Christians. We should repudiate this vicious type of Christian teaching of contempt for Jews in our teachings and proclamations and in our production of new translations of the Christian Scriptures.

This present study of the anti-Roman cryptograms of the Newer Testament is in many ways the "other side of the coin" of *Mature Christianity*. It is a study of a different kind of polemic, a polemic that is largely concealed because the Romans would have retaliated and increased their persecutions of the early Christians if the Romans could have "cracked the code" of the cryptograms that were directed against them.

28   Eckardt, *Reclaiming the Jesus of History*, 69–70. See also Michael J. Cook, "The New Testament: Confronting Its Impact on Jewish-Christian Relations," in *Introduction to Jewish-Christian Relations*, edited by Michael Shermis and Arthur E. Zannoni (Mahwah, NJ: Paulist, 1991) 34–61; Helmut Koester, "The Passion Narratives and the Roots of Anti-Judaism," *Bible Review* 9:1 (1993) 5, 46, and *Jews and Christians Speak of Jesus,* edited by Arthur E. Zannoni (Minneapolis: Fortress, 1994).

29   Lima, OH: Fairway, 2001.

30   Minneapolis: Fortress, 2003.

31   This we have from Mark 6:1–6a and Matthew 13:53–58.

32   The acreages needed for minimum subsistence calculated by Douglas E. Oakman, *Jesus and the Economic Questions of His Day* (Lewiston, NY: Edwin Mellen, 1986) 61 is 1.35 acres per adult. Rainfall and quality of the land would greatly affect such estimates.

33   The members of Jesus' family were not remembered as food producers, since most of the rural and small town people of that place and time were engaged in subsistence tilling of the soil. It was their particular woodcraft skill that distinguished them. They would not, of course, have been the only persons in Nazareth who were skilled at making usable objects out of wood and leather. It is preferable to refer to the skills of Joseph and of his sons in terms of "woodcrafts" rather than as "carpentry," since they obviously did not use the power tools that we today generally associate with the work of carpenters.

34   Much has been written recently about the taxation of rural and small town Jews of the time of Jesus. Marcus J. Borg, for example, in *Conflict, Holiness and Politics in the Teachings of Jesus* states, "Thus Jews in Palestine were subject to two systems of taxation, both of which they were powerless to affect. The one was dictated by Roman policy, over which they had no control, and the second was required by divine revelation. For the small landowner, still constituting the majority of the population, the burden was extraordinary: in addition to his need to save for the sabbatical year, the double system demanded from 35 to 40% of his produce, perhaps even more. The impact of the economic crunch was severe, producing signs of social disintegration, such as widespread emigration, a growing number of landless 'hirelings,' and a social class of robbers and beggars" (32–33).

35   Oakman, *Jesus and the Economic Questions of His Day,* 66–67. See also Richard L. Rohrbaugh, "The Social Location of the Markan Audience," *Interpretation* 47 (1993) 388–390

36   Wengst, *Pax Romana*, 37–40.

37   I am deliberately avoiding the use of Josephus' labels of *am ha-aretz,* Pharisees, Essenes, Zealots, and Herodians for these options. The labels provided by Josephus are certainly very helpful as a supplement to what we can learn from the accounts within the Four Gospels, but they are inadequate. The people in each group were much more diverse than Josephus' labels suggest. See, for example, Eckardt, *Reclaiming the Jesus of History,* 41–42, 237–238, and Ellis Rivkin, *What Crucified Jesus?* (Nashville: Abingdon, 1984) 39–55.

38   This is most clearly seen in Mark 2:15–17 and its parallels in Matthew 9:10–13 and Luke 5:27–32, where tax collectors and their associates are called "sinners" and are contrasted with the "healthy" Pharisees. The implication is that those who cooperate fully with the oppressive Romans are "sick" and need a physician, while the Pharisees and other Jews who do not cooperate with the Romans are healthy and do not need the attention of Jesus the healer. Tax collectors are linked with "sinners" also in Matthew 11:19 and in its parallel in Luke 7:34. Where Matthew 5:46 has tax collectors, its parallel in Luke 6:32 has "sinners." The contrast between tax collectors and sinners and Pharisees is highlighted also in the Lukan parables of the lost sheep and the lost coin in Luke 15:1, 2, 7, 10 and in the Lukan parable of the Pharisee and the tax collector praying in the Temple in Luke 18:9–14. Finally, it is said that the Son of man is going to be delivered over into the hands of "sinners" (Caiaphas and his hired goons) in Mark 14:41 and Matthew 26:45.

39   *What Crucified Jesus?* (Nashville: Abingdon, 1984) 60.

40   Rivkin, 61. See also Horsley, *Jesus and the Spiral of Violence*, 81–85.

41   For an excellent discussion of this, see Horsley, *Jesus and Empire.*

42   A partial list of the most prominent includes Richard A. Horsley, *Jesus and Empire*, cited above; Horsley, *Galilee: History, Politics, People* (Valley Forge, PA: Trinity Press International, 1995); Horsley, editor of *Hidden Transcripts and the Arts of Resistance* (Atlanta: Society of Biblical Literature, 2004); Christopher Bryan, *Render to Caesar: Jesus, the Early Church, and the Roman Superpower* (Minneapolis: Fortress, 2004); Warren Carter, *Matthew and the Margins: A Religious and Socio-Political Reading* (Maryknoll, NY: Orbis, 2000); Warren Carter, "Are There Imperial Texts in the Class? Intertextual Eagles and Matthean Eschatology as 'Lights Out' Time for Imperial Rome Matthew 24:27–31," *Journal of Biblical Literature* 122 (2003) 467–487; Ched Myers, *Binding the Strong Man: A Political Reading of Mark's Story of* Jesus (Twentieth Anniversary Edition, Maryknoll, NY: Orbis, 2008); Walter E. Pilgrim, *Uneasy Neighbors: Church and State in the New Testament* (Minneapolis: Fortress, 1999); Warren Carter, *The Roman Empire and the New Testament* (Nashville: Abingdon, 2006); John Dominic Crossan, *God and Empire: Jesus Against Rome, Then and Now* (New York, NY : HarperCollins, 2007); Richard J. Cassidy, *Christians and Roman Rule in the New Testament: New Perspectives* (New York, NY: Crossroad, 2001); John Howard Yoder, *The Politics of Jesus* (2nd ed., Grand Rapids: Eerdmans, 1994); Seyoon Kim, *Christ and Caesar: The Gospel and the Roman Empire in the Writings of Paul and Luke* (Grand Rapids: Eerdmans, 2008); and Wolfgang Stegemann, Bruce J. Malina, and Gerd Theissen, eds., *The Social Setting of Jesus and the Gospels* (Minneapolis: Fortress, 2002), especially Gerd Theissen, "The Political Dimension of Jesus' Activities," 225–250, and T. Raymond Hobbs, "The Political Jesus: Discipleship and Disengagement," 251–282.

43   The statement in John 7:5 that not even his brothers were believing in him pertains to the Christological claims made concerning Jesus in the Fourth Gospel, not to the proclamations of the Jesus of history.

44   This may be a major portion of the historical basis for the "Messianic Secret" motif in the Gospel According to Mark. In a recent study of Jesus' messianic self-consciousness, Suzanne Watts Henderson, "Jesus' Messianic Self-Consciousness Revisited: Christology and Community in Context," *Journal for the Study of the Historical Jesus* 7:2 (2009) 168–197, suggests "that the historical Jesus construed his messianic role primarily in dynamic relation to the faithful community that would manifest *God's* rule." (italics mine)

45   Within the Synoptic Gospels the word "sinners" (*hamartoloi*) is not applied to everyone, as it is in Paul's letters to the Galatians and to the Romans, but almost exclusively to people such as the Temple officials, tax collectors, and prostitutes who cooperated with the Romans. This is clearly seen in Mark 2:15–17; Matthew 9:10–13; 11:19; Luke 5:29–32; 6:32–34; 7:34, 36–50; 15:l-10, and 18:13. In Mark 14:41 and Matthew 26:45 the motley crowds that came to seize Jesus in the Garden of Gethsemane, together with Caiaphas, Pontius Pilate, and the Roman soldiers who tortured and crucified Jesus are the "sinners" into the hands of which Jesus is going to be betrayed.

46   According to Luke 15:7, there will be "more joy in heaven over one sinner who repents than over ninety-nine righteous persons who do not need repentance."

47   It is interesting to note that by applying the methodologies of literary criticism to Matthew 11:28–30 ("Come to me, all you who are weary and heavily burdened, and I will give you rest ....") Peter W. Macky in *The Centralitv of Metaphors to Biblical Thought: A Method for Interpreting the Bible* (Lewiston, NY: Mellen, 1990) 277–297, describes the

image that Matthew wished to evoke in his readers' imaginations with this artistic metaphor in a way that is similar in many respects to the scenario of the crucifixion of Jesus depicted above. After imagining for his readers what a typical day might have been for the pre-Israelites, weary and heavily burdened as they were while wandering in the desert between Egypt and Canaan, Macky says, "Even more graphic and immediate and powerful for Matthew's readers would be imagining themselves as a victim of Roman oppression, on the way to crucifixion: I have been unjustly condemned because I spoke out against Roman barbarism; now I have been whipped, almost to the point of death, and an unbelievably heavy crossbar has been tied to my shoulders and arms; the feelings of shame and degradation are overwhelming, and when I get just a spurt of energy I'm angry enough to want to kill every soldier around me; but they have the power, so they poke me with their spear-butts, lash me again with their whips, lift me up so I can't lie in peace in the dust. When will it be over? O God let it be over soon! Let me just pass out and feel nothing. By imagining ourselves in such a scene as this one that Matthew and his hearers knew personally, we may begin to feel some of the impact of his symbol" (288). For a thoughtful analysis of the contributions made in recent years by contemporary literary criticism in relation to our continuing quest for the historical Jesus, see Meier, *A Marginal Jew I*, 9–12. In Meier's own words, literary criticism is "a useful way of focusing on what otherwise could get lost in our zealous quest for sources and historical background. It helps us listen to the literary whole and understand how individual parts of the narrative function within that whole. Obviously, though, such an ahistorical approach to 1st-century documents of Christian propaganda that advanced truth claims about Jesus of Nazareth, truth claims for which some 1st-century Christians were willing to die, cannot be the main method employed in a quest for the historical Jesus. Nevertheless, contemporary literary criticism provides a salutary caveat by reminding us to ask what is the literary function of a verse or pericope in a larger work before we glibly declare it a reliable source of historical information. Along with the emphasis on social context, it is a useful addition to the toolbox of the working exegete" (12).

48   In the words of Walter Wink, *Engaging the Powers: Discernment and Resistance in a World of Domination* (Minneapolis: Fortress, 1992) 115, "In parable after parable, Jesus speaks of the 'reigning of God,' using images drawn from farming and women's work. The reign of God "is not described as coming from on high down to earth; it rises quietly and imperceptibly out of the land."

49   *Jesus: The King and His Kingdom*, 37, 40.

50   *Reclaiming the Jesus of History*, 63–64.

51   *Jesus and Empire*, 108–109.

52   It is unfortunate that the message of Jesus regarding the coming of the kingdom of Adonai to replace that of the Romans has not been clearly understood by the majority of Christians during the past sixteen centuries. Much of this lack of understanding can be traced to the firm alliance between Church and State that we call Christendom that has existed for so many of these centuries.

53   According to N.T. Wright, *The Challenge of Jesus: Rediscovering Who Jesus Was and Is* (Downers Grove, IL: InterVarsity Press, 1999), the parable of the sower "is a parable about parables and their effect: this is the only way that the spectacular truth can be told, and it is bound to have the effect that some will look and look and never see, while others find the mystery suddenly unveiled, and they see what God is doing" (41).

54   Matthew: *A Commentary on His Literary and Theological Art* (Grand Rapids: Eerdmans,

1982) 261–265.

55   Buchanan, *Jesus: The King and His Kingdom*, 141–143, suggests that the tares were the Jewish tax collectors appointed by the enemy, Rome. I think that the Roman soldiers are a better option for the tares.

II. Anti-Roman Cryptograms in the Letters of Paul and in Other Pauline Literature

1   Ernst Käsemann, *Perspectives on Paul* (Philadelphia: Fortress, 1971) 138.

2   For example, historian Michael H. Hart in *The 100: A Ranking of the Most Influential Persons in History* (New York: Hart, 1978) 61–65, ranks Paul number six.

3   Oxford: Clarendon, 1956, x.

4   According to Clinton E. Arnold, *Powers of Darkness: Principalities and Powers in Paul's Letters* (Downers Grove, IL: InterVarsity Press, 1992), Paul assumed that the demonic powers of Satan "were working behind the scenes to control the course of events during the passion week" (104), but "Paul himself never connected the powers of darkness with any specific country or territory" (99). I agree that Paul in his seven letters never explicitly connected the "powers of darkness" with any specific country or territory, but, unlike Arnold, I point out that Paul made the connection implicitly through the use of hidden transcripts of anti-Roman cryptograms.

5   *Naming the Powers: The Language of Power in the New Testament* (Philadelphia: Fortress, 1984) 5. See also his *Unmasking the Powers: The Invisible Forces That Determine Human Existence* (Philadelphia: Fortress, 1986) and *Engaging the Powers: Discernment and Resistance in a World of Domination* (Minneapolis: Fortress, 1992).

6   "The Apostle Paul and Empire," *In the Shadow of Empire: Reclaiming the Bible as a History of Faithful Resistance* (edited by Richard A. Horsley, Louisville: Westminster John Knox, 2008) 98, 101.

7   *Paul the Convert* (New Haven: Yale, 1990) xiii.

8   *Introduction to the New Testament, Volume Two: History and Literature of Early Christianity* (Philadelphia: Fortress, 1982) 97–145.

9   Koester, *Introduction*, II, 104.

10   Both nouns in the Greek title for this document are anarthrous. Certainly the document does not claim to include all of the acts or actions of all of the apostles. Although we may be accustomed to the title "The Acts of the Apostles," a better translation of the title would be simply "Acts of Apostles," the designation that I use in this study. The distinction is important. The title "The Acts of the Apostles" suggests that it is a short history of the early Church; "Acts of Apostles" more accurately implies a selective work produced by a skilled literary playwright.

11   For an excellent depiction of these differences, see Krister Stendahl, "Preaching from the Pauline Epistles," in *Biblical Preaching: An Expositor's Treasury*, edited by James W. Cox (Philadelphia: Westminster, 1983) 309–311.

12   Robert Jewett, *A Chronology of Paul's Life* (Philadelphia: Fortress, 1979) 7–24, while warning against "an undifferentiated skepticism regarding the usability of the Book of Acts in historical reconstructions" of Paul's life, concludes that "material from Acts is usable in the chronological experiment only when it does not conflict with evidence in the letters."

13   There is no mention of the Jews at all in Philippians 1:1–3:1. The only possible allusion

to Jews in 1:1–3:1 is Paul's reference to a "crooked and perverse generation" in 2:15, and in the context of Paul's seven letters that expression applies better to actions of Gentiles and of various groups of Christians whom Paul opposed than it does to Jews.

14 "Philippians: Theology for the Heavenly Politeuma," in *Pauline Theology: I Thessalonians, Philippians, Galatians, Philemon,* edited by Jouette M. Bassler (Minneapolis: Fortress, 1991) 91.

15 *Pax Romana,* 202, n. 11.

16 Franz Cumont, *The Mysteries of Mithra,* translated from the second revised French edition by Thomas J. McCormack (New York: Dover, 1956) 33–84.

17 Physical (bending the knee) as well as verbal (confession with the tongue) evidence of submission to the authority of rulers and of the deities of which the rulers were said to be human manifestations apparently was commonly expected of people in antiquity, and not only in the Ancient Near East. Such submission was not necessarily demanded by the ruler directly; it was often required by representatives of the rulers, who thereby extended the power of the ruler and established their own power also. Although efforts are made, for example by Werner Foerster in the *TDNT* article cited in note 24 below, to attempt to document which of the Roman rulers first accepted and which first demanded the appellation *dominus* (Lord), such efforts are actually futile. We simply do not have access to enough information to make such a determination. The statement in Isaiah 45:23b, "To me (Adonai) every knee shall bend, every tongue shall affirm allegiance," suggests that when that text was written (and probably much earlier) many knees were bending to human rulers, their deities, and their representatives, and many tongues were affirming allegiance to human despots. For a summary sketch of absolutist claims of various Roman rulers and their zealous advocates, see Helmut Koester, *Introduction to the New Testament, Volume One: History, Culture, and Religion of the Hellenistic Age* (Philadelphia: Fortress, 1982) 297–322.

18 As a Jew and as an apostle of Jesus the Risen Christ, Paul would most likely have been familiar with Isaiah 45:23b, the core biblical basis for this Christ-hymn. Philippians 2:5–11 is not introduced as a quotation. This is supported also by the view of N.T. Wright in *Paul in Fresh Perspective* (Minneapolis: Fortress, 2005) 72, who says, "I still hold the view that Paul wrote this poem himself, quite possibly for use at this point in this letter, and he certainly used it here in a way that integrates closely with the thrust of the letter as a whole." See also Peter Oakes, *Philippians: From People to Letter* (Cambridge: Cambridge University Press, 2001).

19 That the writer of Acts portrayed the Asiarchs as friends of Paul rather than as his captors is an additional significant difference between Paul and the writer of the Acts literary drama that often is not noted.

20 N. T. Wright, "Paul's Gospel and Caesar's Empire," in *Paul and Politics: Ekklesia, Israel, Imperium, Interpretation: Essays in Honor of Krister Stendahl* (edited by Richard A. Horsley, Harrisburg, PA: Trinity Press International, 2000, 173, in a section with the caption, "Paul's Coded Challenge to Empire: Philippians 3," wrote that Paul's words in Philippians 3:20, "Our citizenship is in heaven, and from it we await the Saviour, the Lord Jesus, the Messiah" are "Caesar-titles," and that "The whole verse says: Jesus is Lord, and Caesar isn't." We might add that the same could be said as implied in the hidden transcript in the Christ-hymn, Philippians 2:5–11.

21 As Ralph P. Martin puts it in *Carmen Christi: Philippians 2:5–11 in Recent Interpretation and in the Setting of Early Christian Worship* (Grand Rapids: Eerdmans, 1983) xviii, "The lordship of Christ is indeed the hymn's Mitte....The summons to Paul's Philippian

readers is that they should submit to Christ's divinely invested authority as Kyrios."

22 For one of many detailed analyses of the possibilities regarding place and time of the writing of these letters, see Gerald F. Hawthorne, *Philippians* (Word Biblical Commentary, vol. 43, Waco, TX: Word, 1983) xxxvi–xliv. Hawthorne, with heavy reliance upon Acts of Apostles, favors Caesarea and the years 59–61. My own choice, based on Paul's own letters, would be Ephesus and the years 55–58.

23 According to this document, Polycarp could have avoided execution had he been willing to say, "Caesar is Lord," and to offer the required incense.

24 "*kyrios, kyria, kyriakos, kyriotēs, kyrieuō, katakyrieuō*," *Theological Dictionary of the New Testament* 3, edited by Gerhard Kittel, translated by Geoffrey W. Bromiley (Grand Rapids: Eerdmans, 1965) 1056.

25 Philadelphia: Westminster, 1955, 141.

26 Parenthetically, we can also say that if Paul intended Philippians 2:9–11 to be not only a strong statement of faith but also an anti-Roman cryptogram, it is probable that the writer of Isaiah 45:23b intended the statement there that to Adonai as Lord every knee shall bend and every tongue confess not only as a strong confession of faith but also as an anti-Babylonian cryptogram.

27 Why was the confessional statement that "Jesus is Lord" called the Roman Symbol? Was it only because it was a confession expressed in Rome? May it at one time have been a subtle statement in Rome that Jesus, not Rome and its Caesar, is truly Lord?

28 Holland Lee Hendrix, "Archaelogy and Eschatology in Thessalonica," in *The Future of Early Christianity:Essays in Honor of Helmut Koester* (Minneapolis: Fortress, 1991) 107–118, suggests the possibility that Paul's prediction in 1 Thessalonians 5:3 of destruction for those who speak about "peace and security" may be a reference to Roman imperial sloganeering, that those who engage in such sloganeering may be the first to fall victim to the sudden wrath of God.

29 Karl P. Donfried in "The Imperial Cults and Political Conflict in 1 Thessalonians," *Paul and Empire: Religion and Power in Roman Imperial Society* (edited by Richard A. Horsley, Harrisburg, PA: Trinity Press International), 1997, 215–223, describes them as "politarchs."

30 It should be noted that the writer of Acts used the terminology "the Holy Spirit" and "the Spirit of Jesus" in Acts 16:6–10 rather than Paul's *ho satanas* when referring to limitations placed on the movements of Paul and his companions. James Denney, The Epistles to the Thessalonians (*The Expositor's Bible*, ed. by W. Robertson Nicoll, New York, NY: Armstrong, 1903) 103–104, when commenting about 1 Thessalonians 2:17–18 and Acts 16:6–10 a century ago wrote perceptively that "the conflict of good and evil is essentially a conflict of persons. Good persons are in conflict with bad persons; and so far as the antagonism comes to a head, Christ, the New Testament teaches, is in conflict with Satan. These persons are the centers of force on one side and on the other; and the Apostle discerns, in incidents of his life which now have been lost to us, the presence and working now of this, and now of that....The obstacles which checked Paul's impulse to preach in Asia and in Bithynia he recognized to be of Divine appointment; those which prevented him from returning to Thessalonica were of Satanic origin. We do not know what they were; perhaps a plot against his life, which made the journey dangerous; perhaps some sin or scandal that detained him in Corinth. At all events it was the doing of the enemy, who in this world, of which Paul does not hesitate to call him the god, has means enough at his disposal to foil, though he cannot overcome, the saints."

31 "Imperial Ideology and Paul's Eschatology in 1 Thessalonians," *Paul and Empire: Religion and Power in Roman Imperial Society* (edited by Richard A. Horsley, Harrisburg, PA: Trinity Press International, 1997), 162, 166.

32 Minneapolis: Fortress, 1999, 33.

33 Richard A. Horsley, *1 Corinthians* (Nashville: Abingdon, 1998) 58, considers "the rulers of this age" cited by Paul in 2:6 to be "human political rulers" of the Roman Empire.

34 See note 3 above in this chapter.

35 James Moffatt, The First Epistle of Paul to the Corinthians (New York: Harper, n.d.) 254, suggested that Paul was speaking metaphorically when he referred to fighting with wild beasts, since "Wild brutes of men sometimes attacked him." Abraham J. Malherbe, "The Beasts at Ephesus," Journal of Biblical Literature 87 (1968) 71–80, agreed that Paul was referring metaphorically to his opponents. Hans Conzelmann, I Corinthians (translated by James W. Leitch, Philadelphia: Fortress, 1975) 277, said that it was "a figurative expression for: 'fighting for his life.'" According to William F. Orr, I Corinthians (Garden City, NY: Doubleday, 1976) 338, "It is therefore likely that he is using vigorous symbolic language to compare his dreadful experiences in Ephesus to life-and-death struggle with ferocious animals."

36 *The Apostolic Fathers* 1, *The Loeb Classical Library* 15 (Cambridge, MA: Harvard, 1965) 230-232, quoted here in my own translation.

37 Sören Kierkegaard, *Edifying Discourses* 4, translated by David F. Swenson and Lilian Marvin Swenson (Minneapolis: Augsburg, 1946) 52, said, "Who would ever finish if he tried to mention all the ingenuity and foolishness which has been expended in explaining or trying to explain this passage, which, ever since it got the reputation of being a riddle, seems to have afforded an uncommonly favorable opportunity of everyone to become an interpreter of the Bible."

38 Walter Bauer, William F. Arndt, F. Wilbur Gingrich, and Frederick W. Danker, *A Greek-English Lexicon of the New Testament and Other Early Christian Literature* (3rd ed. Chicago: University of Chicago Press, 2000) 555.

39 John Dominic Crossan and Jonathan L. Reed, *In Search of Paul: How Jesus' Apostle Opposed Rome's Empire with God's Kingdom* (San Francisco: HarperSanFrancisco, 2004) 232, propose "that Paul had contracted malaria during his youth at Tarsus from a climate that easily produced the chills and fevers, the uncontrollable shivering and profuse sweating, the severe headache, nausea, and vomiting of chronic malarial fever."

40 "Paul's Thorn of Rejected Apostleship," *New Testament Studies* 34 (1988) 550–572.

41 Consider, for example, how Paul cut down the leader within the fellowship of believers in Corinth who was said to have been intimately involved with his own stepmother (1 Corinthians 5:1–8 and 2 Corinthians 2:1-10).

42 These are some of the indications that Paul was probably much more interested in the life and activities of the Jesus of history than we have generally thought.

43 According to Donn McLellan, "Undercover Agents in Worship," *The Lutheran Standard* 25 (November 1, 1985) 4–8, "Jesus Cruz–wearing a concealed recorder–was a regular participant in Sunday evening Bible studies for Central American refugees held at Alzona Lutheran Church (in Phoenix)." See also "ALC Church Ministers to Arrested Refugees," *The Lutheran Standard* 25 (March 1, 1985) 23, and "Indictments Outrage Sanctuary Leaders," *The Lutheran Standard* 25 (February 15, 1985) 22.

44 In addition, we have an increased understanding of the reasons that Paul in the 2 Corinthians 6:14−7:1 segment was so vehemently opposed at that time to the idea of followers of Jesus being mated with unbelievers, whom he identified with darkness and

Belial. For Paul at this time, unbelievers, darkness, and Belial (Satan) may all have been associated in his mind with Rome, Caesar, and the advocates of Roman Civil Religion.

45   Rudolf Bultmann, *The Second Letter to the Corinthians,* translated by Roy A. Harrisville (Minneapolis: Augsburg, 1985) 209.

46   *A Commentary on The Second Epistle to the Corinthians* (New York: Harper, 1973) 286.

47   That Paul and other early Christian writers used subtle anti-Roman cryptograms as messages of hope that soon Jesus Christ rather than Caesar and advocates of Roman Civil Religion would be ruling over them in the heavens, on the earth, and under the earth does not mean that they were in favor of military insurrection or even of guerrilla resistance activity that might include sabotage and attacks on the Roman infrastructure. Analysis of Paul's letters indicates that Paul consistently urged his fellow believers to exhibit good behavior, pay required taxes, and show appropriate respect to those who ruled over them. At the same time, Paul carefully emphasized that the political rulers possessed secondary authority only, authority that was derived from God. These rulers, therefore, should never be permitted to attain ultimate authority over the followers of Jesus Christ. Claims of ultimate authority produced the conflict in which the anti-Roman cryptograms of Paul and of other early Christians became operative.

48   Handley C. G. Moule, *The Epistle of St. Paul to the Romans, The Expositor's Bible,* edited by W. Robertson Nicoll (New York: Armstrong, 1903) 349, said that "civil authority, even with a Nero at its head, was still in principle a thing divine." Most commentators who have written since 1945 have been much more cautious about attributing divinity to civil authority. The majority of these who write in the English language think that by using the words "governing authorities" in Romans 13:1–7 Paul was referring to the Roman Empire. For example, C. K. Barrett, *A Commentary on the Epistle to the Romans* (New York: Harper. 1957) 244, concludes that there is "no difficulty in supposing that Paul is here referring to the (Roman) state, or its administration."

49   "Strategies of Resistance and Hidden Transcripts in the Pauline Communities," *Hidden Transcripts and the Arts of Resistance: Applying the Work of James C. Scott to Jesus and Paul* edited by Richard A. Horsley (Atlanta: Society of Biblical Literature, 2004) 119–122.

50   According to Genesis 3:15, the seed of the woman will bruise the head of the serpent. and the serpent will bruise his heel. The poisonous snake will strike the heel of the man, who will then crush the serpent's head with his heel. (In modern times, the danger from poisonous snakes is a reason for wearing cowboy boots and carrying a rifle.)

51   Paul and his fellow believers were not to engage in insurrection against Rome. Their role was to refuse to submit to the "ungodliness and wickedness of those who by their impure actions suppress the truth" (Romans 1:18), and to submit only to the righteousness of God that is revealed through faith.

52   I use the word "letters" for the seven basic letters of Paul, correspondence in which he addressed specific situations, and "epistles" for the documents attributed to Paul, to Peter, and to others, or written without a designated author that were intended to be sent from house-church to house-church in order to attempt to increase uniformity in practice and in belief among early Christians. I think that this is a helpful distinction that should be used.

53   G. H. C. Macgregor, "Principalities and Powers: the Cosmic Background of Paul's Thought," *New Testament Studies* 1 (1954) 22–23, focuses on the ultimate powers that were responsible for the crucifixion of Jesus, but he does not exclude the visible human rulers. According to Macgregor, "it is the 'principalities and powers' themselves who

are ultimately responsible for the crucifixion. When Paul writes that had they known 'the mysterious wisdom of God' ...'the rulers of this world' ...'would not have crucified the Lord of glory' (1 Cor. ii.7–8), he is not exonerating from blame earthly authorities like Caiaphas, Pilate and Herod; but he is suggesting that behind them stand invisible powers, infinitely more dangerous, of whom the visible human 'rulers' are the mere agents. By 'rulers of this world' the Apostle appears to mean both the cosmic 'principalities and powers' and also their actual human executives; and the very kernel of his doctrine of redemption is that by their tragic miscalculation the 'rulers' became the instruments of their own destruction."

54   As Charles R. Erdman, *The Epistles of Paul to the Thessalonians* (Philadelphia: Westminster, 1935) 86, indicates, "This apostasy, or 'falling away,' seems to mean a defection from the Christian faith ...." According to Gerhard Krodel, "The Second Letter to the Thessalonians, " *Ephesians, Colossians, 2 Thessalonians, The Pastoral Epistles* (Proclamation Commentaries: The New Testament Witnesses for Preaching, Gerhard Krodel, ed., Philadelphia: Fortress, 1978) 88, "The tenses of the verbs in 1:44 clearly indicate that the recipients of our letter were being subjected to persecution."

55   According to Dennis C. Duling, *The New Testament: History, Literature, and Social Context* (4th ed. Belmont, CA: Wadsworth/Thomson, 2003) 259–261, "In any case, a Paulinist writes 2 Thessalonians using 1 Thessalonians as a model. *The best understanding of 2 Thessalonians, therefore, is to see it as a deliberate imitation of 1 Thessalonians, most probably by a member of a Pauline school"* (italics his).

56   James Everett Frame, *A Critical and Exegetical Commentary on the Epistles of St. Paul to the Thessalonians* (New York: Scribner's, 1912) 252–253, suggests that "(The man of lawlessness) is not a proper name but a characterization of a person, and that too a definite person, as the article in each of the four phrases makes plain. It is evident that the figure in question is not Satan but a man, a unique man, however, in whom Satan dwells and operates."

57   Koester, *Introduction* I, 316–317.

58   Ephesus rather than Thessalonica is suggested as the most likely place for the persecution of the Christians addressed in this epistle merely because we have evidence elsewhere of extreme persecution in the province of Asia from 90–96 C.E. In apocalyptic writing, geographical location as well as names of persons are often concealed in order to attempt to protect oppressed people.

59   For example, the preface to 2 Thessalonians in the *New Oxford Annotated Bible*, edited by Herbert G. May and Bruce M. Metzger (New York: Oxford, 1973) 1437, begins with the statement, "The congregation in Thessalonica continued to experience sharp opposition from the synagogue, which regarded the new fellowship as a heretical sect."

60   It is helpful and supportive of the second basic thesis of this book that Martin Dibelius and Hans Conzelmann, *The Pastoral Epistles*, translated by Philip Buttolph and Adela Yarbro (Hermeneia, Philadelphia: Fortress, 1972) 124, thought that the lion in 2 Timothy 4:17 referred to Roman imperial power and pointed out that Josephus in his *Antiquities* 18.228 wrote "the lion is dead" in reference to the death of Tiberius.

61   One of the designations of the Risen Christ in the Apocalypse (Revelation 5:5) was as "the Lion who is from the tribe of Judah, the new stalk shooting up from the root of David." The Risen Immortal Lion would prevail over the mortal transitory one.

III. Anti-Roman Cryptograms in the Synoptic Gospels

1   Expanded and Revised Edition, New York, NY: Crossroad, 1994.

2   It was not, of course, called the Markan community at that time.

3   Philadelphia: Westminster, 1977.

4   According to Mark 8:27–33, it was on the way to the villages in the area of Caesarea Philippi that Peter, speaking for the disciples of Jesus, recognized Jesus as the Christ. It was also supposedly in the same area that Jesus was transfigured in the presence of Peter, James, and John (Mark 9:2–13).

5   The itinerary of the Markan Jesus, according to Mark 7:24–31, took him from the region of Tyre to Sidon farther north, and then to the east side of the Sea of Galilee, through the region of the Decapolis, east of Galilee. These areas, together with Caesarea Philippi, provide locations in a semicircle north and east of Galilee.

6   "The Gospel of Jesus Christ" is the self-designation for this document as given in its first line. One hundred years after its original composition, the document came to be called "The Gospel According to Mark," in order to distinguish it from the three other Gospels known by that time.

7   For this, see J. Louis Martyn, *History and Theology in the Fourth Gospel* (New York: Harper & Row, 1968); rev. ed. (Nashville: Abingdon, 1979); Raymond E. Brown, *The Community of the Beloved Disciple* (New York: Paulist, 1979); and Klaus Wengst, *Bedrängte Gemeinde und verherrlichter Christus: Der historische Ort des Johannesevangeliums als Schlüssel zu seiner Interpretation* (Neukirchen-Vluyn: Neukircher Verlag, 1981).

8   There are indications, for example in Mark 12:13–17 and Matthew 22:15–22, that Herodians tried to persuade the Jesus of history to urge his followers to pay their required taxes and tributes to the Roman state and its representatives without resistance and dissent. As Ellis Rivkin puts it in his *What Crucified Jesus?* (Nashville: Abingdon, 1984) 36–37, "In such a world, where violence stalked the countryside, death frequented the streets of Jerusalem, and riots disturbed the precincts of the Temple; where every flutter of dissidence sent chills of fear up the spines of puppet kings, governors, procurators, and procurator-appointed high priests—even the most nonpolitical of charismatics took his life in his hands when he preached the good news of God's coming kingdom. And if his call to repentance were so eloquent that crowds gathered round to hear and to hope, would not the power of his word invite the kiss of death?"

9   The most pointed example is, of course, Mark 8:31–38 and parallels in which Peter as the spokesperson of the other close followers of Jesus is said to have tried to dissuade Jesus from going to Jerusalem because he would undoubtedly be killed if he proclaimed his message of hope and liberation there.

10   Judas actually cooperated with the oppressive Romans and with Caiaphas and his representatives, according to Mark 14:10–11, 43–46 and parallels. Judas may have attempted without success to persuade Jesus to cooperate with the Herodians and with the Romans in order to avoid violence.

11   Others have interpreted these texts, at least in part, in this same way. For example, Joseph A. Fitzmyer, *The Gospel According to Luke (I-IX)* (Garden City, NY: Doubleday, 1981) 516, suggests that in "all the kingdoms of the world" in Luke 4:5 "Possibly there is an allusion to the Roman empire, but it is not clear." According to I. Howard Marshall, *The Gospel of Luke* (Grand Rapids: Eerdmans, 1978) 172, "The reference to 'all the kingdoms of the world ...and their glory' in Luke 4:5–6 is in contemporary terms at

least to the Roman world (cf. 2:1) ; it is not clear how far Luke thought of territories outside its borders."

12   The same verb (*diakoneō*) is used to denote the actions of the angels in Mark 1:13 and of the mother-in-law of Peter in Mark 1:31.

13   As is noted, for example, by John Dominic Crossan, *God and Empire: Jesus Against Rome, Then and Now* (New York, NY: HarperCollins, 2007) 116, in the Gospel According to Matthew, in which the expression "the Kingdom of the Heavens" is used so frequently, the words "heaven" and "heavens" were simply euphemisms "for God." The Kingdom was not "of the future, of the next world, or of the afterlife."

14   Macon, Georgia: Mercer University Press, 1983. See the more extensive discussion of Buchanan's work in chapter I above.

15   *Jesus and Empire: The Kingdom of God and the New World Disorder* (Minneapolis: Fortress, 2003), 108.

16   Horsley, *Jesus and Empire*, 109.

17   "Jesus and Empire," *In the Shadow of Empire: Reclaiming the Bible as a History of Faithful Resistance* (edited by Richard A. Horsley, Louisville: Westminster John Knox, 2008) 86. For more detail, see Richard A. Horsley, *Jesus and Empire: The Kingdom of God and the New World Disorder* (Minneapolis: Fortress, 2003) chapters 4–5.

18   Pope Gregory I, soon after becoming Pope in 590, during an Easter sermon made the assumption that Mary Magdalene had willingly been a prostitute until she met Jesus. Gregory's assumption was maintained in the Western Church after that, even though nowhere in the Gospel accounts is Mary Magdalene identified as having chosen to be a prostitute.

19   According to I. Howard Marshall, *The Gospel of Luke* 338–339, "It has been suggested that the man may have had a traumatic experience in childhood with the soldiery which led to his insanity."

20   *Mark* (Augsburg Commentary on the New Testament, Minneapolis: Augsburg, 1990) 80. For Ched Myers, *Binding the Strong Man: A Political Reading of Mark's Story of Jesus* (Twentieth Anniversary Edition, Maryknoll, NY: Orbis, 2008), in this "symbolic act of exorcism," the demon "represents Roman military power" 192. "Given his political circumstance in reoccupied Galilee late in the war, Mark obviously cannot speak directly about Rome. Thus he relies upon two forms of more veiled discourse: the Jewish resistance tradition of apocalyptic and the literary devise of parody" 426.

21   R. H. Charles, ed., *The Apocrypha and Pseudepigrapha of the Old Testament in English* 2 (Oxford: Clarendon, 1913) 252.

22   See the comments on Isaiah 43:9 in *Abodah Zarah* of the Babylonian Talmud.

23   Charles, *The Apocrypha and Pseudepigrapha* 2, 252.

24   *New Testament Apocrypha* 2, edited by E. Hennecke, W. Schneemelcher, and R. McL. Wilson (Philadelphia: Westminster, 1964) 293–294.

25   Quoted in C. K. Barrett, ed., *The New Testament Background: Selected Documents* (New York: Harper, 1961) 77–78.

26   As demonstrated, for example, by Howard C. Kee, *Community of the New Age*, 45, 64–70.

27   Cf. Ronald D. Worden, "Taking the Bible on Its Own Terms," *The Christian Century* 101 (1984) 832–834.

28   Perhaps this sprinkling of the pieces of the statue of Caesar in the name of Jesus symbolized the baptism of Caesar into the Christian church and thereby the triumph of Christianity over Roman oppression.

29   According to S. R. F. Price, *Rituals and Power: The Roman Imperial Cult in Asia Minor*

(Cambridge: Cambridge University Press, 1984) 189, Roman Imperial Cult statues, including life-size stone representations, generally adorned various temples. For example, the "imperial images at Ephesus formed part of the cult of Artemis and were accordingly kept in the porch of her temple."

30   Oxford: Oxford University Press, 2005, 44.

31   Edited by Richard A. Horsley, Atlanta: Society of Biblical Literature, 2004, 41–60.

32   "Matthew Negotiates the Roman Empire," *In the Shadow of Empire: Reclaiming the Bible as a History of Faithful Resistance* (edited by Richard A. Horsley, Louisville: Westminster John Knox, 2008), 133.

33   For an interesting use of the Lord's Prayer to illustrate critical methods of interpretation, see Dennis C. Duling, *The New Testament: History, Literature, and Social Context* (4th edition; Belmont, CA; Wadsworth/Thomson, 2003) 66–93.

34   Edited by Richard A. Horsley, Louisville: Westminster John Knox, 2008, 88–89.

35   "Jesus and Empire," *In the Shadow of Empire: Reclaiming the Bible as a History of Faithful Resistance* (edited by Richard A. Horsley, Louisville: Westminster John Knox, 2008), 84–85.

IV. Anti-Roman Cryptograms in John and in the Johannine Epistles

1   For detailed analyses of the polemics against other groups that can be detected in the Gospel According to John and in the First Epistle of John, see Raymond E. Brown, *The Community of the Beloved Disciple* (New York: Paulist, 1979) 59–144, and "'Other Sheep Not of This Fold': The Johannine Perspective on Christian Diversity in the Late First Century," *Journal of Biblical Literature* 97 (1978) 5–22.

2   Klaus Wengst, *Bedrängte Gemeinde und verherrlichter Christus* (Neukirchen-Vluyn: Neukircher Verlag, 1981).

3   It is possible that at the time when John 21 was written there were no more then one hundred fifty-three adult male members (big ones in the unbroken net) of the Johannine community.

4   All of the translations from the Gospel According to John in this chapter are taken from my *The New Testament: A New Translation and Redaction* (Lima, OH: Fairway, 2001).

5   "James C. Scott and New Testament Studies: A Response to Allen Callahan, William Herzog, and Richard Horsley," *Hidden Transcripts and the Arts of Resistance: Applying the Work of James C. Scott to Jesus and Paul,* (edited by Richard A. Horsley, Atlanta: Society of Biblical Literature, 2004), 93.

6   Here in my 21st century translation I can be more explicit than the followers of Jesus living within the oppressive Roman Empire could be. For us, it is not necessary that the hidden transcripts of the early followers of Jesus be so carefully concealed. *Their* oppressors are not *our* oppressors.

7   As Thomas L. Brodie, *The Gospel According to John: A Literary and Theological Commentary* (Oxford: Oxford University Press, 1993), 537, puts it, "Trapped between conflicting fears, he (Pilate) still has to go through the motions of being in charge and of pretending to administer justice."

V. Anti–Roman Cryptograms in Revelation, 1 Peter, and Acts: Three Vastly Differing Responses to Severe Roman Oppression

1   As indicated in note 10 of chapter II of this study, since both nouns in the title of this document are anarthrous, and since the document certainly does not relate all of the activities of all of the apostles of Jesus Christ, the name for the document used in this study is "Acts of Apostles" rather than "The Acts of the Apostles."

2   Most critical commentaries date Revelation within the period of severe persecution of early Christians in the Roman province of Asia during the last seven years of the reign of Domitian (90–96 C.E.). Others, including J. Christian Wilson, "The Problem of the Domitianic Date of Revelation," *New Testament Studies* 39 (1993) 587–605, argue for an earlier date, usually for the latter years of the reign of Nero (64–65), or the short reign of Galba (68–69). 1 Peter is usually dated somewhere between 64 and 96. Since 1 Peter is addressed to "the elect exiles of the diaspora in the regions of Pontus, Galatia., Cappadocia, Asia, and Bithynia," all of which are in the interior areas east of Ephesus, it is likely that it was written in response to the same situation about which Revelation was written.

3   According to Marla J. Selvidge, "The Acts of the Apostles: A Violent Aetiological Legend," *Society of Biblical Literature Seminar Papers Series* 25, edited by Kent Harold Richards (Atlanta: Scholars, 1986) 331, the writer of Acts adds forty-four violent and abusive terms to those employed in the Synoptic Gospels and uses "at least twenty-eight different verbs to describe how a person may be killed."

4   Ernst Haenchen, *The Acts of the Apostles* (Oxford: Basil Blackwell, 1971) 106, showed some awareness of this when he wrote that "Luke was most anxious to impress upon his readers that the Roman authorities treated the Christian missionaries with benevolence and acknowledged them to be politically harmless. Put in the form of a general contention, the idea would scarcely have carried weight; after all, the fate finally suffered by both Peter and Paul spoke clearly against it." In a footnote on 104, Haenchen wrote that "the real business in hand" of the Lukan writer was "to prove Christianity itself innocent of all crimes against Roman law."

5   If we find it difficult to accept the evidence that early Christian writers distorted history in an attempt to try to save Christian lives, we can compare this to the distortions that many political candidates perpetrate during election campaigns in our own society, in spite of the sophisticated communications networks that should make such distortions difficult in our time. Helmut Koester, "The Passion Narratives and the Roots of Anti–Judaism," *Bible Review* 9:1 (1993) 5, describes this distortion of history as an expediency, stating that "For the Christians, whose Messiah had indeed been sentenced to death by a representative of the Roman government, it was expedient to shift the blame to the Jews and to exonerate the Romans."

6   According to Gerhard Krodel, *Acts* (Augsburg Commentary on the New Testament; Minneapolis: Augsburg, 1986) 369, "Coins attest to the fact that Ephesus was temple keeper of the emperor cult (a special privilege which was by no means granted to every city with temples, not even to major ones) ....The honor was extended so that Ephesus was also designated temple keeper of the great Artemis." The association between the great goddess Artemis in Ephesus and the emperor cult with its goddess Roma would easily be made by early Christians who were familiar with cultic practices in that important city late during the first century of the common era. Both the Roman Imperial Cult and the Artemis cult used images made with hands.

7   See Helmut Koester, *Introduction to the New Testament* 11, 249, for a picture of the head and arm of the statue of Domitian found in the vaults of the support structure of this temple in Ephesus. According to Colin J. Hemer, *The Letters to the Seven Churches of Asia in Their Local Setting* (Sheffield: *Journal for the Study of the Old Testament*, 1986) 40, Domitian also extended the boundaries of the temple of the great Artemis.

8   *Introduction to the New Testament* 2, 251.

9   For example, in Acts 16:35; 18:14–16; 19:35–41; 21:37–40; 22:30; 23:10, 17–35;25:16; 26:31.

10   Among other places, in Acts 5:17–18; 6:9–14; 7:54–58; 18:12–13; 21:27–31; 22:22–23; 23:2, 12–15; 24:1–9; 25:2–3, 7, 24.

11   Especially with Cornelius, a centurion of the Italian Cohort in Caesarea, who, with his relatives and close friends, welcomed Peter into his home and was baptized (10:1–48); the Roman proconsul Sergius Paulus in Cyprus, who listened to Paul and believed (13:7, 12); and the Roman officials in the province of Asia itself, who are said to have been friendly to Paul, sending a message urging him not to endanger his life by entering the theater in Ephesus (19:31).

12   Another possibility is that, since the "John" of the Apocalypse is not designated as "the apostle," or as "an apostle, this "John" is an otherwise unknown elder who had that name or used that name as the writer of the document.

13   As Gerhard Krodel indicates in "The First Letter of Peter," in *Hebrews-James-1 and 2 Peter-Jude-Revelation* (Proclamation Commentaries, edited by Gerhard Krodel, Philadelphia: Fortress, 1977) 58, "Babylon is used as a cryptogram representing Rome as the persecutor of the people of God" not only in Rev 14:8, 16:19, etc., but also in "2 Baruch 11:1f.; 67:7f.; 2 Esdras 3:1f.,28, Sibylline Oracles 5:143."

14   *Crisis and Catharsis: The Power of the Apocalypse* (Philadelphia: Westminster, 1984) 124.

15   Actually, according to *A Concordance to the Greek Testament*, edited by W. F. Moulton and A. S. Geden, Fourth Edition revised by H. K. Moulton (Edinburgh: T. &. T. Clark, 1963) 883, the Romans are mentioned explicitly only twelve times in the entire Newer Testament, once in John and eleven times in Acts. Rome is mentioned eight times, five of which are in Acts, two in Paul's letter to the Romans, and one in 2 Timothy. When the cryptograms that are analyzed in this present study are recognized as allusions to Rome and the Romans, the number of Newer Testament documents in which there are references to Rome and the Romans jumps from four to twenty-one. Only Paul's letters to the Galatians and to Philemon, the Epistle to Titus, and the three Johannine Epistles are not on the list.

16   Elaine Pagels, "The Social History of Satan," *Harvard Theological Review* 84:2 (1991) 105–128 proposes (See also chapter 1, note 19 above) that the concept of Satan as the leader of an "evil empire," of "an army of hostile spirits who take pleasure in destroying human beings," developed among what she calls "dissident Jews," which included early followers of Jesus and perhaps, although she does not say this, the Jesus of history himself. Her article identifies some of the ways in which Satan appears in various extracanonical Jewish sources. She points out that this concept of Satan as a leader of an evil empire is not found in classical Jewish sources and is not a factor in traditional Judaism. She carries her analysis farther in "The Social History of Satan, Part II: Satan in the New Testament Gospels," *Journal of the American Academy of Religion* 62:1 (1994) 17–58.

17   According to Revelation 2:9 and 3:9, those who are called "a synagogue of Satan" say they are Jews, but are not Jews. As J.P.M. Sweet, *Revelation* (Philadelphia: Westminster,

1979) 85, puts it, "they claim to serve God, but in fact serve Satan, through their alliance with Rome against Christians...." Sean P. Kealy, *The Apocalypse of John* (Wilmington, DE: Michael Glazier, 1987) 87, says that "there is no suggestion (in Rev 2:9 and 3:9 that all Jewish synagogues were synagogues of Satan."

18 *The Book of Revelation: Justice and Judgment* (Philadelphia: Fortress, 1985) 196. For this reason, any Jews or Christians who did not vehemently oppose the zealous advocates of Roman Civil Religion were also condemned in this document, especially in the "letters to the seven churches" section.

19 Richard L. Jeske, *Revelation for Today: Images of Hope* (Philadelphia: Fortress, 1983) 107.

20 *Crisis and Catharsis*, 123.

21 *Revelation* (Augsburg Commentary on the New Testament; Minneapolis: Augsburg, 1989) 292.

22 *The Revelation of St. John the Divine* (New York, NY: Harper & Row, 1966) 214.

23 Krodel, *Revelation*, 293.

24 Caird, *Revelation*, 162.

25 Fiorenza, *Revelation*, 83.

26 Sweet, *Revelation*, 208.

27 Caird, *Revelation*, 162; Sweet, *Revelation*, 207; Fiorenza, *Revelation*, 84–86.

28 Fiorenza, *Revelation*, 86.

29 John Ferguson, *The Religions of the Roman Empire* (Ithaca: Cornell University Press, 1970) 13–31.

30 Fiorenza, *Revelation*, 80–81. See also Sweet, *Revelation*, 194, and Allan A. Boesak, *Comfort and Protest: Reflections on the Apocalypse of John of Patmos* (Philadelphia: Westminster, 1987) 79–92.

31 *The Rapture Exposed: The Message of Hope in the Book of Revelation* (Cambridge, MA: Westview, 2004) 104–105.

32 Fiorenza, *Revelation*, 109.

33 See above, chapter III, section B.

34 Fiorenza, *Revelation*, 109.

35 Paul J. Achtemeier, *1 Peter: A Commentary on 1 Peter* (Minneapolis: Fortress, 1996) 341, note 79, suggests that "Our author avoids any direct identification of the devil with the power of Rome...."

36 According to Helmut Koester, *Introduction to the New Testament* 1, 316–7, and 2, 288, the Christian community in Rome also suffered severe persecution during the last years of Domitian's life, as 1 Clement in particular indicates. As Koester expressed it, "Domitian's last years became a reign of terror, and his assassination by his friends and freedmen was a great relief to everyone. This fact is demonstrated by the *damnatio memoriae* which was thoroughly executed after Domitian's death: his name was erased on all inscriptions and all his statues were removed" (1, 316–7). Richard Bauckham, *The Bible in Politics* (London; S.P.C.K., 1989), also emphasizes that the murderous policies of Domitian victimized not only Christians, but many non-Christians as well.

37 Gerhard Krodel, "The First Letter of Peter," in *Hebrews–James–1 and 2 Peter–Jude–Revelation* (57–63), states that most early Christian writers carefully and "deliberately played down the (Roman) government's role as persecutor." Krodel considers the Apocalypse and 1 Peter to be exceptions to this, and identifies portions of 1 Peter as a "cryptogram" whose place of origin is probably "in proximity to that of the Book of Revelation." Krodel does not, however, explain the cryptogram in detail. According to Edward Gordon Selwyn, *The First Epistle of St. Peter* (London: St. Martin's, 1958) 237,

"the picture of the lion (in 1 Peter 5:8) ranging at will for his prey suggests the action of swirling tides of irrational prejudice used by a Gestapo rather than the deliberate imperial law." This indicates that Selwyn was aware that the persecutions of the Christians in the Roman province of Asia were not ordered by, but were sanctioned by, the emperor; it was not an empire-wide persecution. The early followers of Jesus, however, had no civil rights and were easy prey of the Gestapo-like tactics of their adversary.

38   This possibility is suggested here merely to help us to compare the three documents of Revelation, 1 Peter, and Acts. We have no way of knowing the sequence of composition of the three documents or whether the writer of Acts had access to the other two.

39   For an excellent analysis of the Lukan writer's development and use of this call story, see Haenchen, *The Acts of the Apostles* 107–110.

40   For this, see Norman A. Beck, *Mature Christianity: The Recognition and Repudiation of the Anti–Jewish Polemic of the New Testament* 207–247, and *Mature Christianity in the 21st Century* 241–284.

41   The Jews were people associated with the "Torah" (Greek "*Nomos*," English "Law"). The Romans were *anomoi* (Greek "not–Law–people," "Lawless"). Therefore, the writer of Acts was saying cryptically in 2:23 to those who could understand the code that the Romans rather than the Jews had crucified Jesus, while at the same time refraining from identifying the Romans explicitly.

VII. Conclusions, Implications, and Future Agenda

1   For more details, see Norman A. Beck, *Blessed to Be a Blessing to Each Other: Jews, Muslims, and Christians as Children of Abraham in the Middle East* (Lima, OH: Fairway, 2008).

Bibliography

"ALC Church Ministers to Arrested Refugees." *The Lutheran Standard* 25 (March 1, 1985): 23.

Achtemeier, Paul J. *1 Peter: A Commentary on 1 Peter*. Minneapolis: Fortress, 1996.

Arnold, Clinton E. *Powers of Darkness: Principalities and Powers in Paul's Letters*. Downers Grove, IL : InterVarsity, 1992.

Bammel, Ernst, and C. F. D. Moule, eds. *Jesus and the Politics of His Day*. Cambridge: Cambridge University Press, 1984.

Barrett, C. K. *A Commentary on the Epistle to the Romans*. New York: Harper, 1957.

———, *A Commentary on the Second Epistle to the Corinthians*. New York: Harper, 1973.

———, ed. *The New Testament Background: Selected Documents*. New York: Harper, 1961.

Bassler, Jouette M., ed. *Pauline Theology: 1 Thessalonians, Philippians, Galatians, Philemon* .Minneapolis: Fortress, 1991.

Bauckham, Richard. *The Bible in Politics*. London: S. P. C. K., 1989.

Bauer, Walter, William F. Arndt, F. Wilbur Gingrich, and Frederick W. Danker. *A Greek–English Lexicon of the New Testament and Other Early Christian Literature*. 3rd edition, Chicago: University of Chicago Press, 2000.

Beck, Norman A. *Anti-Roman Cryptograms in the New Testament: Symbolic Messages of Hope and Liberation*. New York, NY: Peter Lang, 1997.

———, *Blessed to Be a Blessing to Each Other: Jews, Muslims, and Christians as Children of Abraham in the Middle East*. Lima, OH: Fairway Press, 2008.

———. *Mature Christianity in the 21st Century: The Recognition and Repudiation of the Anti-Jewish Polemic of the New Testament*. New York, NY: Crossroad, 1994.

———. *Mature Christianity: The Recognition and Repudiation of the Anti-Jewish Polemic of the New Testament*. Susquehanna, PA: Susquehanna University Press, 1985.

———. *The New Testament: A New Translation and Redaction*. Lima, OH: Fairway Press, 2001.

Blockson, Charles L. *The Underground Railroad in Pennsylvania*. Jacksonville, NC: Flame, 1981.

Boadt, Lawrence. *Ezekiel's Oracles against Egypt: A Literary and Philological Study of Ezekiel 29-32*. Rome: Biblical Institute Press, 1980.

Boesak, Allan A. *Comfort and Protest: Reflections on the Apocalypse of John of Patmos*. Philadelphia: Westminster, 1987.

Borg, Marcus J. *Conflict, Holiness and Politics in the Teaching of Jesus.* Lewiston, NY: Mellen, 1984.

———. *Jesus: A New Vision.* San Francisco: Harper, 1987.

———, *Meeting Jesus Again for the First Time.* San Francisco: Harper, 1994.

——— "Portraits of Jesus in Contemporary North American Scholarship." *Harvard Theological Review* 84:1 (1991): 1-22.

———, "A Renaissance in Jesus Studies." *Theology Today* 45 (1988): 280–292.

Bradford, Sarah. *Harriet Tubman: The Moses of Her People.* 2d ed., 1886. Reprint. New York: Corinth, 1961.

Brodie, Thomas L. *The Gospel According to John: A Literary and Theological Commentary.* Oxford: Oxford University Press, 1993.

Brown, Raymond E. *The Community of the Beloved Disciple.* New York: Paulist, 1979.

———, "'Other Sheep Not of This Fold': The Johannine Perspective on Christian Diversity in the Late First Century." *Journal of Biblical Literature* 97 (1978): 5–22.

Bryan, Christopher. *Render to Caesar: Jesus, the Early Church, and the Roman Superpower.* Oxford: Oxford University Press, 2005.

Buchanan, George Wesley. *Jesus: The King and His Kingdom.* Macon, GA: Mercer University Press, 1983.

Buckmaster, Henrietta. *Let My People Go: The Story of the Underground Railroad and the Growth of the Abolition Movement.* Boston: Beacon, 1959.

Bultmann, Rudolf. *The Second Letter to the Corinthians.* Translated by Roy A. Harrisville. Minneapolis: Augsburg, 1985.

Burk, Denny."Is Paul's Gospel Counterimperial? Evaluating the Prospects of the 'Fresh Perspective' for Evangelical Theology," *Journal of the Evangelical Theological Society* 51/2 (June 2008): 309-337.

Caird, G. B. *Principalities and Powers: A Study in Pauline Theology.* Oxford: Clarendon, 1956.

———. *The Revelation of St. John the Divine.* New York: Harper & Row, 1966.

Carter, Warren, "Are There Imperial Texts in the Class? Intertextual Eagles and Matthean Eschatology as 'Lights Out' Time for Imperial Rome (Matthew 24:27-31)," *Journal of Biblical Literature* 122 (2003): 467-487.

———. "James C. Scott and New Testament Studies: A Response to Allen Callahan, William Herzog, and Richard Horsley." in *Hidden Transcripts and the Arts of Resistance: Applying the Work of James C. Scott to Jesus and Paul,* edited by Richard A. Horsley. Atlanta: Society of Biblical Literature, 2004.

———. *Matthew and the Margins: A Religious and Socio-Political Reading.* Maryknoll, NY: Orbis, 2000.

———, "Matthew Negotiates the Roman Empire," *In the Shadow of Empire: Reclaiming the Bible as a*

History of Faithful Resistance. Edited by Richard A. Horsley, Louisville: Westminster John Knox, 2008, 117-136.

———. *The Roman Empire and the New Testament. Nashville: Abingdon, 2006.*

Cassidy, Richard J. *Christians and Roman Rule in the New Testament: New Perspectives.* New York, NY: Crossroad, 2001.

———, *Jesus, Politics, and Society: A Study of Luke's Gospel.* Maryknoll, NY: Orbis, 1978.

———, *Society and Politics in the Acts of the Apostles.* Maryknoll, NY: Orbis, 1987.

Charles, R. H., ed. *The Apocrypha and Pseudepigrapha of the Old Testament in English.* Vol. 2. Oxford: Clarendon, 1913.

Charlesworth, James H. *Jesus Within Judaism.* Garden City, NY: Doubleday, 1988.

———, ed. *The Old Testament Pseudepigrapha.* 2 vols. Garden City, NY: Doubleday, 1983–85.

Collins, Adela Yarbro. *Crisis and Catharsis: The Power of the Apocalypse.* Philadelphia: Westminster, 1984.

Collins, John J. *The Apocalyptic Imagination: An Introduction to the Jewish Matrix of Christianity.* New York: Crossroad, 1984.

Cone, James H. *The Spirituals and the Blues.* New York: Seabury, 1972.

Conrad, Earl. *Harriet Tubman.* Washington, DC: Associated, 1943. Reissue. New York: Erricksson, 1969.

Conzelmann, Hans. *1 Corinthians.* Translated by James W. Leitch. Philadelphia: Fortress, 1975.

Cook, Michael J. "The New Testament: Confronting Its Impact on Jewish-Christian Relations." In *Introduction to Jewish-Christian Relations,* edited by Michael Shermis and Arthur E. Zannoni. Mahwah, NJ: Paulist, 1991.

Crossan, John Dominic. *God and Empire: Jesus against Rome, Then and Now.* New York, NY: HarperCollins, 2007.

———. *The Historical Jesus: The Life of a Mediterranean Jewish Peasant.* San Francisco: Harper, 1991.

Crossan, John Dominic, and Jonathan L. Reed, *In Search of Paul: How Jesus' Apostle Opposed Rome's Empire with God's Kingdom.* San Francisco: HarperSanFrancisco, 2004.

Cumont, Franz. *The Mysteries of Mithra.* Translated from the second revised French edition by Thomas J. McCormack. New York: Dover, 1956.

Denney, James. *The Epistles to the Thessalonians. The Expositor's Bible.* Edited by W. Robertson Nicoll. New York: Armstrong, 1903.

Dibelius, Martin, and Hans Conzelmann. *The Pastoral Epistles.* Translated by Philip Buttolph and Adela Yarbro. Hermeneia. Philadelphia: Fortress, 1972.

Dixon, Christa K. *Negro Spirituals: From Bible to Folksong.* Philadelphia: Fortress, 1976.

Donfried, Karl P. "The Imperial Cults and Political Conflict in 1 Thessalonians," *Paul and Empire: Religion and Power in Roman Imperial Society*. Edited by Richard A. Horsley, Harrisburg, PA: Trinity Press International, 1997, 215-223.

Douglass, Frederick. *Life and Times of Frederick Douglass*. Boston: DeWolfe, 1892. Reissue. New York: Collier, 1962.

DuBois, W. E. B. *The Souls of Black Folk*. New York: Fawcett, 1961.

Duling, Dennis C. *The New Testament: History, Literature, and Social Context*. 4th ed. Belmont, CA: Wadsworth/Thomson, 2003.

Duling, Dennis C., and Norman Perrin. *The New Testament: An Introduction: Proclamation and Parenesis, Myth and History*. 3rd ed. Fort Worth, TX: Harcourt Brace, 1994.

Eckardt, A. Roy. *Reclaiming the Jesus of History: Christology Today*. Minneapolis: Fortress, 1992.

Ehrman, Bart D. *Jesus: Apocalyptic Prophet of the New Millennium*. Oxford: Oxford University Press, 1999.

Eichrodt, Walter. *Ezekiel: A Commentary*. Philadelphia: Westminster, 1970.

Elliott, Neil. "Strategies of Resistance and Hidden Transcripts in the Pauline Communities," *Hidden Transcripts and the Arts of Resistance: Applying the Work of James C. Scott to Jesus and Paul*. Edited by Richard A. Horsley, Atlanta: Society of Biblical Literature, 2004, 97–122.

———, "The Apostle Paul and Empire," *In the Shadow of Empire: Reclaiming the Bible as a History of Faithful Resistance*. Edited by Richard A. Horsley. Louisville: Westminster John Knox, 2008, 97–116.

Erdman, Charles R. *The Epistles of Paul to the Thessalonians*. Philadelphia: Westminster, 1935.

Ermatinger, James W. *Daily Life in the New Testament*. Westport, CN: Greenwood Press, 2008.

Esler, Philip F. *Community and Gospel in Luke-Acts*. Cambridge: Cambridge University Press, 1987.

Ferguson, John. *The Religions of the Roman Empire*. Ithaca: Cornell University Press, 1970.

Fiorenza, Elisabeth Schüssler. *In Memory of Her*. New York, NY: Crossroad, 1983.

———, *The Book of Revelation: Justice and Judgment*. Philadelphia: Fortress, 1985.

Fisch, S. *Ezekiel: Hebrew Text & English Translation with an Introduction and Commentary*. London: Soncino Press, 10th edition, 1985.

Fisher, Miles Mark. *Negro Slave Songs in the United States*. New York: Citadel, 1953.

Fitzmyer, Joseph A. *The Gospel According to Luke (I–IX)*. Anchor Bible 28A. Garden City, NY: Doubleday, 1981.

Foerster, Werner. *"kyrios, kyria, kyriakos, kyriotēs, kyrieuō, katakyrieuō."* *Theological Dictionary of the New Testament*. Vol. 3. Edited by Gerhard Kittel. Translated by Geoffrey W. Bromiley. Grand Rapids: Eerdmans (1965): 1039-1098.

Frame, James Everett. *A Critical and Exegetical Commentary on the Epistles of St. Paul to the Thessalonians.* New York: Scribner's, 1912.

Gara, Larry. *The Liberty Line: The Legend of the Underground Railroad.* Lexington: University of Kentucky, 1967.

Grelot, P. and A. Lacocque. *Daniel.* Paris: La Traduction Oecumenique de la Bible, 1975.

Gundry, Robert H. *Matthew: A Commentary on His Literary and Theological Art.* Grand Rapids: Eerdmans, 1982.

Haenchen, Ernst. *The Acts of the Apostles.* Oxford: Basil Blackwell, 1971.

Harris, Kim, and Reggie Harris. *Music and the Underground Railroad.* Album and tape. Philadelphia: Ascension, 1984.

Hart, Michael H. *The 100: A Ranking of the Most Influential Persons in History.* New York: Hart, 1978.

Harvey, A. E. *Jesus and the Constraints of History.* Philadelphia: Westminster, 1982.

Hawthorne, Gerald F. *Philippians.* Word Biblical Commentary, vol. 43. Waco, TX: Word, 1983.

Hemer, Colin J. *The Letters to the Seven Churches of Asia in Their Local Setting.* Sheffield: *Journal for the Study of the Old Testament*, 1986.

Henderson, Suzanne Watts. "Jesus' Messianic Self-Consciousness Revisited: Christology and Community in Context." *Journal for the Study of the Historical Jesus* 7:2 (2009): 168-197.

Hendrix, Holland Lee. "Archaeology and Eschatology at Thessalonica." *The Future of Early Christianity: Essays in Honor of Helmut Koester.* Minneapolis: Fortress, 1991.

Hennecke, E., W. Schneemelcher, and R. McL. Wilson, eds. *New Testament Apocrypha.* Vol. 2. Philadelphia: Westminster, 1964.

Herzog, William R. II. "Onstage and Offstage with Jesus of Nazareth: Public Transcripts, Hidden Transcripts, and Gospel Texts." *Hidden Transcripts and the Arts of Resistance: Applying the Work of James C. Scott to Jesus and to Paul.* Edited by Richard A. Horsley, Atlanta: Society of Biblical Literature, 2004.

Hobbs, T. Raymond. "The Political Jesus: Discipleship and Disengagement," *The Social Setting of Jesus and the Gospels* Edited by Wolfgang Stegemann, Bruce J. Malina, and Gerd Theissen, Minneapolis: Fortress, 2002, 251–282.

Horsley, Richard A. *Galilee: History, Politics, People.* Valley Forge, PA: Trinity Press International, 1995.

———, *1 Corinthians* Nashville: Abingdon, 1998.

———, "Jesus and Empire," *In the Shadow of Empire: Reclaiming the Bible as a History of Faithful Resistance.* Edited by Richard A. Horsley, Louisville: Westminster John Knox, 2008, 75–96.

———. *Jesus and Empire: The Kingdom of God and the New World Disorder.* Minneapolis: Fortress, 2003.

————. *Jesus and the Spiral of Violence*. San Francisco: Harper, 1987.

————, *The Liberation of Christmas: The Infancy Narratives in Social Context*. New York: Crossroad, 1989.

————, *Sociology and the Jesus Movement*. New York: Crossroad, 1989.

Horsley, Richard A., ed. *Hidden Transcripts and the Arts of Resistance: Applying the Work of James C. Scott to Jesus and Paul*. Atlanta: Society of Biblical Literature, 2004.

————, *Paul and Empire: Religion and Power in Roman Imperial Society*, Harrisburg, PA: Trinity Press International, 1997.

————, *Paul and Politics: Ekklesia, Israel, Imperium, Interpretation: Essays in Honor of Krister Stendahl*. Harrisburg, PA: Trinity Press International, 2000.

Horsley, Richard A., and John S. Hanson. *Bandits, Prophets, and Messiahs*. Minneapolis: Winston, 1985.

Ignatius. "Letter to the Romans: The Apostolic Fathers I." *The Loeb Classical Library*. Vol. 15. Cambridge, MA: Harvard, 1965.

"Indictments Outrage Sanctuary Leaders." *The Lutheran Standard* 25 (February 15, 1985): 22.

Jeske, Richard L. *Revelation for Today: Images of Hope*. Philadelphia: Fortress, 1983.

Jewett, Robert. *A Chronology of Paul's Life*. Philadelphia: Fortress, 1979.

Juel, Donald. *Mark* Augsburg Commentary on the New Testament, Minneapolis: Augsburg, 1990.

Käsemann, Ernst. *Perspectives on Paul*. Philadelphia: Fortress, 1971.

Kealy, Sean P. *The Apocalypse of John*. Wilmington, DE: Michael Glazier, 1987.

Kee, Howard Clark. *Community of the New Age: Studies in Mark's Gospel*. Philadelphia: Westminster, 1977.

Kierkegaard, Sören. *Edifying Discourses* 11. Translated by David F. Swenson and Lilian Marvin Swenson. Minneapolis: Fortress, 1962.

Kim, Seyoon. *Christ and Caesar: The Gospel and the Roman Empire in the Writings of Paul and Luke*. Grand Rapids: Eerdmans, 2008.

Kittel, Gerhard, ed. *Theological Dictionary of the New Testament* 3. Translated by Geoffrey W. Bromiley, Grand Rapids: Eerdmans. 1965.

Koester, Helmut. "Imperial Ideology and Paul's Eschatology in 1 Thessalonians," *Paul and Empire: Religion and Power in Roman Imperial Society*. Edited by Richard A. Horsley, Harrisburg, PA: Trinity Press International, 1997.

————, *Introduction to the New Testament, Volume One: History, Culture, and Religion of the Hellenistic Age*. Philadelphia: Fortress, 1982.

————, *Introduction to the New Testament, Volume Two: History and Literature of Early Christianity*. Philadelphia: Fortress, 1982.

———. "The Passion Narratives and the Roots of Anti–Judaism." *Bible Review* 9:1 (1993): 5, 46.

Krodel, Gerhard. *Acts*. Augsburg Commentary on the New Testament. Minneapolis: Augsburg, 1986.

———, *Revelation*. Augsburg Commentary on the New Testament. Minneapolis: Augsburg, 1989.

———, "The First Letter of Peter." *Hebrews–James–1 and 2 Peter–Jude–Revelation*. Proclamation Commentaries. Edited by Gerhard Krodel. Philadelphia: Fortress, 1977.

———, "The Second Letter to the Thessalonians." *Ephesians, Colossians, 2 Thessalonians, The Pastoral Epistles*. Proclamation Commentaries. Edited by Gerhard Krodel. Philadelphia: Fortress, 1978.

Lacocque, André. *The Book of Daniel*. Atlanta: John Knox, 1979.

Lesbaupin, Ivo. *Blessed are the Persecuted*. Maryknoll, NY: Orbis, 1987.

Lohfink, Norbert F. *Option for the Poor*. Berkeley: Bibal, 1987.

Lovell, John. "The Social Implications of the Negro Spiritual." *The Social Implications of Early Negro Music in the United States*. Edited by Bernard Katz. 1939. Reissue. New York: Arno, 1969.

McCant, Jerry W. "Paul's Thorn of Rejected Apostleship." *New Testament Studies* 34 (1988): 550–572.

Macgregor, G. H. C. "Principalities and Powers: the Cosmic Background of Paul's Thought." *New Testament Studies* 1 (1954): 22–23.

McLellan, Donn. "Undercover Agents in Worship." *The Lutheran Standard* 25 (November 1, 1985): 4–8.

Macky, Peter W. *The Centrality of Metaphors to Biblical Thought: A Method for Interpreting the Bible*. Lewiston, NY: Mellen, 1990.

Malherbe, Abraham J. "The Beasts at Ephesus." *Journal of Biblical Literature* 87 (1968): 71–80.

Marshall, I. Howard. *The Gospel of Luke*. Grand Rapids: Eerdmans, 1978.

Martin, Ralph P. *Carmen Christi: Philippians 2:5–11 in Recent Interpretation and in the Setting of Early Christian Worship*. Grand Rapids: Eerdmans, 1983.

Martyn, J. Louis. *History and Theology in the Fourth Gospel*. New York: Harper & Row, 1968. Rev. ed. Nashville: Abingdon, 1979.

May, Herbert G., and Bruce M. Metzger, eds. *The New Oxford Annotated Bible With the Apocrypha: Revised Standard Version*. New York: Oxford, 1973.

Meier, John P. *A Marginal Jew: Rethinking the Historical Jesus*. Vol. 1. Garden City, NY: Doubleday, 1991.

Miller, Ruth. *Blackamerican Literature: 1760–Present*. Beverly Hills, CA: Glencoe, 1971.

Moffatt, James. *The First Epistle of Paul to the Corinthians*. New York: Harper, n.d.

Montgomery, James A. *A Critical and Exegetical Commentary on the Book of Daniel.* New York: Scribners's, 1927.

Moule, Handley C. G. *The Epistle of St. Paul to the Romans. The Expositor's Bible.* Edited by W. Robertson Nicoll. New York, NY: Armstrong, 1903.

Moulton, W. F., and A. S. Geden, eds. *A Concordance to the Greek Testament.* 4th ed. Revised by H. K. Moulton. Edinburgh: T. & T. Clark, 1963.

Myers, Ched. *Binding the Strong Man: A Political Reading of Mark's Story of Jesus.* Maryknoll, NY: Orbis, 2008.

Oakes, Peter. *Philippians: From People to Letter.* Cambridge: Cambridge University Press, 2001.

Oakman, Douglas E. *Jesus and the Economic Questions of His Day.* Lewiston, NY: Mellen, 1986.

Orr, William F. *1 Corinthians.* Garden City, NY: Doubleday, 1976.

Osofsky, Gilbert, ed. *Puttin' On Ole Massa: The Slave Narratives of Henry Bibb, William Wells Brown, and Solomon Northup.* New York: Harper, 1969.

Owens, J. Garfield. *All God's Chillun: Meditations on Negro Spirituals.* Nashville: Abingdon, 1971.

Pagels, Elaine. "The Social History of Satan, the 'Intimate Enemy': A Preliminary Sketch." *Harvard Theological Review* 84:2 (1991): 105–128.

———, "The Social History of Satan, Part II: Satan in the New Testament Gospels." *Journal of the American Academy of Religion* 62:1 (1994): 17–58.

Patterson, Lindsay, ed. *The Negro in Music and Art.* New York: Publishers, 1967.

Perkins, Pheme. "Philippians: Theology for the Heavenly Politeuma." *Pauline Theology I: Thessalonians, Philippians, Galatians, Philemon,* Edited by Jouette M. Bassler. Minneapolis: Fortress, 1991.

Perrin, Norman, and Dennis C. Duling. *The New Testament: An Introduction.* 2nd ed. New York: Harcourt Brace Jovanovich, 1982.

Pilgrim, Walter E. *Uneasy Neighbors: Church and State in the New Testament.* Minneapolis: Fortress, 1999.

Price, S. R. F. *Rituals and Power: The Roman Imperial Cult in Asia Minor.* Cambridge: Cambridge University Press, 1984.

Rivkin, Ellis. *What Crucified Jesus?* Nashville: Abingdon, 1984.

Roetzel, Calvin J. *The World That Shaped the New Testament.* Atlanta: John Knox, 1985.

Rohrbaugh, Richard L. *The New Testament in Cross-Cultural Perspective.* Eugene, OR: Wipf & Stock, 2006.

———."The Social Location of the Markan Audience." *Interpretation* 47 (1993): 380–395.

Rossing, Barbara R. *The Rapture Exposed: The Message of Hope in the Book of Revelation* Cambridge, MA: Westview, 2004.

Sanders, E. P. *Jesus and Judaism*. Philadelphia: Fortress, 1985.

———. *The Historical Figure of Jesus*. New York: NY: Penguin, 1993.

Schottroff, Luise, and Wolfgang Stegemann. *Jesus and the Hope of the Poor*. Maryknoll, NY: Orbis, 1986.

Scott, James C. *Domination and the Arts of Resistance: Hidden Transcripts*. New Haven: Yale University Press, 1990.

———, *Weapons of the Weak: Everyday Forms of Peasant Resistance*. New Haven: Yale University Press, 1985.

Segal, Alan F. *Paul the Convert*. New Haven: Yale, 1990.

Segal, Phillip. *The Halakhah of Jesus of Nazareth According to the Gospel of Matthew*. Lanham, MD: The University Press of America, 1987.

Selvidge, Marla J. "The Acts of the Apostles: A Violent Aetiological Legend." *Society of Biblical Literature Seminar Papers Series* 25. Edited by Kent Harold Richards. Atlanta: Scholars, 1986.

Selwyn, Edward Gordon. *The First Epistle of St. Peter*. London: St. Martin's, 1958.

Siebert, Wilbur H. *The Underground Railroad: From Slavery to Freedom*. New York: Macmillan, 1898.

Stambaugh, John E., and David L. Balch. *The New Testament in Its Social Environment*. Philadelphia: Westminster, 1986.

Stauffer, Ethelbert. *Christ and the Caesars*. Philadelphia: Westminster, 1955.

Stegemann, Wolfgang, Bruce J. Malina, and Gerd Theissen, eds. *The Social Setting of Jesus and the Gospels*. Minneapolis: Fortress, 2002.

Stendahl, Krister. "Preaching from the Pauline Epistles." *Biblical Preaching: An Expositor's Treasury*. Edited by James W. Cox. Philadelphia: Westminster, 1983.

Sterling, Dorothy. *Lucretia Mott: Gentle Warrior*. Garden City, NY: Doubleday, 1964.

Still, William. *The Underground Railroad*. Philadelphia: Porter, 1883.

Sundberg, Albert C. "On Testimonies." *Novum Testamentum* 3 (1959): 268–281.

Sweet, J. P. M. *Revelation*. Philadelphia: Westminster, 1979.

Swidler, Leonard. *Yeshua: A Model for Moderns*. Kansas City: Sheed & Ward, 1988.

Taylor, Walter F. "New Quests for the Historical Jesus." *Trinity Seminary Review* 15 (1993): 69–83.

Theissen, Gerd, "The Political Dimension of Jesus' Activities," Wolfgang Stegemann, Bruce J. Malina, and Gerd Theissen, eds. *The Social Setting of Jesus and the Gospels*. Minneapolis: Fortress, 2002, 225-250.

Villard, Oswald Garrison. *John Brown, 1800–1859: A Biography Fifty Years After*. Boston: Houghton Mifflin, 1910.

Walsh, Michael. *The Triumph of the Meek.* San Francisco: Harper, 1986.

Wengst, Klaus. *Bedrängte Gemeinde und verherrlichter Christus: Der historische Ort des Johannesevangeliums als Schlüssel zu seiner Interpretation.* Neukirchen-Vluyn: Neukircher Verlag, 1981.

—, *Pax Romana and the Peace of Jesus Christ.* Translated by John Bowden. Philadelphia: Fortress, 1987.

Wilson, J. Christian. "The Problem of the Domitianic Date of Revelation." *New Testament Studies* 39 (1993): 587–605.

Wink, Walter. *Engaging the Powers: Discernment and Resistance in a World of Domination.* Minneapolis: Fortress, 1992.

—, *Naming the Powers: The Language of Power in the New Testament.* Philadelphia: Fortress, 1984.

—, *Unmasking the Powers: The Invisible Forces That Determine Human Existence.* Philadelphia: Fortress, 1986.

Worden, Ronald D. "Taking the Bible on Its Own Terms." *The Christian Century* 101 (1984): 832–834.

Wright, N. T. *Paul in Fresh Perspective.* Minneapolis: Fortress, 2005.

—, "Paul's Gospel and Caesar's Empire," *Paul and Politics: Ekklesia, Israel, Imperium, Interpretation: Essays in Honor of Krister Stendahl.* Edited by Richard A. Horsley, Harrisburg, PA: Trinity Press International: 2000.

—, *The Challenge of Jesus: Rediscovering Who Jesus Was and Is.* Downers Grove, IL: Intervarsity Press, 1999.

Wright, N. T., and Stephen Neill. *The Interpretation of the New Testament 1861–1986.* New York: Oxford University Press, 1988.

Yoder, John Howard. *The Politics of Jesus: Behold the Man! Our Victorious Lamb.* 2nd ed. Grand Rapids: Eerdmans, 1994.

Zannoni, Arthur E., ed. *Jews and Christians Speak of Jesus.* Minneapolis: Fortress, 1994.

Index of Authors

Achtemeier, Paul J., 173
Arndt, William F., 165
Arnold, Clinton E., 162

Balch, David L., 154
Bammel, Ernst, 154
Barrett, C. K., 69–70, 166, 169
Bassler, Jouette M., 163
Bauckhan, Richard, 173
Bauer, Walter, 165
Beck, Norman A., 28, 29, 157–158,170, 174
Blockson, Charles L., 6, 153
Boadt, Lawrence, 154
Boesak, Allan A., 173
Borg, Marcus J., 24–25, 156–157, 159
Bradford, Sarah, 153
Brodie, Thomas L., 170
Bromiley, Geoffrey W., 164
Brown, Raymond E., 168, 170
Bryan, Christopher, 17, 99, 154, 156, 160, 170
Buchanan, George Wesley, 26–27, 38, 42, 91–92, 157, 161, 162, 169
Buckmaster, Henrietta, 153
Bultmann, Rudolf, 166
Burk, Denny, 156
Buttolph, Philip, 167

Caird, G. B., 47–49, 64, 129, 162, 165, 173
Callahan, Allen Dwight, 156
Carter, Warren, 38, 99–100, 111, 154, 156, 160, 170
Cassidy, Richard J., 154, 160
Charles, R. H., 96, 169
Charlesworth, James H., 155, 157
Collins, Adela Yarbro, 125, 128–129, 172, 173
Collins, John J., 155
Cone, James H., 6, 153
Conrad, Earl, 153

Conzelmann, Hans, 165, 167
Cook, Michael J., 158
Cox, James W., 162
Cravens, O. Fred, 2, 6, 153
Crossan, John Dominic, 24, 154, 157, 160, 165, 169
Cumont, Franz, 54, 163

Danker, Frederick W., 165
Denney, James, 164
Dibelius, Martin, 167
Dixon, Christa K., 6, 153
Donfried, Karl P., 164
Douglass, Frederick, 153
DuBois, W. E. B., 153
Duling, Dennis C., 167, 170

Eckardt, A. Roy, 26, 27–29, 38, 42, 157, 158, 159, 161
Ehrman, Bart D., 154
Eichrodt, Walter, 154
Elliott, Neil, 50, 72, 156, 162, 166
Elliott, Susan M. (Elli), 156
Erdman, Charles R., 167
Ermatinger, James W., 154
Esler, Philip F., 154

Ferguson, John, 173
Fiorenza, Elisabeth Schüssler, 23, 127, 133, 157, 173
Fisch, S., 154
Fisher, Miles Mark, 6, 153
Fitzmyer, Joseph A., 168
Foerster, Werner, 60–61, 163, 164
Frame, James Everett, 167

Gara, Larry, 153
Geden, A. S., 172
Gingrich, F. Wilbur, 165
Grelot, P., 154

Gundry, Robert H., 44, 162

Haenchen, Ernst, 171, 174
Hanson, John S., 154, 157
Harris, Kim, 4, 6, 153
Harris, Reggie, 4, 6, 153
Hart, Michael H., 162
Harvey, A. E., 22-23, 157
Hawthorne, Gerald F., 164
Hemer, Colin J., 172
Henderson, Suzanne Watts, 160
Hendrix, Holland Lee, 164
Hennecke, E., 169
Herzog, William R. II, 17, 99, 156, 170
Hobbs, T. Raymond, 160
Horsley, Richard A., 17, 25–26, 29-30, 38,
        42, 93, 94, 100, 105, 154, 156,
        157, 159, 160, 161, 162, 163, 165,
        166, 169, 170

Isaac, Jules, 158

Jeremias, Joachim, 21
Jeske, Richard L., 128, 173
Jewett, Robert, 162
Josephus, 35
Juel, Donald, 96, 169

Käsemann, Ernst, 162
Kealy, Sean P., 173
Kee, Howard Clark, 84, 168, 169
Kierkegaard, Sören, 165
Kim, Seyoon, 154, 156, 160
Kittel, Gerhard, 164
Kittredge, Cynthia Briggs, 156
Klijn, A. F. J., 155
Koester, Helmut, 50–51, 63, 116–117, 158–
        159, 162, 163, 165, 167, 171, 172,
        173
Krodel, Gerhard, 129, 130, 167, 171, 172,
        173

Lacocque, André, 154
Leighton, Christopher M., 157
Leitch, James W., 165
Lesbaupin, Ivo, 154
Lohfink, Norbert F., 154
Lovell, John, 6, 153

McCant, Jerry W., 67, 165
Macgregor, G. H. C., 166–167
McLellan, Donn, 165
Macky, Peter W., 160–161
Malherbe, Abraham J., 165
Malina, Bruce J., 160
Marshall, I. Howard, 168-169
Martin, Ralph P., 163–164
Martyn J. Louis, 168
Marx, Karl, 43
May, Herbert G., 167
Meier, John P., 21, 26, 156, 157, 161
Metzger, Bruce M., 14, 155, 167
Miller, Ruth, 153
Moffatt, James, 165
Montgomery, James A., 11, 154
Moule, C. F. D., 154
Moule, Handley C. G., 166
Moulton, H. K., 172
Moulton, W. F., 172
Myers, Ched, 19, 156, 160, 169

Neill, Stephen, 156–157
Nicoll, W. Robertson, 164, 166

Oakes, Peter, 163
Oakman, Douglas E., 154, 159
Orr, William F., 165
Osofsky, Gilbert, 153
Owens, J. Garfield, 6, 153

Pagels, Elaine, 26, 155, 157, 172
Parkes, James, 158
Patterson, Lindsay, 153
Perkens, Pheme, 53, 163
Perrin, Norman, 21, 22
Philostratus, 98
Pilgrim, Walter E., 63, 160, 165
Price, S. R. F., 169–170

Reed, Jonathan L., 165
Richards, Kent Harold, 171
Rivkin, Ellis, 35, 159, 160, 168
Roetzel, Calvin, J., 154
Rohrbaugh, Richard L., 154, 159
Rossing, Barbara R., 132, 173

Sanders, E. P. 22, 157
Schneemelcher, W., 169
Schottroff, Luise, 154
Scott, James C., 16–17, 155-156
Segal, Alan F., 50, 162
Segal, Phillip, 23, 157
Selvidge, Marla J., 171
Selwyn, Edward Gordon, 173–174
Shermis, Michael, 158
Siebert, Wilbur H., 153
Stambaugh, John E., 154
Stauffer, Ethelbert, 61, 164
Stegemann, Wolfgang, 154, 160
Stendahl, Krister, 162
Sterling, Dorothy, 153
Still, William, 153
Sundberg, Albert C. 154–155
Sweet, J. P. M., 172–173
Swenson, David F., 165
Swenson, Lilian Marvin, 165
Swidler, Leonard, 23–24, 157

Taylor, Walter F., 157
Theissen, Gerd, 160

Villard, Oswald Garrison, 153

Walsh, Michael, 154
Wengst, Klaus, 6–7, 14, 26, 27, 38, 53, 108,
        154, 155, 157, 159, 163, 168, 170
West, Gerald, 156
Wilson, J. Christian, 171
Wilson, R. McL., 169
Wink, Walter, 49–50, 161, 162
Wintermute, O. S., 12, 155
Worden, Ronald D., 169
Wright, N. T., 156, 161, 163,

Yarbro, Adela, 167
Yoder, John Howard, 17, 156, 160

Zannoni, Arthur E., 158–159

Studies in Biblical Literature

This series invites manuscripts from scholars in any area of biblical literature. Both established and innovative methodologies, covering general and particular areas in biblical study, are welcome. The series seeks to make available studies that will make a significant contribution to the ongoing biblical discourse. Scholars who have interests in gender and sociocultural hermeneutics are particularly encouraged to consider this series.

For further information about the series and for the submission of manuscripts, contact:

Peter Lang Publishing
Acquisitions Department
P.O. Box 1246
Bel Air, Maryland 21014-1246

To order other books in this series, please contact our Customer Service Department:

(800) 770-LANG (within the U.S.)
(212) 647-7706 (outside the U.S.)
(212) 647-7707 FAX

or browse online by series at:

WWW.PETERLANG.COM

Studies in Biblical Literature